THE VOICE OF ANFIELD

George Sephton is a stadium announcer, match-day DJ and voiceover artist. He is popularly known as 'The Voice of Anfield'.

THE VOICE OF ANFIELD

George Sephton

ALLEN&UNWIN

First published in hardback and trade paperback in Great Britain in 2021 by
Allen & Unwin, an imprint of Atlantic Books Ltd.

This paperback edition first published in Great Britain in 2022 by
Allen & Unwin, an imprint of Atlantic Books Ltd.

10 9 8 7 6 5 4 3 2 1

A CIP catalogue record for this book is available from the British Library.

Paperback ISBN: 978 1 83895 270 9
E-book ISBN: 978 1 83895 269 3

Designed and typeset by benstudios.co.uk
Printed and bound by CPI Group (UK) Ltd, Croydon, CR0 4YY

Allen & Unwin
An imprint of Atlantic Books Ltd
Ormond House
26–27 Boswell Street
London
WC1N 3JZ

www.allenandunwin.com/uk

To my wife Liz and the rest of my wonderful family,
without whom none of this would have meant anything

Contents

Foreword by
Sir Kenny Dalglish

George Sephton is part of the brickwork of Liverpool Football Club and was witness to so many iconic moments. He has lived through a huge chunk of our history, from when Liverpool were in the Second Division, when he used to come to Anfield with his father, all the way to being crowned World Club and Premier League champions. It's been a roller-coaster ride, and George has been there for all the ups and downs – but mainly the ups.

George has made an impression on so many people at the club and in the wider Liverpool community. I remember as a player when George would put up the scores at half-time. The players never got the chance to listen to him or the records he played, as we were either warming up in the dressing room or getting a bollocking at half-time, but we knew he was often the bearer of great news when the half-time and full-time scores came through.

When I started at Liverpool Football Club, everyone was important, irrespective of their role, and everybody was treated respectfully, from the tea ladies to the manager. Football clubs have always been an important part of their local community, and Liverpool fans have always been made to feel special and have always been appreciated. The fans would be in the ground before the game started, singing along to George's records. People could always relate to his voice, even before they could see his face.

He's got a great sense of humour, too. I remember the home game against Burnley in 2015. I was at the ground early and walking around in front of the Kop with my wife Marina. It was my birthday, and Anfield was fairly quiet, with just a few stewards about. Suddenly, I heard The Beatles' 'When I'm Sixty-Four' blaring out of the ground's PA, which made me laugh. I couldn't see George, but I knew it was him!

George Sephton has been an integral part of Liverpool Football Club and the community for more than fifty years. And that is the greatest compliment I can pay him.

'Sleeve Notes'

The voice of George Sephton has been heard at Anfield for so long that you could be forgiven for imagining him poised with a wind-up gramophone and a 78-rpm record of Gerry with his ukulele and a single Pacemaker, on a comb and tissue paper, piping Alan A'Court and Alf Arrowsmith on to the field.

As you know, George actually arrived in the booth when Bill Shankly was still manager, in the heady days of Heighway and Hughes, Keegan and Toshack. Those were afternoons, when, as a schoolboy (sorry, George), I was taking my spec every week on the left side of the Kop goal.

I've supported Liverpool since they were in the Second Division, and from 1977, when I began to travel the world to sing songs, I have tried to cheat the time difference, the short- or long-wave radio signal or, more recently, the cable television rights to follow the Reds wherever I went. Few things say 'I'm home' more than hearing George read out the team sheet when you return to Anfield after a spell away.

I would have tried to write more songs that the Kop could have adapted as chants, but, as you know, few things rhyme with 'Carragher', and nothing at all rhymes with 'El Hadji Diouf'. So, having failed to persuade George to play my song '45' in praise of then-new signing, Mario Balotelli, I'll settle for him occasionally spinning one of my discs in the pre-match record session. It's probably as close as I'll ever get to hearing my name sung at Anfield.

George has been part of the drama of home games, in the best and worst of times, some of them too sad for words, but he also has a sense of humour for the occasion. I was there the night George played the visitors off the park with 'Arrivederci Roma' after a testy UEFA Cup tie. And I wish we could all be there together to hear him cue up 'You'll Never Walk Alone' when the title trophy is held aloft at Anfield again. I think we can trust George to blow the dust off the needle on that afternoon.

Elvis Costello, July 2020

(With apologies to William Shakespeare)

Ninety-six families, alike in dignity
(In fair Liverpool, where we lay our scene),
From ancient grudge break to new mutiny,
Where civil blood makes civil hands unclean.

Prologue

I f I'd known half a century ago that I'd still be the 'Voice of Anfield' all these years later, I would have been careful to keep records, count matches and create a full and accurate catalogue of the people I've met, the players I've seen and the music I've played.

The routine has changed, the technology has transformed and the club has evolved into the global giant it is now. In the seventies and eighties, I'd arrive at Anfield a couple of hours before kick-off carrying a heavy box of vinyl records – some from my own collection, some borrowed from friends and some from Crease's record shop near Goodison Park. I'd got on to several record companies' mailing lists, and I asked them for advance copies of new records, pointing out they supplied club DJs who had crowds much smaller than mine.

The advent of CDs made life a lot easier, and by then some big music stores were happy to give me CD singles. HMV let me pick a selection from the Top 40 (and the occasional album) in exchange for an advert in the match-day programme and regular plugs from me at half-time. That carried on until they had to trim their sails. I now play tunes from a memory stick, mostly downloads plus material ripped from my personal CD collection. The mixture is pretty standard and taken from several sources: the current charts, fan favourites, meaningful songs (for example, when a great artist has just passed away) or sent to me direct by bands from around Merseyside. I'm proud of my reputation for giving local talent an airing, and there are a few artists around who had their first exposure at Anfield on a Saturday afternoon.

There is, of course, one constant: 'You'll Never Walk Alone'. I was standing on the Kop one afternoon in October 1963 when it was first played, and nearly six decades later it's taken on a life of its own. The hairs on my neck still stand up when the first three words are heard: 'When you walk . . .' It isn't a song any more. It's a hymn. It's an anthem. It's a message of comfort and hope and reassurance that binds the worldwide Red family together.

Nowadays, I am normally in the DJ room, at the junction of the Kop and Sir Kenny Dalglish Stand, four hours before kick-off. I only start playing music when the gates open, two hours before kick-off – the previous two are a safety buffer. First, to make sure I'm alive and well and in place. Second, to make sure that the technical stuff is working: the microphones, CD decks, USB ports, scoreboard, VAR display and TV monitor, which is linked directly to the cameras all around the ground.

Until the new Main Stand opened in 2016, I would park up in Anfield Road or Stanley Park and then enter the ground via the reception desk in the old Main Stand. I would always hang around in there so I could chat to whomever I needed to see. I habitually popped into the press room and into the office next door to the manager's room down the back corridor. On match days, this was the communications hub, where the team sheets were collated and printed for distribution to

2

the media. Even after all these years, I still can't believe I can walk into Anfield and take part in what's going on! I keep telling people that until you've been to the stadium, you can't understand the feeling generated by the place.

Since the new Main Stand opened, my routine has changed completely. I'm lucky enough to have a parking space opposite the Shankly Gates. I go straight into the Sir Kenny Dalglish Stand, up to the third floor and down the corridor behind all the executive boxes to my room. Most of the staff (but not all!) know who I am and greet me by name, but I have no interaction whatsoever with the current squad. That's a shame for me personally, but it's the way of the world.

This book is one of parallel stories: my day-to-day working life, the exploits of Liverpool Football Club and – of course – the music, which has probably kept me sane (well almost), as well as bringing so much joy into my life. Regulars at Anfield will know I have extremely eclectic tastes, and I have always refused to be pigeonholed. As the late, great Helen Reddy once said to me, 'What would the world be if all the flowers were the same colour?'

PART ONE

The Fifties and Sixties

Growing Up on the Kop

My mum and dad (Amy and Ted) were married in a church in Goodison Road, of all places, in 1934, and I was born nine months after the end of the Second World War. I was their only child. I never knew my grandparents.

My dad was a lifelong Liverpool supporter. He was a big strapping centre-forward who had a trial for the Reds in 1923 when he was fourteen years old. He stood on the Kop, week in week out, for years until he was crippled with arthritis and had to give up in the late fifties. In 1950, his beloved Reds got to the FA Cup final. He was desperate to go but had to enter the ballot for tickets, which you did by sending a postcard to Anfield with your name and address on the back. He and my poor mum wrote fifty postcards, but he didn't strike lucky. His only remaining option was to buy a ticket from a tout. He was a plumber, and my mum was an usherette, and they just didn't have the money that the touts were asking, so he couldn't go! That episode instilled in me a lifelong hatred of ticket touts.

The Empire Theatre is a historic part of Liverpool's cultural history, and it holds a special place in my heart. My mum worked there for a while, and her sister Dorothy did too, in the box office. Dorothy was allowed two free tickets on Monday night for every show that ran for a week or more. My parents did well out of that arrangement and so did I when I was a youngster. My parents used the tickets once in a while, then I sometimes went with my mum before being let loose with schoolmates.

Those were the days of the package tours when promoters like Larry Parnes would put on a bill of British and American stars. One particular gig I went to with my mum on 11 November 1956 turned out to be more significant than any of us could have realized. Top of the bill was Lonnie Donegan, the singer, songwriter and musician referred to as the 'King of Skiffle'. He had thirty-one UK Top 30 hits, including three number ones, and he was the first British male singer with two US Top 10 hits. The importance of that gig was that a young lad called James Paul McCartney was in the audience with his dad. The story goes that it was Donegan's concert that influenced young Paul to take up the guitar. The following year he met up with another lad by the name of John Lennon at a church fete in south Liverpool and the face of popular music changed for ever. Paul was still a pupil at the Liverpool Institute High School for Boys when I arrived there in 1957. He's four years older and his brother Mike two years older than me. Mike also went to the Institute, as did a lad by the name of George Harrison, who overlapped me by three years. George used to call me 'Bugs' because of my Bugs Bunny teeth! This was the era of rock 'n' roll, and the 'Inny' was full of baby boomers who took to the new music. My form master (Mister Edwards, aka 'Jake') was the poor devil who returned early to his form room after lunch one time and, finding a lad with a guitar, uttered the immortal words, 'McCartney! Put that thing away! It'll never get you anywhere!'

I was one of those teenagers who spent a lot of time in my bedroom with my record player, radio and homework, listening to hours of music on Radio Luxembourg and, later, Radio Caroline. I wasn't a very sociable guy and was never a 'mixer'. My father remarried a couple of years after my mum passed away, and my new stepmother, who had her own ideas about family life, marched me to the youth club in Aintree, a couple of miles from home in Walton. It was run by the Methodist Church there, and we were never allowed to hold dances unless we called them 'socials'. Coming up to Christmas 1961, we decided to hold one such event and blow our kitty on a band – except they were called groups then! We had £8 to spend. We got The Undertakers, one of the burgeoning number of groups in Liverpool, to play. They were fantastic and were soon making hit records. But my abiding memory of the event was a casual remark from a fellow committee member. 'Eight quid! That's a pity! If we'd had ten quid, we could have got The Beatles!' If we'd known what was on the horizon, we would have found the extra £2!

A couple of years after the Donegan gig, Cliff Richard was booked to appear at the Empire with his band The Shadows, who had just changed their name from The Drifters to avoid clashing with an American group of the same name. I really fancied seeing Cliff (he was cutting-edge rock 'n' roll in those days!), so I went into Liverpool and wandered round to the Empire. There was a queue that started just inside the big double doors leading to the box office before weaving its way into Lord Nelson Street at the side of the theatre and up the hill, disappearing into the far distance.

I had a quick look through the doors at the head of the queue and spotted a familiar face at the second window. My Aunt Dorothy! She was at the window that said 'Billy Cotton Band Show', which, strangely enough, no one was queueing for. She worked out very quickly what I was after and discreetly moved sideways to the next window. She came back with two precious Cliff Richard tickets, and I was on my way. The poor devils at the front of the line realized what was going on and were giving me some murderous looks as I made my escape. Luckily for me, none of them dared to break ranks and lose their position in the queue.

I saw Roy Orbison on the same bill as The Beatles and Gerry and the Pacemakers in London in 1963. That was the famous tour when Roy started off as top of the bill and finished up as the support act to The Beatles. The birth of Beatlemania. I was doubly happy, as it was the only time I got to see the wonderful Louise Cordet (my teenage idol), who was also on the bill, in the flesh. And I saw the show on the day Gerry's last single before 'You'll Never Walk Alone' was released! Forty years later, I got to know Gerry and Louise. If only I'd known then what was in store for me.

On 6 July 1964, I was in the crowd on the far side of Water Street in the centre of Liverpool looking up at the town hall balcony watching The Beatles, alongside Lord Mayor Louis Caplan, waving to the thousands of people who had come to see the lads return home for the premiere of their first feature film *A Hard Day's Night*. That summer I was a clerk at the Trustee Savings Bank city branch in Fenwick Street. Friday was the day when we had evening opening. Normally, it was a pain for an eighteen-year-old who wanted to be out and about, but that night it worked in my favour. As soon as we'd cashed up, I went through the back alleys between Fenwick Street and Water Street and grabbed an ideal spot in the corner between two buildings directly opposite the town hall, just in time for The Beatles to emerge. Four decades later, I sneaked out of a function at the town hall and stood on that same balcony looking down from where The Beatles had waved to their fans.

They say that the song that's number one on your fourteenth birthday defines your musical tastes for life. I'm not sure that's always entirely accurate, but in my case it's not too far from the truth. On 22 February 1960, I turned fourteen, and a catchy little tune called 'Why' by Anthony Newley was number one. Newley was a TV actor turned singer who appeared in several movies and married Joan Collins. More important to me was that number four in the same chart was 'Way Down Yonder in New Orleans' by Freddy Cannon – not the greatest piece of music ever written but part of the tidal wave of rock 'n' roll which was engulfing the world. The music was being imported in large quantities by the merchant sailors who criss-crossed the Atlantic and brought cases full of the newfangled 45-rpm records which would soon contribute to the birth of the Merseybeat sound. It may be that I was a late developer. The songs at number one on my fifteenth and sixteenth birthdays were both by Elvis Presley.

Meanwhile, the sleeping giant that was Liverpool Football Club had been, for a few short weeks, in the care of an ambitious Scotsman by the name of Bill Shankly. A decade of underachievement would soon be over, and we would regain the status of champions and reach the holy grail of FA Cup triumph, a trophy that had thus far eluded us.

My first visit to Anfield was in January 1960. Liverpool had been drawn at home in the FA Cup against the mighty 'Busby Babes' of Manchester United. After queueing for several hours around Stanley Park, and having been kicked by a passing police horse, I had the precious piece of paper in my hand and went to my first match. We lost 3–1, but I was hooked. Between then and the time I started working at the club, I spent many hours standing on the old Kop. It could be hard work. If you got in too late to find a spot in front of a crush barrier, you could go home with some serious damage. I had my ribs cracked twice in those heady days.

In 1965, Shankly's Liverpool got to the cup final at Wembley for the first time in fifteen years. By now my poor dad was crippled with arthritis and could barely get out of his chair, so we watched the game on a black-and-white TV in our front room. We went through all sorts of emotional somersaults until Ian St John scored a wonderful flying header to win the game. At the final whistle my dad turned painfully to face me and said, 'This is the greatest day of my life!'

I'm of an age that I've seen almost every one of the top players since the Second World War. I never saw Tom Finney play, but I did see Stanley Matthews when he was in his forties playing for Stoke City. And I was at the World Cup games in Liverpool in 1966 and saw Pelé, Lev Yashin, Eusébio, Bobby Charlton, Garrincha and Ferenc Puskás, to name but a few, in the flesh. Later on, I saw Johan Cruyff playing for Ajax at Anfield. Luckily, I was at the famous 1966 World Cup quarter-final when the Eusébio-inspired Portugal came back from 3–0 down to beat North Korea 5–3.

I was also standing in the Park End at Goodison when Brazil's Garrincha scored the most amazing free-kick I can remember. My mate Bob Hands and I were behind the goal. A wall was formed by the Portuguese defenders, and we could just glimpse the top of Garrincha's head as he lined up to take the kick. He was facing the dead centre of the wall. The only reason we knew when he was striking the ball was because of the roar of expectation from the Brazil fans in the Main Stand. Suddenly, the ball appeared like a guided missile round the *far end* of the wall. It circled back round and hit the back of the net, having flown through 180 degrees. Although I was to witness quite a few more over the years, it remains one of the finest goals I've ever seen.

PART TWO

The Seventies

1970–71

Music plays a huge part in my life, and 1970 was a watershed year. The sixties had come and gone, and in April a bomb dropped: The Beatles had split up. I was choked. The phrase 'end of an era' is overused, but not in this case. My mood was lifted when I got tickets to see Simon and Garfunkel play at the Royal Albert Hall in London. They were probably at their peak, and their masterpiece 'Bridge over Troubled Water' was number one in the UK charts. I just missed out on their first concert but got the best seats for the 'by popular demand' second gig. In 1970, you bought tickets by sending a cheque and a stamped envelope. Happy days!

My soon-to-be-wife Liz and I were sitting amongst the likes of two Bee Gees, a couple of the Dave Clark Five and one or two TV stars. There was a tall, long-haired guy next to me whom I didn't recognize, but when Simon and Garfunkel were about to sing 'Bridge over Troubled Water', he suddenly stood up and made his way to the stage. He was Larry Knechtel, the pianist on the actual record.

Liz had to work Saturdays but came with me to midweek games whenever she could. So it was that in spring of 1971 she came with me to see Liverpool play Newcastle. Before kick-off, the guy on the Tannoy made a blooper when reading out the teams. I made a sarcastic remark, and Liz remarked, 'Could you do any better?'

I don't know what possessed me, but as soon as we got home I wrote to Peter Robinson. His title was club secretary, but he was effectively in charge of running the club. I wish I still had a copy of that letter. Although it filled an A4 page, it boiled down to, 'I can do better. Why not give me a go?'

Before long, I got a letter from Peter asking me to come in and see him. We met in his temporary office in the midst of the chaos that was the building work being carried out on the Main Stand. I was nervous, as you can imagine, but I must have said the right thing because I was asked to put some ideas down on paper and, soon afterwards, was given a 'trial' and then offered the job. Unbeknownst to me, a young man by the name of Alan Harrison was telling his relative on the Anfield board of directors that he too could make a good fist of the stadium announcer's job. However, he was soon told that someone else had been appointed but was promised that when I moved on the job would be his. Half a century later, he's still waiting. Alan is the voice of AFC Liverpool, the semi-professional club set up by supporters of Liverpool FC in 2008, and I'm pleased to call him a friend. The new club was set up as a not-for-profit organization and is run on a one-member, one-vote basis. I'm honoured to be one of their first patrons, alongside Karen Gill, David Price, Joey Jones and John Aldridge. I look forward to the day when they get their own stadium and attain their rightful place in the upper echelons of non-league football. Chairman Chris Stirrup and all of the others who run the club work tirelessly for the place and deserve every success that comes their way.

Before my big day starting work at my beloved Anfield, I had a couple of traumatic moments to get through. My friend Mike Hulm was a devoted Evertonian. In the autumn of 1970, he phoned me to say he was getting married the following spring. The date? Saturday, 8 May!

'You do realize that's cup final day, don't you?' The line went quiet! For some reason, the significance of the date hadn't hit him. Just to complicate things, the semi-final draw had brought us together: Everton v. Liverpool at Old Trafford. We went to see the game together in Manchester.

FA Cup Semi-final – Liverpool v. Everton, Old Trafford, 7 March 1971

Mike was in a no-win situation. If Liverpool won, he would be devastated to lose such a big game to his team's arch-rivals, but if Everton won, he would be unable to make the trip down to Wembley.

The game was a tight affair. Alan Ball put Everton ahead just after the ten-minute mark. It stayed that way till half-time, but midway through the second half Alun Evans equalized for Liverpool before 'Little Bamber', aka Brian Hall, won it for the Reds. It's fair to say that Mike drove home with mixed feelings!

By the time Mike's wedding came around, several guests had remarked about the 'fixture clash', so the event was brought forward from an afternoon to a morning start. A portable TV was found, and the speeches were shorter than usual, with the result that proceedings ended about five minutes before the Wembley kick-off. There was a mini stampede in the direction of the back room where the TV was ready and waiting.

Arsenal won 2–1 after extra time, with all three goals coming in the added half hour. Steve Heighway scored for Liverpool first, before Arsenal equalized with a scrambled goal from substitute Eddie Kelly – the first time a substitute had ever scored in an FA Cup final. Charlie George scored the winner in the second half of extra time. If I close my eyes, I can still see Charlie lying on his back – arms outstretched – inviting the adulation of his teammates. And I can still feel the sick feeling in the pit of my stomach.

The bride and groom, incidentally, had gone on their merry way during half-time.

1971–72

Blackburn Rovers v. Liverpool, Ewood Park, 3 August 1971

With my debut at Anfield fast approaching, my best man Dave Callaghan and I decided to pop up to Ewood Park in Blackburn to see Liverpool's pre-season friendly against Rovers. The stadium was barely one third full, but it was an eye-opening experience. We stood on the terracing directly in front of the directors' box with our backs resting on the wall. *Right in front of Shanks and Bob Paisley.* We spent the whole match trying to eavesdrop on what they were saying, but all we could hear was the occasional 'Oh Bob' and 'Eh Bill!' Suffice to say, it wasn't the most riveting of games, although the team contained some familiar names: Ray Clemence, Chris Lawler, Alec Lindsay, Larry Lloyd, Tommy Smith, Emlyn Hughes, Steve Heighway, Brian Hall, Peter Thompson, Bobby Graham, John Toshack. The only goal was scored by John Toshack.

Liverpool v. Nottingham Forest, Anfield, 14 August 1971

My first day as stadium announcer! My nerves were completely shredded. I had spent the week borrowing records (good old seven-inch vinyl) from friends and work colleagues at the Harrison Line, a shipping company, in Liverpool. My record collection was probably enough to see me through, but I was determined to turn up with more than enough music to keep me going. Following the Boy Scout motto 'Be Prepared' has never let me down. Some of the music I got together was, looking back, embarrassing. The New Seekers, Lobo, New World, Dawn, White Plains: not exactly cutting edge. Other than that lot, however, was some serious rock music: T. Rex, Atomic Rooster and Slade. One track in the charts at the time was 'Won't Get Fooled Again' by The Who. I still play that to this day, although I use the glorious eight-minute version.

In those days, the stadium announcer's 'perch' was on the TV gantry, suspended from the roof of the Main Stand. To get there I had to climb the fire escape at the side of the stand and walk along a gangway through the roof of the stand and down a vertical ladder on to the gantry. I got down the ladder with difficulty (I was carrying enough borrowed vinyl to restock HMV) and put my record box down.

Looking out over the Anfield crowd, knowing that I was going to be talking to them in a few minutes, I froze. I had a decision to make. I could either get on with it, bite the bullet and get the music going or go home, pack a suitcase and disappear. Everyone I knew was aware of my debut and quite a lot of them were at Anfield to hear it! In 1971 there was quite often a good crowd of people on the terrace even before I made my way up to my position. My instructions from Peter Robinson had been to 'Get there for 1.15', and I carried on in that vein for quite a few years. The system on the Kop was exactly the same then as when I'd stood there in the sixties. If you wanted your usual spot, you had to get there early and claim it.

I gritted my teeth and turned on the mic and record decks. I had decided to do the whole thing just as my predecessors had done it. I'd play a couple of tunes, have a quick chat, play some more tunes, then a bit more chat, passing on the usual bits of information: next game, 'beware of pickpockets', etc.

We were playing Nottingham Forest, and when the team sheet arrived it contained an unfamiliar name: Kevin Keegan! This young lad had arrived from Scunthorpe United during the summer for the princely sum of £35,000 and had impressed Bill Shankly in training. Needless to say, he made an immediate impact. He scored in a 3–1 win and thus began his legendary partnership with John Toshack.

The following Tuesday was my second game working at the hallowed ground. Wolves were the visitors, and I managed to cut my hand badly by banging it on the desk when Liverpool scored. And people thought I was laid-back and low-key.

Manchester United v. Arsenal, Anfield, 20 August 1971

I thought I had a couple of weeks off after the Wolves match (according to the fixture list), but no – Manchester United were banned from playing their first two home matches in Manchester after hooligans had thrown knives into the away section at a match at the end of the previous season, so their opening 'home' games would be played at Anfield and Stoke's Victoria Ground. So forgotten is this story that even some Manchester United players who took part in the 3–1 victory over Arsenal can't remember it.

I can still see the half-empty ground. It was spooky. Liverpool were given 15 per cent of the gate receipts from the 27,649 fans who attended the game, and United were instructed by the FA to pay Arsenal compensation, as the gate was below the 48,000 that had attended the fixture at Old Trafford the previous year. (Until the 1980s, gate receipts for league games were shared.)

The rest of 1971 fell into a pattern: working in the shipping office and turning up to Anfield for matches. The reserve team played their home matches at the stadium back then, and it was fascinating to watch some of the kids coming through. A young lad by the name of Phil Thompson signed up as a professional that year, and I frequently bored my weekday colleagues with tales of his progress. Looking back, I was spot on. He went on to win everything domestic football has to offer, as well as captaining club and country before ending up as Gérard Houllier's assistant manager and acting manager when Houllier was ill during the fabulous trophy haul of the 2000–01 season.

There were no thoughts on my mind in those days of trying to create an atmosphere inside Anfield. I was basically providing background music interspersed with important announcements until I read out the two teams and then, of course, played 'You'll Never Walk Alone'! Everything is different now. I try my best to ramp up the excitement before games by playing some of the crowd's favourite Liverpool songs (for example, 'Allez Allez Allez' or 'The Fields of Anfield Road') or some loud rock tracks to get the feet stomping and the circulation going. The atmosphere at Anfield in the twenty-first century can be as good as it ever was, but the advent of the all-seater stadium means that people arrive later, so I have less time to get them going.

The big-selling tune in the charts in 1971 was George Harrison's wonderful 'My Sweet Lord', which always went down well at Anfield. I only recently discovered that George came to a game at the stadium, heavily disguised, in 1986 when he was in Liverpool for the funeral of Ringo Starr's mum.

Liverpool's youth team were playing an FA Youth Cup tie at Anfield on 5 April 1972. There was a reasonable-sized crowd in and a nice atmosphere. Over on the other side of the Pennines, Huddersfield Town, who appeared destined for relegation, were entertaining Leeds United, who were at the top end of the First Division and our fiercest rivals for the title. Midway through the first half, Peter Robinson phoned me. Leeds were a goal down. Peter told me to wait for a break in play and tell the crowd what was going on. I did and an almighty cheer went up from below me, as the crowd were all on the Main Stand side of the ground. Halfway through the second half, the phone rang again. Peter was on the line. 'Leeds are winning now,' he said, 'so in the interest of fairness, you'd better announce that too.'

As soon as the ball went out of play, I turned on the Tannoy and let everyone know that Leeds were 2–1 up. This announcement was greeted by a collective groan. After the game, I went down to the Main Stand reception to hand in the keys. As soon as I was in sight of Eileen on the reception desk, she shouted in my direction, 'Leg it! Shanks is after you!' I ran for the car. Apparently, the manager had come down after the game shouting, 'Where is he? He ruined the atmosphere!' Three days later, we had a First Division game at Anfield, and who should be the first person I bumped into?

You guessed it. Shanks! I froze, but he just looked up and said, 'Good morning, son.' Panic over.

Roger Hunt's Testimonial – Liverpool v. England, Anfield, 11 April 1972

Roger Hunt was Liverpool's top goalscorer eight years in a row from 1962 to 1969, and after winning two league titles and an FA Cup he moved on to Bolton. Hunt scored a total of 286 goals in 492 first team games for the Reds. He returned to a hero's welcome for his testimonial. Torrential rain didn't keep the crowd away.

The Liverpool team consisted of every player from the 1965 FA Cup-winning side: Tommy Lawrence, Chris Lawler, Gerry Byrne, Ron Yeats, Tommy Smith, Willie Stevenson, Geoff Strong, Peter Thompson, Ian Callaghan, Ian St John and Roger Hunt. The opposition consisted of most of England's 1966 World Cup-winning team. It was a special night, with fourteen goals scored and Hunt hitting a hat-trick.

During the interval, I noticed a line in the running order that I'd not seen earlier. Tucked in there just after the celebrity five-a-side game at half-time was a little note that read: 'Say thanks to Roger'. This was a superstar footballer, idolized by everyone in attendance, and suddenly I had to think of an appropriate way to thank him. Luckily, someone had just handed me a piece of paper that told me the attendance that night was the biggest of the season. I said to the crowd that I thought the best way of showing our appreciation was to hear that attendance figure. It worked. I got a huge cheer and a metaphorical pat on the back from Peter Robinson after the game.

I was in awe of some of the people who sat near me in the players' lounge after Roger's testimonial game. I was at a table with the staff from the old souvenir shop, most of whom I knew, and I occasionally wandered over to say a few words to some of the players, including Roger himself.

I ended my first year at Anfield not knowing if I would be brought back for the 1972–73 season. When I finally got round to plucking up the courage to ask Peter Robinson if I was still in the job, he said something along the lines of, 'Of course! You're part of the furniture now!'

Arsenal v. Liverpool, Highbury Stadium, 8 May 1972

The Reds travelled to Arsenal's Highbury Stadium knowing that a win would see them crowned champions. In the event they drew 0–0, and Derby County lifted the league trophy. Their players were all sunning themselves on a beach in Spain, having completed their season and gone on a club holiday, assuming that they had no chance of winning the league. I wasn't at the Arsenal game, and the days of TV blanket coverage hadn't arrived, so the only evidence I have is the radio commentary and the complaints from several Reds who travelled to the game, but I've always understood that a dodgy refereeing decision disallowed a perfectly good goal and denied me (not to mention the squad, staff and many thousands of fans) a trophy in my first season.

1972–73

Liverpool v. Stoke City,
Anfield, 21 October 1972

On the face of it, this was a bog-standard, run-of-the-mill, unremarkable match between two of the oldest clubs in English football. Liverpool won 2–1, with the winner coming from Ian Callaghan in the ninetieth minute after Emlyn Hughes had equalized Stoke's opener.

The significance of the game, which nobody realized at the time, was that it turned out to be the last competitive game for Stoke's goalkeeper, the great Gordon Banks – six years on from his heroics in helping England to win the World Cup and two years after making the 'Save of the Century' in Mexico against the mighty Brazil! The day after the game, Gordon was involved in a car crash that resulted in him losing the sight in one eye and bringing a stellar career to a premature end.

European Cup – Liverpool v. AEK Athens,
Anfield, 24 October 1972

The 1972–73 season saw Liverpool in the UEFA Cup and my linguistic skills being put to the challenge when we were drawn against AEK Athens. I had done pretty well so far with the foreign teams, but that was thanks to my school, and one teacher in particular – Jack Sweeney, who taught Spanish and Russian. When you've got a grasp of those two, you can cope with a lot of what's put in front of you. Greek, however, was a whole new ball game. We didn't have squads then. There were eleven players named on the night, and they wore one to eleven on their shirts. I arrived at Anfield to be presented with a match programme that contained eleven Greek names, which seemed just about manageable. But when the team sheet arrived later, five of those names had changed and five substitutes were also listed! I got through as best I could.

As the match progressed, I could hear, out of my left ear, the two guys doing match commentary for the old hospital radio network. It was remarkable how much possession Tommy Smith and Joey Jones had that night if you happened to be listening on that network. (Incidentally, Liverpool won 3–0!)

The bestselling single in the UK in 1972 was 'Amazing Grace' by the Royal Scots Dragoon Guards. It was an unlikely hit, given that it was an old hymn tune in the middle of the glam rock era. We have used it ever since to honour Bill Shankly and Bob Paisley, and I played this version at Anfield several times over the years. Bob Paisley's wife Jessie also asked me to play it when we paid tribute to her husband after he died.

Liverpool had a very successful end to the 1972–73 season when they were crowned First Division champions and UEFA Cup winners. The league was more or less sewn up by beating

Leeds United several days previously but was put beyond doubt thanks to a tedious 0–0 draw with Leicester City on the last day of the season. There was relief rather than jubilation at the final whistle, but we were now champions, and the lap of honour was a joy to watch. The players summoned up the energy to parade the trophy around all four sides of the ground, followed by Shanks wearing a scarf borrowed from someone on the terraces. I was delighted, remembering the last-game drama at Highbury just twelve months previously.

Liverpool's first European trophy was earned in a two-legged final against Borussia Mönchengladbach, a team that would come to figure prominently in the club's history. The first leg took place at Anfield on 9 May. Well, at least that was the plan! The weather was atrocious, but the match kicked off on time. After twenty-seven minutes in torrential rain, play became impossible, and the referee took the players off the pitch. After frantic discussions, it was decided that the match would be replayed the next day. I was told to announce that anyone on the standing terraces would be asked to pay ten pence to get in the following night. Obviously, it was impossible to refund the cash they'd paid on the way in (there were no tickets issued to those standing on the terraces in those days), and the club couldn't let everyone in for free the following night. Imagine the chaos!

By the time kick-off arrived the following night, the canny Bill Shankly, having seen the German line-up in action, had made a change up front, bringing John Toshack into the team. Liverpool won 3–0 on the night, with two goals from Kevin Keegan and one from Larry Lloyd. We all left Anfield thinking the job was done, but the second leg in Germany a fortnight later saw Borussia go 2–0 up, leaving Liverpool to defend manfully, come out aggregate winners and bring home that huge cup.

I never understood the principle of the two-legged final and was relieved when UEFA finally saw sense and introduced a one-off final at a neutral venue. In this case, we left Anfield with a sense of restrained euphoria, not really knowing if we'd won the trophy or not. Two weeks later, the vast majority of the crowd went home disappointed having seen their team beaten. A fifty-fifty split in the crowd would have at least made for a better atmosphere. Nevertheless, it was still a tremendous achievement to win our first European trophy.

1973–74

The 1973–74 season kicked off with a home win against Stoke in front of nearly 54,000 optimistic fans who were hoping for more of the same success that we'd enjoyed the previous season, but it wasn't to be. I was a happy man, having become a father for the first time when my son Rob was born on 7 August.

As champions of England we were in the European Cup and stumbled through the first round 3–1 on aggregate against the Luxembourg champions Jeunesse Esch, who, frankly, should have been put to the sword. One of Shanks's 'Boot Room Boys' watched the match from my room on the TV gantry and said they were the worst team he'd ever seen at Anfield. They were, but they were so disorganized they managed to accidentally 'park the bus'. Anyway, we were through.

Next up was an eye-opening footballing lesson from Red Star Belgrade, who twice beat us 2–1. Home *and* away. The Anfield crowd, in typical fashion, clapped the Yugoslavs off the field at the end of the second leg. They have always recognized and applauded skilful players. Lessons were learnt behind the scenes and eventually it was Liverpool's brand of football that was feared and admired all over Europe.

The biggest selling single in the charts in 1973 was
'Tie a Yellow Ribbon Round the Ole Oak Tree' by Tony
Orlando and Dawn. I played it for a good while and
often wonder what the guys on the Kop thought about
it. There was no such thing as social media in those
days. If I played something so twee now, my inbox
would be full by the time I got home.

FA Cup Final – Liverpool v. Newcastle, Wembley Stadium, 4 May 1974

In many ways, 1974 was an eventful year. Leeds won the league,
but Liverpool battled their way to the FA Cup final at Wembley,
where they played Newcastle. The Liverpool team sheet from
that day is fascinating: Ray Clemence, Tommy Smith, Alec
Lindsay, Phil Thompson, Peter Cormack, Emlyn Hughes, Kevin
Keegan, Brian Hall, Steve Heighway and John Toshack; sub.
Chris Lawler. It was Bill Shankly's last great team.

Alan Kennedy and Terry McDermott for the Magpies would
both impress their opponents' backroom staff and play a huge
part in Liverpool's future. The arrogant Malcolm Macdonald,
Newcastle's number nine, had been telling anyone who would
listen that they would give Liverpool the runaround. They
didn't! Liverpool won comfortably by three goals to nil. Kevin
Keegan got two and Steve Heighway the third. Little did we
know at the time that we were watching footballing history
unfolding in front of us. Shanks was leading out the Reds for
the last time.

The weeks between the cup final and Shankly's retirement were quite traumatic for me too. In an effort to restart my career, by moving into IT, I'd gone out of my way to get myself some additional qualifications. I did three more GCE exams and one A level. Then I took a course in basic IT and passed the entrance exam for one of the industry's professional bodies. Eventually I put my new qualifications to good use and was offered a job as a trainee computer programmer in Skelmersdale. Most trainees were fresh out of college or university, but my new boss had issues with wet-behind-the-ears ex-students and was impressed when he heard that I, at the grand old age of twenty-eight, had been taking exams. I had, incidentally, been told by some charmer at the Job Centre that I was far too old to get into IT and should stick to being a shipping clerk.

I left my 'safe' clerical job on the Friday after the cup final. I'd decided that I couldn't afford to take any sort of cut in income during the close season, so I was working a few hours every week for a TV rental firm in Kirkby. My job was to call on people whose payment was in arrears and 'have a word'. Saturday afternoon was suddenly free, so I set off for my first call.

I knocked on the guy's front door and vaguely remember him objecting to being disturbed on a Saturday afternoon, but things are a bit unclear after that. Apparently, my poor wife, who was waiting for me in the car, suddenly saw me flying horizontally down the guy's front path. She didn't have a driving licence then, so I drove us back to the town centre and flagged down a passing police car. I dripped blood on his bonnet and gave him the address of my attacker. Liz persuaded me to go to A & E, where they discovered my jawbone was broken clean in two! My (ex-)customer was arrested for assault and released on bail. The following morning, Liz rang Kirkby

Police Station to inform them that I was in hospital with a broken jaw. They told her that when they arrested Chummy, he said, 'I never touched 'im – 'e must have tripped over the step on the way out!' The police went round to pay another visit. This time they ripped up the assault charge and did him for grievous bodily harm. His defence now was, 'I can't 'ave broken 'is jaw. I was wearing me carpet slippers when I kicked 'is 'ead in!' You really couldn't make it up.

I was in Walton Hospital for a week. They operated on my jaw and wired me back together again. Sadly, I missed Ron Yeats's testimonial match at Anfield the following Monday, but luckily my opposite number from Goodison was there as a spectator and he stood in for the night. My new employers were very understanding and held my new job open for a couple of weeks until I could start. I was living on painkillers for a while, but I got through nevertheless. Eventually, the guy who had hospitalized me had his day in court. He told the magistrate some cock-and-bull story about a peeping Tom in the neighbourhood. He had only been concerned about his wife's safety. This, incidentally, was the same wife who told Liz that he used to give her a good hiding on a regular basis. The magistrate swallowed all this hook, line and sinker. He was fined £50 and ordered to buy me a new pair of glasses.

I settled into my new job, which turned into a forty-year career in IT. Meanwhile, the new season approached, and I was ready to go again, having had the wires removed from my jaw. I also got back to eating solid food again. That old cliché about 'eating your dinner through a straw' had turned out to be not too far from the truth for a while!

Liverpool Football Club called a press conference on 12 July 1974, and Sir John Smith stunned the football world by announcing that Bill Shankly had indicated his intention to retire. As the news filtered out, the city of Liverpool was in shock. This was a watershed for the club. No doubt about that. From my personal standpoint, of course, Shanks had been Liverpool's manager ever since I'd started going to Anfield and was a figure whose presence had dominated the club while I'd been working there. I'd had that one run-in with him, but by and large we were like ships passing in the night along the back corridors of the old Main Stand. I was still, as a fan, in awe of the man.

I don't think anyone thought that the club could carry on at the same level. How wrong we were. The board's decision to keep the manager's job in-house and appoint Bob Paisley was a master stroke. Bob's record is the best of any manager in the English game.

Shanks's final signing before retirement was the supremely talented Ray Kennedy. He'd been playing up front for Arsenal, but at Anfield he was converted into a world-class midfielder.

1974–75

The 1974–75 season came round, and new manager Bob Paisley's first competitive game was the Charity Shield at Wembley against the league champions, Leeds United. Their manager Brian Clough was in the middle of his short (forty-four day) reign at Elland Road. Sadly, this match is remembered above all for the double sending off – Kevin Keegan of Liverpool and the late Billy Bremner of Leeds United. I was brought up never to speak ill of the dead, so I'll say no more than this: Kevin is such a nice guy that whatever Bremner did to him to provoke him to defend himself must have been horrendous. For the record, Liverpool won on penalties after a 1–1 draw.

Bob Paisley's first signing at Liverpool was a master stroke. Phil Neal came in from Northampton and went on to win a sackful of medals at club level and a huge number of England caps, captaining both club and country. He settled on Merseyside, where he still lives today.

There was another great night at Anfield on 17 September in the European Cup Winners' Cup. The unfortunate Strømsgodset of Norway shipped *eleven* goals at the hands of *eleven* different goalscorers. The joke going around the club later was that Brian Hall, the only outfield player not to score that night was on the wrong end of a tongue-lashing from his manager for not pulling his weight!

The song of 1974 was 'Waterloo', the Eurovision winner bringing Abba to the attention of the world for the first time.

The year 1975 was memorable inasmuch as my second son Laurie was born in March, and I saw Helen Reddy in concert for the first time. Twenty years later, I got to interview the great lady for my radio programme on Dune FM, but that was just a pipe dream at that time. Looking back at the end of the 1974–75 season, there were none of the great 'I was there' games. Derby County won the league for the second time in four years. Yes, Derby County.

Scanning the league table, two things stand out. First, there was no sign of Manchester United – they were in the old Second Division. Second, so many of the teams in the league back then have been languishing in the lower divisions in recent years: Derby, Stoke City, Middlesbrough, Queens Park Rangers, Leeds United, Birmingham City, Coventry City, Luton Town and Carlisle United.

The only full house at Anfield was for the visit of neighbours Everton, and both Merseyside giants finished in the top four. Liverpool were rebuilding for the post-Shankly era, and Bob Paisley's first season in charge ended trophyless, but it really was the end of the beginning and not the beginning of the end.

1975–76

When football returned after the summer break, Liverpool didn't exactly hit the ground running, losing 2–0 away at Queens Park Rangers in west London. They dug in, however, and by the turn of the year were level on points with the reinvigorated Manchester United, the Reds topping the table on goal difference. We had also despatched Hibs, Real Sociedad and Śląsk Wrocław in the UEFA Cup.

> The bestselling single of the year in 1975 was 'Bye Bye Baby' by the Bay City Rollers.

Bob Paisley, in his second season as manager, saw Liverpool narrowly clinch the league title ahead of contenders Queens Park Rangers, and so began the club's Golden Age. In the climax to the season, Liverpool needed to either win or secure a low-scoring draw against relegation-threatened Wolves. With fourteen minutes left to play, and despite constant pressure in the second half, the Reds trailed to a Steve Kindon strike for Wolves. The title was slipping away, but three late goals from Kevin Keegan, John Toshack and Ray Kennedy in front of the away support ensured Liverpool's ninth title and Bob Paisley's first trophy. Not for the last time, my celebration involved a quiet cup of tea at home with my wife. QPR captain Gerry Francis had been invited into the BBC studios to watch Liverpool's game against Wolves, and I can still see his face as he made a speedy exit at the final whistle.

In the UEFA Cup, Liverpool overcame Dynamo Dresden in the quarter-finals and Barcelona in the semis, to set up a final with Club Brugge. Liverpool won the first leg 3–2 on 28 April after being 2–0 down in the first half. Three weeks later, a 1–1 draw in the Olympiastadion in Bruges saw them lift the cup for the second time. Once again, the trophy was clinched away from home on live TV, so there was a low-key celebration at home. I heard a story that Tommy Smith was in a state of collapse after carrying the UEFA Cup on a lap of honour. I'm lucky enough to have held that trophy – it's very heavy. I imagine Tommy was exhausted!

The emergence of Phil Neal, Phil Thompson and Ray Kennedy in the Liverpool side saw them make their England debuts in the Centenary International against Wales on 24 March 1976. Also in the side were Ray Clemence and, captaining England for the first time, Kevin Keegan. Those five would go on to play for the national team for many years to come.

The bestseller of 1976 was the super-cute Eurovision winner 'Save Your Kisses for Me' by Brotherhood of Man.

1976–77

In all kinds of ways, 1977 was a *very* eventful year. I spent a lot of time in the IT department of the *Manchester Evening News*, installing their first computerized advertising system. The hours were long, and the travelling was a pain. I went through four rush hours a day sometimes, getting out of Liverpool and into Manchester, then repeating the process in reverse at night. My Liverpool duties meant that I had some hair-raising journeys from central Manchester to Anfield late in the afternoon. And I was the brunt of more than my fair share of banter, especially when United beat us at Wembley in the FA Cup final.

Looking back, I wonder how I squeezed my daily life into twenty-four hours. Even now I regularly watch *Traffic and Travel* on the breakfast news while shaking my head and wondering how the hell Liz and I coped. But we did. And we raised three great kids of whom I am immensely proud.

There were more complications too. One night I was rushing to the car park in Manchester's Quay Street in a desperate bid to get home at a civilized time. My kidney donor card must have fallen out of my pocket. A clerk from the Manchester Magistrates

Court near the multistorey found it and mailed it back to me. My worried wife rang me at work when the letter arrived. She wanted to know why I was getting mail from the magistrates. I asked her to open it, thinking it might be an unpaid parking fine or some such. It wasn't – it was my donor card.

Later the same day, Liz took a call from a senior police officer at Merseyside Police headquarters. He asked her if I could phone him back, which prompted another anxious call from her while I was at work: 'What have you been up to?' Once again, the answer was, 'Nothing!' The guy who rang was in charge of a unit who were trying to cut down on pickpocketing at Anfield (which was rife) and just wanted to agree the wording of an announcement I was putting out at the next home game. Just to finish off her day, the phone rang again: 'Hi, it's Gerry Marsden!' Convinced it was a prankster, she put the phone down sharpish. But it *was* Gerry. He'd rung with a view to me playing some tracks from his new album!

European Cup Quarter-final – Liverpool v. St Etienne, Anfield, 15 March 1977

The first thing I remember about this game is the fact that I very nearly didn't make it there. Because I was working in the IT department of the *Manchester Evening News*, I was still having to negotiate the horrendous rush-hour traffic to get to Anfield. I eventually turned into Gilroy Street, heading for my usual car parking space. To my horror, there was a solid queue of people from the Kop turnstiles right across my path and down Back Rockfield Road. After waiting in the hope that someone would take pity on me, I climbed out of the car and stood on the running board. I was driving a Citroën 2CV at the time. I shouted as loud as I could for the crowd to let me through, which did the trick.

The atmosphere when I finally got inside Anfield was electric. There had been a growing feeling as the season went on that Liverpool had a genuine chance of lifting the European Cup for the first time. We had won the UEFA Cup twice in the past four seasons, and we were ready to step up to the next level. This was the second leg of the tie, and the French team held a 1–0 lead from the first leg.

We needed to score two and keep a clean sheet. Sounds simple, but it didn't work out that way. Kevin Keegan netted in the first minute, and the Kop were in cloud cuckoo land. No more goals were scored before half-time, but St Etienne came out fighting after the break and equalized: 1–1 on the night but ahead on aggregate and with that precious away goal.

With half an hour to go, Ray Kennedy scored. We were now level on aggregate, but the French side still had the advantage of the away goal, which would send them through to the semi-final if the score remained the same. With just fifteen minutes to go, the collective feeling in the ground was that our dream was about to die. What happened next is part of Liverpool history. 'Supersub' David Fairclough emerged from the dugout, and, with six minutes left on the clock, he made his now famous run and scored to put Liverpool back in the driving seat. The crowd were delirious. However, those last ten minutes were nerve-racking, a trademark of Liverpool games to this day. The final whistle eventually came, and we were through. The rest, as they say, is history!

Liverpool won the First Division that spring. By one of those ridiculous coincidences that the fixture list sometimes throws up, we played Manchester United at Anfield in the First Division on 3 May just a couple of weeks before we were due to play them again in the FA Cup final at Wembley. United fielded, shall we say, an unfamiliar line-up, no doubt resting players for the final. We only saw them off by the one goal, but a win's a win.

I was shocked when BBC commentator John Motson suddenly appeared in my room before the game. He introduced himself (unnecessarily!) and got his cameraman to record me reading out the teams before the match. The following night, I appeared on TV for the very first time. The footage is still available on the Bob Paisley DVD, and it is hysterical. I was wearing a tank top, kipper tie and spotted shirt, and I had a perm. I'm not sure how I was allowed out like that, but then again it was the seventies.

In those days, the Double involved winning the league and FA Cup in the same season. Sadly, it was Manchester United who were waiting for us, and it was they who took the cup home. No more to be said – it was a bad day at the office. Many years later, I met Tommy Docherty, United's manager at the time, and told him I could still see him skipping round the Wembley turf with the lid of the FA Cup on his head.

Back in work on the Monday morning, I was subjected, as you would expect, to a barrage of banter. As it happened, the IT project at the *Manchester Evening News* was at a critical point, so I had no choice but to turn up and smile graciously, magnanimous in defeat. Most of the ribbing was in good humour, which was just as well, as I wasn't in the best of moods. But I finally let rip later in the day. I'd taken refuge in the data-entry room, quietly keying in some coding updates. The three other people in the room were all women in their twenties. One of them broke off to talk to her colleague at the next station. She was telling the story of her weekend. Her husband, apparently, was a United fan who couldn't get a ticket for the Wembley final. He had resigned himself to watching the game on TV, unaware that his mother-in-law had been invited round for the afternoon. Conversely, she had been blissfully unaware that it was cup-final day or, indeed, that Manchester United were playing. I have no time for people like that. Fair enough, if you're not a football fan, then go and do something else and leave us dedicated fans to follow our teams. But the FA Cup final is a national event, like the Olympic Games or Wimbledon or the Grand National. The poor guy was taken aback when his ma-in-law turned up, and I gather that the atmosphere was a bit frosty.

After the interloper had gone home, the woman decided that she should invite her poor mother back again the following Wednesday night. Hubby's patience ran out at that point. My colleague now told the assembled group, who were listening enthralled, 'Apparently, there's some other football match on Wednesday.'

My blood pressure was now through the roof! I left my desk and went to hers. 'SOME OTHER FOOTBALL MATCH! SOME OTHER FOOTBALL MATCH! It's the European Cup final! The English champions playing against the German champions! On your behalf! The biggest game in club football anywhere in the world! And you think it's just SOME OTHER FOOTBALL MATCH!'

I went back to my office and waited for my boss to call me, fully expecting my P45. For whatever reason, the call never came. I have a sneaking feeling that if and when she complained, she got short shrift from her boss, who I'm absolutely sure agreed with me.

The following Wednesday, I got home from work a matter of seconds before kick-off. This was far and away the most important game in Liverpool Football Club history. We were about to cement our position in the top echelons of world football.

European Cup Final – Liverpool v. Borussia, Mönchengladbach, Stadio Olimpico, 25 May 1977

Liverpool finally arrived at the promised land – the European Cup final! A thunderbolt from Terry McDermott, a high-pressure penalty from Phil Neal and a header from Tommy Smith did the business in a 3–1 win in Rome.

Liverpool had won their first European Cup. It was almost unbelievable for someone who had been watching them for twenty years like me and must have brought even greater satisfaction to anyone who had been following Liverpool since the forties. I wished my dad, who had passed away nine years previously, could have witnessed it, although he was of the generation who thought that the FA Cup and not European silverware was the holy grail.

Back in work in Manchester the following morning, the atmosphere had completely changed. I didn't have to say a word, but I did show my face at some office windows in the building that I hadn't visited previously. 'Smug' doesn't come close!

The downside of the Rome final, of course, was the fact that Kevin Keegan was now a wanted man. He went to Hamburg in the off-season, and the feeling around Anfield was that we had lost the heart of the team. Bob Paisley, however, had other ideas. He went to Glasgow Celtic with the club cheque book and came back with Kenny Dalglish!

1977-78

In September 1977, Liverpool had several players selected for England alongside former star Kevin Keegan. The new national team manager Ron Greenwood took the sensible step of building his first side around a group of top-class players who were used to playing together. I was quietly chuffed at the number of familiar names in the squad. I've always been a proud supporter of the national team. I was born and raised in England, my parents were English, English is my native tongue and I have always lived in England. Who else would I support? I get slightly bored with the Scouse-not-English brigade. I wouldn't live anywhere else but Liverpool, and I wouldn't want to live anywhere else but England!

One last minor incident while working at the *Manchester Evening News* gave me cause for grief. I was finished for the day, so I phoned home and said, 'I'll be home in an hour!' When I got to the multistorey car park, I was held up in a queue to exit thanks to a barrier which had stuck in the down position. By the time I got out, I was thirty minutes behind schedule. There were no mobile phones in those days, so I was in a quandary. Luckily, I spotted a telephone box and phoned home to say I was late. Just as I finished the call, I saw a group of 'unfriendly' locals heading my way and realized that my car had one of those tinted signs on the windscreen (popular at the time) which said, in big letters, 'LIVERPOOL – CHAMPIONS OF EUROPE'. You would not believe the speed I got up to running back to the car! I did what they used to call a Le Mans start and flew out of Manchester as fast as my little Citroën could muster. Phew!

Hooliganism in English football was rife in that era. I have to say, though, that I hate the phrase 'football hooligan', which was (and to an extent still is) used to imply that the 'beautiful game' is the root cause of the violence. People speak as if the guys causing trouble at the weekend spend the rest of the week picking wildflowers and reading books of romantic poetry. Nothing could be further from the truth. There's a certain Neanderthal element in society that has a natural predilection for violence. They need an outlet for their violence, and that outlet needs to be clearly defined. One such outlet, of course, is the fan base of the opposing club on a match day. I know for a fact that my feelings are reciprocated at other clubs. More than once, I have walked through the middle of a brawl after a football match without any fears for my safety. The two sides were only interested in pitting their strength against each other, and very rarely were innocent parties targeted. I have never been able to understand the logic of hooligans. I just wish they'd all go away and leave the genuine football fans to get on with watching the game.

UEFA Super Cup – Liverpool v. Hamburg, Anfield, 8 December 1977

Hamburg won the Cup Winners' Cup to join Liverpool in the Super Cup. A 1–1 draw in the first leg set things up nicely for the return match at Anfield. Phil Thompson scored first then a Terry McDermott hat-trick and late shots from David Fairclough and Kenny Dalglish saw the Germans off 7–1 on aggregate. I always wondered if Kevin Keegan had second thoughts about his move to Hamburg that night!

It was Terry McDermott's birthday, so the medal and the match ball were probably the icing on his cake! My night didn't end so well, however. Liz had the family car that day, so I needed to catch a bus home. Just as my bus appeared on the horizon, there was a sudden push from the rear of the queue, and I was jolted forward. I lost my rag with the young lads behind me: 'There's no need to push – there's plenty of room on the bus!'

Then I realized what was going on. As I've mentioned, I used to make regular announcements to the Anfield crowd to warn them about pickpockets, emphasizing the need to be careful at bus stops and to never leave anything worth stealing in your back pockets. I should have taken notice. I was in a bus queue with my wallet in my back pocket! One of the young lads behind me had pushed me, his mate had lifted my coat and the third had taken my wallet. I picked on the lad nearest to me who was protesting his innocence and pulling out his empty trouser pockets to back up what he was saying. I knew what had happened and dragged him off towards the pub 100 yards away near the traffic lights, where I knew there was a payphone just inside the door. Before we got there, the traffic lights turned red, and the bus, now full, stopped. The door opened and I heard a voice shout, 'Oi! Where are you taking him?' I looked round and realized that the people on the bus were either all close personal friends of the lad I was dragging into the pub or had got the wrong end of the stick and didn't like what they were seeing. Either way, I was about to be lynched. I picked the lad up, threw him at the bus and legged it into the pub. Luckily, no one followed me and, equally luckily, I had enough change left to pay for my bus fare home.

Someone in the office told me a few days later about a similar incident on another bus in the same area. Apparently, a passenger had suddenly stood up and shouted, 'There's pickpockets on board!' A lad next to him had gone through the same routine of pulling out his trouser pockets and denying any involvement. This time, however, he got his comeuppance. A big guy at the back of the bus had come forward, picked the lad up by the lapels and, in one movement, opened the bus door and knocked him flying on to the pavement. While he'd lain there spitting out several of his teeth, his assailant had closed the bus door and told the driver to carry on: 'Get a move on, mate. I want my tea!' I always like to think that lad was the same one who took my wallet!

> Wings' iconic 'Mull of Kintyre' took the charts by storm in 1977.

Graeme Souness arrived from Middlesbrough on 10 January in one of the big transfers of 1978 – £350,000, a club record at the time. He was a terrific player, and I was pleased to see him in our ranks, although I was mindful of the fact that his arrival would probably mean the end of Ian Callaghan's career. I had been at Anfield when Ian had made his debut, the general feeling on the Kop being one of amazement that the great Billy Liddell was being replaced by this wet-behind-the-ears teenager! How little did we know. To this day, Ian is still the player with the most Liverpool appearances under his belt. But Souey was here and would make his mark in no uncertain terms.

A couple of years back, I interviewed Ian Rush at a Liverpool Supporters Club in Sweden. One of the questions from the floor that night was, 'Who was the best captain you ever played under?' Without hesitation, Ian said, 'Graeme Souness.'

Graeme was a great guy to have on your side. He took no prisoners. He made life easier for his teammates and led by example. And he was technically brilliant. He could land a pass on a sixpence. I only ever saw him with his guard down once. I was going into Liverpool Maternity Hospital when he was coming out, having just witnessed the birth of one of his children.

It wasn't long, of course, before Graeme won his first trophy as a Liverpool player. At Wembley, four months to the day after his arrival at Anfield, Liverpool took on Club Brugge in the European Cup final.

The first half was as dull as ditchwater. Brugge tried their best to snuff out Liverpool's attacks and succeeded until fifteen minutes into the second half when a Souness through ball to Kenny Dalglish was chipped over the keeper. Liz and I were sitting in the corner of the stands at that end of Wembley, and we were directly in line with the shot, the goal and Kenny's vault over the advertising hoardings with a grin as wide as the River Clyde.

Ten minutes before the end of the match, Jan Sørensen intercepted a Hansen back pass and took a shot, but thankfully he missed the target. I sat next to Alan Hansen for a game at Wembley in 1995 and told him that this moment had taken five years off my life. The match finished 1–0 – Liverpool had retained the European Cup, the first British team to do so. My abiding memory is of slumping back into my seat after the trophy presentation. I was shattered. And I had a 250-mile drive in front of me.

1978–79

The draw for the following year's European Cup was made early the next season. It couldn't happen now, but back then there was no seeding or league format, and we were drawn against the new English champions, Nottingham Forest. They were at their peak and duly dumped us out of the European Cup at the first hurdle. Much to everyone's amazement, they went on to win the competition, although Liverpool exacted revenge by retaking the English crown.

Liverpool v. Tottenham Hotspur, Anfield, 2 September 1978

By a monumental stroke of luck this was my eldest son Rob's first experience of top-division football. He was just five but was already showing an interest. I had taken him with me to one or two reserve matches and youth games, and decided that he was old enough to hit the big time. I negotiated a deal with my mate Dave (the best man at our wedding) whereby I got the tickets and he took Rob with him. That match against

Spurs was one of the standout games of my Anfield career. Spurs had just made headlines by signing two big stars from the Argentina team that had won the World Cup during the summer, Osvaldo 'Ossie' Ardiles and Ricardo 'Ricky' Villa. On paper, Tottenham looked unbeatable, but a rampant Reds side thrashed them 7–0. One of the Sunday papers used to mark players performances on a sliding scale of one to ten. That day the entire Liverpool team were marked at ten out of ten. It was a joy to watch.

In 1978, 'Grease', from the movie of the same name, was the word!

Liverpool started 1979 by struggling to get past lowly Southend United in the FA Cup after a replay. They eventually lost out to not-so-lowly Manchester United, also after a replay, at the semi-final stage. This disappointment was eclipsed by the joy of wrapping up the league title on 8 May by beating Aston Villa 3–0 at Anfield, before finishing off the season with two away wins. Interestingly, the crowd at that Villa game was only the third biggest of the season, and, as in previous years, a simple lap of honour was seen to be enough of a celebration. If memory serves, that was the season when Bob Paisley went around the dressing room casually pushing the winners' medals into players' hands. How times have changed!

1979–80

I went to see Abba in Stafford on Monday, 12 November 1979 at Bingley Hall, a huge barn-like building used for agricultural fairs, county shows and the like that had been turned into a concert venue. It was conveniently situated in the centre of England near the M6 and thrived until the purpose-built National Exhibition Centre (opened in 1976) came into its own.

I was hooked on Abba from the word go. I still rate them up there with the best all these years later and rue the day they split up. As a live band, they were amazing. Polished and professional and with bags of stage presence. If you've ever seen one of the documentaries about the history of the band, you will know that the four of them came together thanks to a series of coincidences in the same way that The Beatles did, and by the time they burst on to the world stage in 1974 they were all experienced performers. The two guys blended as composers, and the two girls' voices dovetailed perfectly. Their repertoire by the time I saw them was overflowing with some great songs. This was probably the best gig I'd ever been to until I went to see Paul McCartney at the Liverpool Arena in 2018.

Being in good seats very near the front of the auditorium for the Abba show, my eardrums took a battering from the sound system. When we got back to the car, we discovered that fog had descended, so I drove home unable to hear anything and only able to see very little – not recommended!

The big song of 1979 was 'Hot Stuff' by Donna Summer. It was the brainchild of Italian producer Giorgio Moroder, who was to loom large over the music scene for some time to come.

We won our twelfth league title in May 1980, which was some consolation for us losing in the semi-finals of the FA Cup to the eventual runners-up Arsenal after a four-game marathon. Yes, *four* games. There was no such thing as a penalty shoot-out in the FA Cup in 1980, and it took three replays before Arsenal beat us by one goal. I was at the original game at Hillsborough and the first replay but couldn't get to the other two, which was probably just as well. The two games I did actually go to were tedious, and I thought the extra games were not helping the players' energy levels in our quest to be champions again.

I probably wasn't far wrong. We more or less sealed the title by thrashing Aston Villa 4–1 in the last home match of the season but lost 1–0 to mid-table Middlesbrough in the last game. As it happened, our nearest contenders, Manchester United, lost too, but even so they would have had to win by a thirty-goal margin, such was our superior goal difference.

Liverpool also lost in the semi-finals of the League Cup to Nottingham Forest, who then lost in the final to a Wolves team led by former Liverpool captain Emlyn Hughes.

PART THREE

The Eighties

1980–81

The start of the new season in August was a welcome relief from the doom and gloom generated by the economic climate, although money worries seemed to be keeping attendances down. The league campaign would eventually prove disappointing, but the opposite applied to our European adventures. We sailed through the first two rounds of the European Cup. First, we put ten past Oulun Palloseura of Finland after a surprising draw in the away leg, followed by home and away wins and two clean sheets against Alex Ferguson's Aberdeen.

On 28 September, I went to see none other than Wonder Woman at the Empire. The theatre had been refurbished and pulled off a major coup to mark its reopening by booking *Wonder Woman* actress Lynda Carter. When we arrived thirty minutes before curtain-up, there was a queue outside the theatre, and no one was being allowed in. The reason for the hold-up was that during the sound checks a strange rumbling sound had been heard that had the sound engineers baffled. They'd tried everything they knew to find the source but had failed. The rumbling would subside, they'd have 'one last

57

test' and it would suddenly start again. Eventually, the old guy sweeping up backstage overheard them. He immediately spotted the problem: 'It's the trains, mate!' What the technical whizz-kids didn't know was that Merseyrail had just opened an underground line under the city!

Late that year, on 8 December 1980, John Lennon was murdered by Mark Chapman outside the Dakota Building in New York City, where he and Yoko had an apartment. He was forty. I remember listening to the early morning news on the BBC the following day, and I can still to this day recall the shock, the sick feeling in the pit of my stomach and the subsequent loathing for Chapman which I still hold. An evil little man had robbed the world of one of its few true stars. Forty is no age to die, and when you listen to what Paul McCartney has produced in the intervening years you can only but wonder what Lennon would have come up with.

On the Sunday afternoon following John's murder, several thousand Scousers congregated at St George's Hall. It was a disorganized and spontaneous gathering. No one seemed to know what to do, but everyone took comfort from the size of the crowd. Someone somewhere had set up speakers, and I remember '(Just Like) Starting Over' being played several times, while the crowd also sang 'She Loves You' Liz was working, so I took the boys with me. They were five and seven years old respectively and were trying their best to understand the gravity of what had happened. At least one of them did, writing an entry in his school diary which pinpointed the hot-dog stall as the highlight of the day.

Wings' 'Coming Up' was top of the pile in the US in 1980.

League Cup Final – Liverpool v. West Ham, Wembley Stadium, 14 March 1981

I'd not even considered going to this game. A workmate (John Spencer) had vaguely enquired about the chance of taking his daughter to the match, and I managed to get hold of two tickets, which the club thought were for me. He was chuffed, as was his little girl. He understood my situation. Liz was expecting our third child and was not very well. I decided to do the decent thing and stay with her rather than go to London for the match. He said that if I changed my mind at the last minute, there would be two spare seats in his car.

The best-laid plans, etc. At 4 p.m. on the eve of the game, Rob came home from school and gave me a look that I'll never forget! His teacher had demanded to know why I wasn't taking him to Wembley. I was devastated and suddenly overcome with guilt.

Because it was the night before the game, every ticket had gone, but someone up there was looking out for me, and I was saved. Liverpool reserves had a match at Anfield that night, and when I turned up, I heard the magic words, 'Are you looking for tickets, George?' Karen Manning, Bob Paisley's PA, had drawn the short straw that night and was on the Main Stand reception. In the minutes before I arrived, she had been tidying the reception desk and had discovered two tickets stuck under one of those old-fashioned blotter pads that adorned every desk in those days. The minor problem was the fact that they were top-price tickets! I tentatively asked, 'How much are they?'

'Twenty-seven pounds each!' That was a lot of money in 1981! I reached into every corner of every pocket in my jacket and coat, rummaging around for money. I had fifty-five quid! I was in, with a pound left over. I phoned Liz, and within ten minutes she'd organized for her best mate Lorraine to sit with her all day. I took up the offer of the two spare seats in John's car. We were good to go!

Up bright and early the next day, we hit the motorways and arrived at Wembley in good time. Rob was beyond excited. Seven years old and off to the magical, mystical Wembley for the first time! Sadly, the overuse of Wembley Stadium in the twenty-first century has destroyed the magic. In 2019, Spurs fans had season tickets for the place, and teams who reach the FA Cup semi-finals nowadays play at Wembley for the right to, er, play at Wembley! But in those days it was still special.

The seats were immediately behind the Royal Box – dead centre. Without actually marrying into the British royal family, you couldn't get a better view. Sadly, one person who didn't have such a good view was Bill Shankly, football royalty. Twenty minutes before kick-off there was a bit of a kerfuffle to our right and about three or four rows nearer to the pitch. People were standing, others were applauding – Shanks had arrived. And to my amazement we had better seats than he did!

The irony of the whole situation got to me, I must admit. Anyway, we settled back and enjoyed the game. Or at least until West Ham equalized Alan Kennedy's early goal and we had to go home empty-handed. Justice was done the following week when we won the replay. Nevertheless, it was a great day out for father and son.

European Cup Final – Liverpool v. Real Madrid, Parc des Princes, 27 May 1981

Three years after grinding out victory against Club Brugge at Wembley, Liverpool were back in the European Cup final – this time in Paris. My friend Dave and I were on the lookout for a cheap and fast trip to Paris for the game. I had a young family, and he had a wife who just didn't understand the desire of the diehard Liverpool fan to actually follow his team when they reached a big final. Dave had been to Wembley with me one time, and she'd never quite got over that, so her stress levels when we wanted to go to Paris were on a par with what Neil Armstrong's wife's were when Neil set foot on the moon. I think she crossed the Mersey once to visit someone on the Wirral but had to lie down in a dark room for quite a while afterwards.

Luckily, Peter Robinson came to my rescue. He rang me at work one day and said that UEFA wanted me to go to Paris to make any announcements if they were needed in English. Was I available? Too right I was available. Dave had given up on the trip anyway, so I think he was quite relieved to be off the hook.

I was told to report to Liverpool Airport on the morning of the game. I was booked into a nice hotel near the Gare du Nord and, once there, the French Football Association would look after me.

My flight included some office staff, a few reserve-team players and a mishmash of celebrities, plus Bill Shankly. I found myself standing in the departure lounge trying in vain to make small talk with Shanks, John Peel and John Gorman from the band The Scaffold. When we boarded, I was about four rows from the front, directly behind Phil Thompson's wife. Bill Shankly was a few rows further back. It was fascinating to watch people coming aboard, looking for a spare seat. Several people headed for the empty chair next to Shanks, realized who was in the seat next to it and scurried past. Everyone was in awe of him, and most people would have loved to have spoken to him, but they didn't have the bottle to sit next to him. The last man to board was an ordinary-looking bloke, a bit nervous, and he soon realized there was only one seat left, right next to the great man. After landing in Paris, we were directed to various coaches, and I found myself on the same one as John Peel. And Bill Shankly.

I was dropped off at my hotel, while Peely and Shanks went further into the city centre. John Peel told me a few years later, by which time I'd got to know him, that a highlight of his life was carrying Bill's bag into his hotel. I had the opposite experience, as Shanks (unbeknownst to me) followed me off the plane into the car park at Liverpool Airport the following day, and I was told off by Liz for not carrying his luggage!

In my hotel, I went through the usual rigmarole: checked in, unpacked, showered, changed and went down to the lobby to hopefully find whoever it was from the French FA who was detailed to 'look after me'. I sat in the hotel lobby for a while, twiddling my thumbs and watching several groups leave in various minibuses and taxis. I suddenly realized that nearly everyone had gone. As luck would have it, the last group were guests of the club's shirt sponsors, KP Nuts, and their managing director, who knew me, so I was able to blag a lift to the stadium. Phew!

I was dropped off as near as was possible and got my bearings. There were three rings of security around the Parc des Princes. The inner ring was made up of the normal stadium stewards and security staff. The next was a ring of gendarmes and, finally, the outside ring was manned by the CRS – the French riot police! One particular guy was directly between me and the alleyway that led to the stadium. I don't speak more than a little tourist French, and I struggled to make any sort of impression on him. Eventually he got bored with me and cocked his rifle. Suddenly I had a bayonet pointing in my direction. I came to the conclusion that I was flogging the proverbial dead horse. Looking at my watch, I decided that my best chance of seeing any football that night was to head to the Metro station in the far corner of the square and get the underground to the Gare du Nord in the hope that I could get back to my hotel room before kick-off.

Halfway across the square, I was surrounded by a few Liverpool lads in their late teens and early twenties. One of them grabbed my lapels: 'Listen, froggie. We want tickets. *Billets. Vous comprendez*, like?'

I was speechless for a moment. Then I replied, 'Sorry, mate. I'm in the same boat as you. I can't get in either.'

He let go of my lapels. 'Sorry, pal. We thought you were a French ticket tout.'

I had a decision to make now. My friend with the bayonet or some irate Scousers with no tickets! I decided to head back to the CRS. Luckily for me, I picked the exact moment when the officer guarding that particular route to the stadium chose to have a cigarette break. And I had found my check-in receipt from my hotel inside my passport. Clearly printed on it was 'George Sephton – Liverpool FC'. I waved this under the nose of the gendarme who appeared to be in charge at the second ring. It did the trick, and he let me through. Next step was getting past the barbed wire and stadium security. Another stroke of luck: I saw the son of one of the club directors walking towards me. I said that if he bumped into Peter Robinson or the chairman, could he please tell them I was stuck outside. Five minutes later, Peter emerged, muttering under his breath about the French FA. He gave me a lapel badge which said 'UEFA – Access All Areas'. I was in.

After all the shenanigans outside the stadium, I got to my post (standing next to a mic stand at the end of the players' tunnel) just in time to see the kick-off. The local announcer didn't speak English but made it clear he thought I'd been having a nap at the hotel rather than heading for the stadium. I made it equally clear that I wasn't impressed at the insinuation. The bottom line, though, was that the hassle was all worthwhile, as we came home with our third European Cup!

On 28 July 1981, there was a leaving do at Tommy Smith's nightclub for Karen Manning, Bob Paisley's PA who had found me the cup tickets. Karen had been Bob's right-hand woman since 1974, but she was off to work in London and would be missed by everyone at the club. She was (and still is!) one of those people who are universally liked – attractive, vivacious and wonderful company. By absolute coincidence, her party was the night before the wedding of Prince Charles and Lady Diana Spencer. All in all, a good time was had.

The importance of the night became apparent when we found out that the great Ray Clemence was leaving for Tottenham Hotspur. I'm not usually privy to such things, but I think he wanted a longer contract than Liverpool were prepared to offer him at the time. He was fast approaching his thirty-third birthday, and this was before the days of the big-money footballer. He needed to set himself up for the future. Shortly after retiring from a successful career with Spurs, he joined the staff and went on to enjoy a stellar coaching career. He is still the best keeper I've seen in a Liverpool shirt, and Liverpool have a history of great keepers: Tommy Lawrence, Clem, Pepe Reina, Alisson Becker and, of course, Bruce Grobbelaar! Sadly, I'm not (contrary to popular belief) old enough to have seen Elisha Scott.

Clem was also one of the unluckiest keepers in football. His England career ran in parallel to Peter Shilton's. At any other period, Clem would have certainly accumulated a much larger number of England caps. But as far as Liverpool were concerned, he was the main man. He was renowned for his concentration levels, which are vital when playing behind a rock-solid defence. He would often be unoccupied for long periods during a game but would always be switched on when needed. His reactions were lightning quick, and his defence were inspired by having him behind them. He also had the knack of saving vital penalties. As it turned out, the clean sheet against Real Madrid in the European Cup final had been his last act as a Liverpool player. When Ray passed away in November 2020 the deluge of tributes in the media was incredible. The same words and phrases cropped up over and over again: 'respected', 'loving family man', 'talent', 'ability', 'Liverpool's best', 'great' and so on. His funeral was a quiet ceremony due to the Covid restrictions in force at the time but Ray's wife Vee, God bless her, sent me a private link so that I could watch the ceremony online. I was very privileged but it was a privilege I sincerely wish I hadn't needed.

That night in Smithy's club was also my first encounter with Bruce Grobbelaar, and I was overwhelmed. He is one of *the* great characters in football. I'd heard stories about his antics at the Melwood training ground, where he was said to have hung upside down from a crossbar and shouted to Clem that his days were numbered! In my case, I wanted to say hello and make sure I was pronouncing his surname right. His response was to tell me to refer to him as the 'Jungle Man from Africa'!

Bruce's backstory is unbelievable. Born in Zimbabwe, he played for a club side in Bulawayo before crossing the border to join Durban City in South Africa when he was in his late teens. During national service in Zimbabwe a year later, he saw active duty in the Bush War. That experience would be enough to harden any man. After the army, he signed for Vancouver Whitecaps, and while on loan from them to Crewe was recruited by Liverpool. He spent fourteen years with the club, and to this day he's a genuine favourite with Liverpool fans everywhere.

1981–82

Every dad wants a daughter. My wish was granted on 14 August 1981, the tenth anniversary of my start at Anfield, when Kim Rachel Sephton came into our lives! The Toxteth riots were just coming to an end at that time. They had started the previous month when police had carried out what appeared to be a straightforward arrest, intercepting a motorcyclist in the area. However, a confrontation had followed between some locals, a crowd gathered and things got exponentially out of hand. Liverpool Maternity Hospital was not far from the epicentre of the trouble on the streets. The riots themselves were largely under control by then, although organized protests were still going on when Kim was born and caused me and my two sons some problems when we all visited Liz and Kim the following day.

Around that time, I was working as a freelance analyst/programmer. My previous contract had come to an end just before Kim was born, and I didn't immediately put myself up for any more work on the grounds that I was better off staying at home for a while, helping out with the kids. I was eventually offered a three-month contract in Grimsby.

Grimsby Town were then in the old Second Division, and they had only one midweek home game during the time I was there, against Norwich City. I wrote a polite note to the club secretary explaining who I was and what I was doing in Grimsby. Would it be possible, I asked, to have a look around behind the scenes? No response.

Come the day of the game and I'd still heard nothing, but my client said he was going to Blundell Park to watch the match. Did I fancy it? I said yes but then decided there was nothing to be lost by following up on my letter to Grimsby Town, so I rang them up. I got as far as my name and the word 'Liverpool' before the lady on the switchboard cut me short and said there would be two tickets waiting for me on the gate that night – result! When we arrived at the stadium, I found someone on the main gate with a box of tickets. Two of them had my name on them. We were in! When I pulled the two tickets out of the envelope, I read the magic words 'Directors' Box'. Things were definitely looking up. My companion, a lifelong Grimsby follower who was used to standing on the terraces, was on cloud nine.

I have to admit that we made the most of the hospitality, and we had a great view from the middle of the second row of the box. The eyes of the press boys were on Grimsby forward Kevin Drinkell, who was the centre of transfer speculation, although he didn't actually move on from Grimsby until 1985, when, coincidentally, he ended up at Norwich City. In front of us in the stand was Joe Royle. At the time, he was a Norwich player but was injured and approaching the end of his playing days. The following year, he was appointed manager at Oldham Athletic and subsequently returned to Goodison Park to manage his home-town club Everton. It was, all in all, an enjoyable night out in the autumn sunshine.

The shine, however, was taken off it the following day when I arrived back down to earth with a bump at my office near the docks, where I was always greeted by the overwhelming smell of fish. The local paper was spread out on my desk: 'Scouts from several clubs were out in force at Blundell Park last night – even the mighty Liverpool had a representative in the directors' box!'

I went pale. The lady on the switchboard had put two and two together and got five! She thought I was one of Liverpool's scouting staff! I spent several days in a nervous state, expecting to get an irate phone call from Anfield, but I don't think news of my visit ever got back to them. At least, if it did, nothing was ever said.

I moved to a much nicer guest house on the seafront in Cleethorpes for the last couple of weeks of my contract in Grimsby. My room at the front of the building even had a balcony overlooking the North Sea. It was like being on holiday – albeit without my family. My mood, however, was shattered on my first morning there. My wife and one of my children had some sort of horrible bug, and I was on the verge of going home to help out. After an almost sleepless night, I woke up early, just in time to hear the 6 a.m. news read by Radio 4's Brian Perkins: 'Bill Shankly, the ex-manager of Liverpool Football Club, has died.'

I'm not sure I can find adequate words to describe how I felt. I'd thought Shanks was invincible! He was like everyone's favourite uncle: loved, revered, admired, idolized and with the entire Red half of the city of Liverpool forever in his debt. And he'd been at Anfield ever since I'd been going there. I hoped for a minute this was one of those nightmares where you wake up and find that everything's fine after all. It wasn't.

Liverpool had lost one of its adopted sons and one of its most respected citizens.

The following weekend, Liverpool played Swansea at Anfield. It should have been a happy occasion, because ex-Liverpool star John Toshack was the Swansea manager, and he had worked miracles getting them promoted from the lower reaches of the Football League. We were, of course, going to have a minute's silence to respect Shanks's memory. Silences have been replaced nowadays by applause on most occasions. I feel this is less respectful than silence but easier for the poor stadium announcer to manage and less susceptible to the problems caused by the odd drunk, heckler or disrespectful latecomer. The Swansea game was a case in point. I called for the minute's silence to begin and the crowd went quiet. The two teams and their managers stood to attention. John Toshack then stunned us all by removing his Swansea tracksuit top to reveal a Liverpool shirt. It was a wonderful gesture, but then I would have expected nothing less from such a man. It was at that point that things started going wrong. Many Swansea fans were still in Anfield Road, waiting to get into the away end. They were not used to having to queue to get into a match or, for that matter, participating in a great occasion like this. The Welsh supporters were blissfully unaware of what was happening inside the stadium and were enjoying their day out, chanting and singing as you would expect. The Liverpool fans became aware of the noise and took it as a lack of respect for our late manager. Booing was suddenly heard from the Reds fans, and the minute's silence basically collapsed in chaos. It was very disappointing.

Shanks's funeral took place at his local church in West Derby shortly afterwards. It was the saddest of sad days. Liverpool would never be the same again.

All in all, 1981 was a mixed bag for music. It was the age of synth-pop, New Wave and the New Romantics. Adam and the Ants were big, as were the likes of Soft Cell, The Human League, Orchestral Manoeuvres in the Dark and Roxy Music. And, of course, Depeche Mode. Pop stars were feted for their costumes as much as for their music, especially as the music video was now becoming prevalent. The average age of my audience at Anfield at the time of writing, which I believe is mid to late thirties, suggests that their favourite music probably falls slap bang in the eighties and nineties.

Shakin' Stevens's revival of the fifties classic 'This Ole House' was the UK's top seller in 1981.

League Cup Final – Liverpool v. Tottenham Hotspur, Wembley Stadium, 13 March 1982

This was a memorable day out for yours truly. I'd decided to take Laurie (a week on from his seventh birthday), and my friend Dave Callaghan came with us, too. Dave was muttering darkly about 'children of that age going to Wembley', but I told him that if he didn't like it, it was tough, because it was my car and my tickets. On the eve of the match, I'd had a visit from an agent from the company who leased my car. The salesman who'd supplied me had lied, and the deal was not the one that I thought I'd agreed to. After a long conversation, I'd given up and said he could have his car back. I arranged to drop it off in Liverpool the following Monday night after work. Unfortunately for the leasing company, we beat Tottenham 3–1, and when we got back to the car after the game we discovered that several pairs of hob-nailed boots had been to work on it. All four doors were now concave, as was the boot. Dave was mortified, and I was taken aback at the sight of my nice motor, which was less than six months old. On the upside, it wasn't my problem any more. We had something to eat and then, for reasons I can't remember, stopped off at Downing Street before heading home. I put the back seats down, and Laurie slept all the way home. On the Monday evening, I called into the company's office in Paradise Street, handed over the keys and headed for the train. I paused at a safe distance to watch the salesman's face when he saw the state of what had once been a company asset.

The match itself was a classic Liverpool comeback: a goal down after eleven minutes and about to lose out when the midfield master Ronnie Whelan scored an equalizer three minutes from time. We dominated extra time, and Ronnie scored again before Ian Rush finished the job off with a minute to go. Two months later, Liverpool rounded off the league championship by the same score against the same opponents. In August, we returned to Wembley, and a Rush goal won us the Charity Shield, again against Spurs, who must have been sick of the sight of us, especially Ray Clemence, who was now in the Tottenham goal and would have wanted to do better against his old team. That was the first match of Bob Paisley's last season.

Significant tunes in 1982 included 'Centerfold' by The J. Geils Band and 'Ebony and Ivory' by Stevie Wonder and Paul McCartney.

1982–83

Bob Paisley was the most successful English football manager of all time. During nine years in charge at Liverpool, he won honours at a rate of 2.2 per season. Brought up in Hetton-le-Hole in the north-east of England, he played for the famous old amateur club Bishop Auckland and arrived at Liverpool in 1939, but the Second World War interrupted his football career and he didn't make his debut until 1946. That season he won a championship medal, but who knows what more he could have achieved if it hadn't been for Adolf Hitler! Bob retired as a player in 1954 and became reserve-team coach and club physiotherapist. When Bill Shankly took over as manager in 1959, he made Bob his right-hand man. In 1974, Shanks retired and Bob reluctantly accepted the manager's job. He retired from that role in 1983 and was succeeded by Joe Fagan. He died in 1996, aged seventy-seven, after suffering from Alzheimer's disease for several years.

Bob was the quiet man in the back-room team, and I can't remember him saying anything other than a brief hello to me during his time at the club. I did, however, have one memorable encounter with him after he'd retired. I managed to broker a speaking engagement for him at the Lancashire Egg Producers Association up in Chorley, where a good friend of mine was the chairman. I was busy getting ready to move house the next morning, so my friend's son collected Bob from his home in Liverpool, and I turned up later on to take him home. That hour-long journey provided me with a fascinating insight into the great man, and I still treasure my time alone with him. Incidentally, Bob was a very canny after-dinner speaker. Apparently, he got to his feet and went straight into a Q and A session. The locals were delighted, and he didn't have to prepare a speech.

My two sons had attended a Bobby Moore Soccer School course in Liverpool in 1982, and they signed up again in 1983. I was working in Manchester at the time and couldn't get out of work to come and watch them, but Liz was happy to chauffeur them back and forth every day. Each night I'd get a report from her and the lads on the day's events. The phrase 'Alan the coach' popped into the conversation intermittently.

I left work at lunchtime on the Friday and drove over to watch the last session and the presentations. I parked up and made my way towards the pitches, where I could see a lot of youngsters playing football in the sun. When I spotted Liz, I noticed a familiar face behind her. I was shocked. 'That's Alan A'Court!' I said.

She looked around, unmoved: 'Yes, Alan the coach.'

I was almost speechless: 'But that's Alan A'Court!'

Her expression still didn't change. All week I'd been unaware that my children were being coached by one of the Liverpool greats.

Alan A'Court was my dad's hero, up there alongside Billy Liddell. I didn't see much of him as a player, as he was nearing the end of his career when I started watching the Reds. I had, however, met him once when I was in senior school. He was good friends with my maths teacher, who persuaded him to pay us a visit. Now, at last, I had the chance to have a long chat, although I wished I'd taken some time off work to go with my sons once or twice during the week.

The big tune of 1983 was 'Every Breath You Take' by The Police.

1983–84

Nineteen *Eighty-Four*, the dystopian novel by George Orwell, describes a world in which the general population are the victims of perpetual war, government surveillance and propaganda. Luckily, the real 1984 was in fact a vintage year for football and music on Merseyside, with Liverpool winning a magnificent three trophies. 'Smokin'' Joe Fagan had taken over the managerial hot seat when Bob Paisley retired, and after a stuttering start to the season, went on to resurrect the glory days.

On the music front, 1984 was the year that saw the arrival of Frankie Goes to Hollywood and Orchestral Manoeuvres in the Dark, and Paul McCartney was making waves with his solo material. Elsewhere, Stevie Wonder's classic 'I Just Called to Say I Love You' was released, and Wham!, Duran Duran and Queen were huge. Looking through the list of the top 100 tunes of that year, I can still sing along with all of them quite happily. I defy you to try that with recent charts. It may be that the eighties were the peak of pop music as we know it.

League Cup Final – Liverpool v. Everton, Wembley Stadium, 25 March 1984

The first leg of the Treble was the League Cup. This was the year of the famous all-Merseyside final when Liverpool and Everton fans headed south to Wembley to demonstrate to the rest of the footballing world exactly how to put a local rivalry to one side and actually enjoy playing your nearest rivals. The TV companies were astonished to see Reds and Blues travelling in the same cars, coaches and trains together. After the build-up to the big day – the colourful procession down the motorway to Wembley and all the hype – it was sad that two hours of football couldn't produce a goal, the destination of the trophy finally being decided by a single Graeme Souness goal at Maine Road in Manchester three days later. From my point of view, it was nice to enjoy a day out at Wembley with my wife and two sons. The downside was that the traffic coming home was so dense that we realized before we got anywhere near the motorway that we had no chance of getting to my stepmother's house to collect our two-and-a-half-year-old daughter before midnight. In fact, the traffic was moving so slowly that Liz had time to leave the car, find a phone box, ring my stepmother and get back in while we had moved no more than fifty yards.

European Cup Final – Liverpool v. AS Roma, Stadio Olimpico, 30 May 1984

Liverpool wrapped up the league in the spring, and there was a feeling of euphoria around the club and the city. The bleak days of the riots were behind us, and the Liverpool International Festival was opened in May by Her Majesty the Queen. The infamous 'managed decline' of Liverpool by Thatcher's government had been abandoned (or at least swept under the carpet!), and Michael Heseltine was dubbed 'Minister for Merseyside' to help regenerate the place. The world-famous Albert Dock was being developed and things were on the up. If I think back to 1984, I have an overriding image of day after day of bright sunshine.

Next, all eyes were focused on the Olympic stadium in Rome for the European Cup final against AS Roma at their home ground. Having the final of the biggest club competition at the home stadium of one of the participants is a recipe for trouble. I can't believe that a plan B couldn't have been put in place to prevent that eventuality, but UEFA obviously weren't fazed by it.

In the run-up to the final, I was phoned at work by Peter Robinson. UEFA wanted me to attend again, but after the trouble I'd had in Paris three years previously, it was decided that I would to go to the Liverpool team hotel on the afternoon of the game and travel in on the team bus. This was every schoolboy's dream, short of actually playing for the Reds!

I was determined to make the most of my free time on the day of the final, so a couple of us managed to take in the Colosseum before heading up to St Peter's Basilica. Late afternoon, I caught a cab to the team hotel and found Peter Robinson. When the time came to set off for the stadium, we all piled aboard the coach. I didn't really know where to sit but settled for a seat at the front on the opposite side to the driver.

When it was nearly time to leave, the Aussie midfielder Craig Johnston came and sat next to me. He was beyond nervous to the point of being seriously distracted. I tried to start a conversation with him, but he spent most of the journey trying to remember if he had sorted out his mates' tickets. I was trying to take some photographs but was frankly embarrassed to use my 'cheap and cheerful' camera when I knew that Craig was a dedicated photographer who had professional-standard equipment at home. I had a lot of time for Craig. He wasn't the most naturally talented of footballers, but he more than made up for that with his work ethic and would run for ever to help his team.

Driving to the stadium, we had an escort of motorcycle outriders, and every so often we would stop at traffic lights, which is when the locals, who were lining the pavement in some places, would peer into the coach. They were excitedly scanning the occupants, and one by one recognized the likes of Ian Rush, Kenny Dalglish and Alan Hansen. Once or twice their prying eyes settled on me, and I swear that some of them went home in the belief that one of Liverpool's squad was overweight and in no condition to play ninety minutes.

There was a point in the journey when the coach reached the top of one of the seven hills and the Stadio Olimpico suddenly appeared in the distance. The team, who had been having a sing-song to calm their nerves, suddenly went very quiet. We descended to the stadium and decamped to the tunnel leading towards the dressing rooms. The playing squad all dumped their bags on benches and headed off to the pitch to get a feel of the surface and to soak up the atmosphere. At this point, I wished them good luck and turned around, hoping to find some clues as to where I would be spending the evening. While I was doing this, I heard a voice behind me: 'Where are you going now?' It was the diminutive guy in a UEFA blazer who had been on the coach.

'Well,' says I, 'I presume I'll be on the TV gantry or wherever the public address system is?'

'No. No. You have no pass – you must leave!'

I was getting slightly annoyed by this time. 'Look,' I said. 'You've just sat next to me all the way into Rome without saying a word. I don't have a pass. Because your lot messed up in Paris three years ago, that's why I was on the coach! So that I didn't need a pass!'

'Wait one minute!' he said, glaring at me before he headed off. I assumed he'd gone to check my story.

When he'd gone, Tom Saunders, who was sitting alone in the dressing room, called me over and produced a small wad of tickets from his inside pocket. Tom was another of Bill Shankly's trusted 'Boot Room Boys'. He was a teacher by profession and had been heavily involved in schoolboy football at local and national levels. Shanks was a great one for spotting talent and had persuaded Tom to join Liverpool full-time as youth development officer in 1968.

'Take this,' he said, putting a ticket in my hand. 'If this clown does throw you out, at least you'll see the game!'

At this point, my UEFA antagonist reappeared, accompanied by a member of the Carabinieri, who, sadly for me, was armed. He repeated his earlier speech, this time with back-up! 'You must go out!' I didn't argue. There was no point, and in any case I had that ticket from Tom, which was now safe in my inside jacket pocket!

I made my way out of the stadium and into the crowds milling round in the car park. As I was trying to fathom out where I needed to go next, I bumped into Jim Kennefick, the trusted lieutenant of Peter Robinson. Jim had previously worked for Aer Lingus, but in 1984 he was working for the Reds in a job which involved keeping the team's sponsors happy. He wondered aloud why I was outside in the car park when I was supposed to be inside and near a microphone. I told him the tale and showed him my ticket.

'Typical,' he said. 'Tell you what, give me that ticket and you take this.' 'This' turned out to be his lapel badge, which said 'UEFA – Access All Areas'! I pinned it to my jacket and headed back inside, thanking him as I went. This time nobody tried to stop me! The TV gantry was up several flights of steps, but I made it in time to introduce myself to the resident announcer and settle down to watch the game.

In the fifteenth minute, Phil Neal scored the opener when he pounced on an uncleared ball following a cross by Craig Johnston. Roma equalized just before half-time and consequently came out the stronger in the second half, but Mark Lawrenson was in top form, helping to repel the Italian's attacks. Steve Nicol replaced Johnston in the seventy-second minute and could have won it in the eighty-fifth minute, but his shot was saved. Extra time was scoreless, so it was on to a penalty shoot-out. At this point, my knees went to jelly, and I had to find a seat at the back of the gantry to recover my composure. A confident-looking Nicol put the first penalty over the crossbar, and Roma took the lead. Phil Neal equalized before Bruno Conti shot over the crossbar. Graeme Souness and Ubaldo Righetti converted their respective penalties, and then Ian Rush scored his, making it 3–2. Francesco Graziani was next up. While he prepared to take his kick, Bruce Grobbelaar famously wobbled his legs in the Liverpool goal, hoping to distract him. He succeeded! Graziani blazed his penalty over the crossbar, and Alan Kennedy stepped up to score the winner. I've heard Alan swear at several dinners since that he didn't volunteer to take a penalty. His version of events is that Joe Fagan said, 'Are you OK?' and he thought Joe was asking him how he was feeling after a gruelling encounter in the Roman sun. Joe actually meant, 'Are you OK to take a penalty?'

When Alan scored, I leapt from my seat, suddenly full of adrenalin. By the time I'd come back to my senses, every Italian on the gantry had disappeared, including my host in the announcer's room. As soon as the trophy was presented, I had to get to the stadium car park and find the coach that was taking me to the airport. My luggage had been loaded up by my room-mate at the hotel. For the first mile or two driving away from the Stadio Olimpico, we had to crouch below the level of the windows on the coach. Several missiles headed our way and one, luckily, bounced *off* my window. We flew straight home to Liverpool, and I was delighted to find my entire family waiting for me at the airport. They, like me, were too excited for words that we had won the European Cup again.

1984–85

The summer was spent basking in the warm glow of being European champions, but when the new season came around, I felt that there was a slightly muted atmosphere at Anfield. The first home game was played on a sunny day in August, and the whole place had the feeling of a pavement café. I remember telling someone at the time that I thought the problem was down to the success we'd had the previous season. Watching Liverpool in those days was like reading a crime thriller for the umpteenth time – you basically knew what the ending was going to be. We would control the game and come out on top. Or at least that's what we thought. In fact, the 1984–85 season would have a tragic ending that none of us could have foreseen.

1984 was the year of 'Ghostbusters' by Ray Parker Jr.

In the lead-up to our traumatic European Cup final in Brussels, we had to watch Everton be crowned champions and even had the ignominy of being beaten by them at Goodison Park in the last league match of the season. This was followed by a remarkable night in Rotterdam when Everton beat Rapid Vienna to win the UEFA Cup Winners' Cup. My attitude was simple. I'd rather Everton had that level of success than some of our other rivals. When push comes to shove, they're still a city club after all, and because of that a lot of my friends are supporters. I went to school with their chairman Bill Kenwright for goodness' sake.

On the day of my trip to Brussels, my family came to the airport to see me off. While I was collecting my travel documents at the desk, Rob was standing behind me. The lady at the desk leaned over and looked at him with a benign smile. 'Are you going with your dad?'

Up to that moment, the thought of him going hadn't occurred to either of us. Nevertheless, his face fell. I promised him that 'next time' he would go with me. Of course, the ban from European football that was placed on Liverpool following this final meant that we didn't get the chance till 2001 in Dortmund, and by that time he was a grown man and working in California.

European Cup Final – Liverpool v. Juventus, Heysel Stadium, 29 May 1985

I am still heartily sick about people pontificating about the Heysel Stadium disaster. More than once I've had to look someone in the eye and say, 'Were you there?' The answer is usually, 'No.' But I *was* there! In 2004, the disaster was described by the newly appointed UEFA chief executive Lars-Christer Olsson as 'the darkest hour in the history of the UEFA competitions'.

As in 1981 and 1984, I got a call from Anfield to say that UEFA wanted me to be at the final. I was to fly out on the morning of the game, find my way to the team hotel, which was quite central, and again travel to the stadium on the team coach.

On the team coach, I was sitting in front of Peter Robinson and Chris Pile, our substitute keeper, was behind him. Chris was just seventeen years old and would not have expected to find himself anywhere near the squad for the European Cup final. Sadly, the regular reserve keeper Bob Bolder had been injured in a match at Bradford a few days earlier, and there was no chance of Liverpool being allowed to bring in another keeper as cover, so Chris was lumbered with the job! Or perhaps he was lucky? I suppose it depends on your point of view.

Joe Fagan, just about to end his long career with Liverpool, came and sat down next to the lad: 'How's this for an experience?' Joe was beaming, but Chris didn't look convinced. I remember his face was bright red.

As soon as we parked the coach and headed into the stadium, the omens were not good. In Rome, the bus could park inside the stadium, out of sight of the crowds, but here it was about fifty yards away from the stadium entrance. Fans were lined up outside but didn't seem to be stewarded, and there was little or no police presence. If one of those supporters had been hostile, he or she could easily have got to the players and caused some damage. On top of this, the Liverpool dressing room was in a dreadful state – ancient and unkempt. I was unimpressed.

The guy assigned to look after me escorted me along the touchline, up the stairs and into the PA announcer's room. In there I found the Heysel Stadium's own announcer and my opposite number from Turin. It was immediately obvious that things were not going to go well. The room was in the corner of the stadium between the Main Stand and the terracing where the main body of the Italian fans were. I was looking down at the guys in black-and-white scarves. The first thing to say is that they were wearing their scarves round their faces like masks and not round their necks like usual football fans. Then I realized that they were split into small groups. Some were prising chunks of brick out of the crumbling walls. Some were systematically breaking the crush barriers. They were tooling up for a fight! I was horrified.

Sometime later, a guy ran from the Italian terraces and fired what turned out to be a starting pistol into the air. Then a scuffle happened at the far end of the ground. Italian fans charged at Liverpool fans, who retreated. Some Liverpool fans then charged back towards the Italians, who were pressed up against a wall that was presumably of the same quality as the rest of the squalid place and collapsed under the strain.

I looked on helplessly. It was painfully obvious that people had been hurt in the process, but a few minutes later we were told that a body had been found in the rubble. Then a few more minutes passed, and we discovered that five Italians had now been declared dead. Eventually the number rose to thirty-nine.

I was traumatized. My Italian counterpart was sobbing uncontrollably. Then another message arrived to say that UEFA were holding a meeting somewhere in the depths of the Main Stand. I'm not sure about the timings after that, but roughly half an hour or so passed before a UEFA official entered our room accompanied by a policeman. It should be said that the police presence around the Heysel Stadium was small, to say the least, until the trouble started.

The UEFA guy came straight for me. He glared at me, almost nose to nose. 'You,' he said through gritted teeth. 'You will tell your people that we have decided to play the game, but if anyone else comes on the pitch, the referee will abandon the game right away!'

I looked him in the eye. 'Are you mad?' This was not well received. 'If you do that, as soon as someone scores, the other team's fans will be on the pitch trying to get the game abandoned!'

'Do as you are told!'

I said one word: 'No!'

At this point, he beckoned the policeman forward. I realized the policeman was armed and wondered how threatening he might become.

'DO AS YOU'RE TOLD!'

Again, my reply was simple: 'NO!'

I told him that there had already been one bloodbath and I wouldn't be party to another. Just as I was wondering how far I would be pushed, Phil Neal appeared with his Juventus counterpart Gaetano Scirea. The two captains had been despatched to our room to address their respective followings. Luckily for me, Phil had heard the exchange between me and the UEFA man and laid into him. Whatever Phil said carried more weight than anything I could say, and it did the trick. The threat to abandon the game was dropped.

The bare facts of the game are quite straightforward. Juventus took the lead in the fifty-sixth minute when Michel Platini scored the only goal from a dodgy penalty given away by Gary Gillespie.

Watching the game was a living nightmare, one of those where you hope to wake up sweating and frightened only to realize that what has just happened isn't real. What I would have given to wake up and find myself in my own bed at home! Trying to concentrate on the actual football was nigh impossible. Heysel had a broad running track, and it resembled a battle scene from a war movie. The dead and seriously injured had been taken away, but the walking wounded were spread out underneath my window.

Towards the end of the match, I started to plot my escape. I'd arrived that morning from Liverpool Airport on a chartered plane that had included some reserve players, office staff and one or two 'friends of friends'. The coach that had brought us into the city was parked in the car park diametrically opposite to the corner where I was watching the game. Everyone else on the plane was in the stand opposite my seat. About ten minutes from the end, I decided to get myself organized. I had a small shoulder bag with a couple of souvenirs for home that I could jettison if need be. My jacket had an inside zip pocket, where I'd put my passport and cash. Many years previously, when I was sixteen and just starting out (or so I hoped) on a career in banking, I'd attended a lecture about personal security given by an ex-member of the Flying Squad at Scotland Yard. He'd said that a secure inside pocket that would fasten was a sure-fire deterrent to pickpockets. So it was that night.

I calculated that soon after the final whistle, the Italians would spend a minute or two celebrating their victory. The stadium staff would then have to find and assemble the podium for the presentations, someone would have to round up the VIPs who would make the presentations, both teams would get their medals, and Juve would go on some sort of half-hearted lap of honour. I decided I had about ten minutes to get clear of the stadium and on to my precious transport back to the airport.

At the final whistle, I ran as fast as I could! I could still run in those days, and I amazed myself with the head of steam I worked up. For the last few yards, I was aware of the first Italians leaving the stadium and headed into the car park. My coach had gone! Apparently, everyone else had decided to leave before the end to get away from any more trouble. They had collectively forgotten about yours truly. In a mild state of panic, I walked up and down the rows of coaches looking for help. Once again, someone up there must have been looking after me, because I spotted the club's press officer sitting on the front seat of a coach. I persuaded him to tell his driver that I was a club employee. He did, and I was very quickly on board. Arriving at Brussels Airport, we were driven straight on to the tarmac. No customs check, no passport control, nothing! On board, dear old Peggy Higby, the ticket-office manager, started taking a roll call. Every seat was taken, and there were about a dozen people sitting on the floor in the aisle. Halfway through her check, however, the Tannoy burst into life and the captain said the magic words, 'We have a window of opportunity to take off. I suggest we use it.' No one argued and we flew home with an overloaded plane – unthinkable now.

Luckily for me, the guy sitting next to me on the plane was due to drive past my house on his way home and gave me a lift. I remember waking the kids when I got in and seeing their excited smiles, even though it was the middle of the night. Don't forget, this was still a decade or so before widespread mobile phones, and my family wasn't at all sure of what had happened to me in Brussels. Likewise, I was unaware of what had been happening at home. At that time, Liz used to help out at a friend's hairdressing salon in Southport on Wednesday evenings. My stepmother was due to babysit but, as usual, was running late. She phoned to say she was on her way, so Liz headed off. On the way to my house, my stepmother, who had the tact and sensitivity of the proverbial bear with a sore head heard the news on her car radio, burst through my front door and announced to my offspring, 'There's been a big disaster at the football match in Brussels and hundreds of people have been killed, but I'm sure your dad will be fine, so don't worry!' Liz arrived at the salon just in time to get a phone call from my eldest along the lines of, 'Mum! Mum! Dad's been killed in Brussels!' Liz knew that the news must have come from my stepmother and calmed my poor lad down. She then found a TV in the back room of the salon and found out the facts for herself. She rang home: 'Listen. There has been a dreadful crush in Brussels, and thirty-nine people have been killed, but they're all Italian!'

By this time, all three of my children were sobbing, so she apologized to her friend and came straight back home. Twenty-five minutes later, she was greeted by three smiling children and her mother-in-law sipping tea in the armchair. While she had been driving home, the TV cameras had zoomed in on me while I was appealing for calm, and they now knew I was alive and seemingly well. Fortunately, the cameras didn't catch the sight of the various injured and angry Italians on the running track beneath my window, who were by now venting their spleens on me because I was obviously English.

When I'd been trying my best to get through to the fans, my overriding thought had been that I was on TV and my family at home would see me – that moment will haunt me for ever. When I arrived home, I swore I was going to burn my passport and never go abroad again. I didn't burn it, of course, because when I calmed down, I took stock and remembered that we were booked into a holiday park in the Netherlands a couple of weeks later. We enjoyed the trip, but nonetheless the memories of that terrible night will never leave me.

1985–86

Kenny Dalglish became player-manager of Liverpool in 1985 after the resignation of Joe Fagan. At the relatively young age of thirty-four, he took over a side that he was still playing in and that included several players in their last seasons. It therefore took him a bit of time to make changes to the team during the season, but it ended with them winning the league and FA Cup Double and reaching the League Cup semi-finals.

They also began their campaign in the newly created Screensport Super Cup. Because the ban on English clubs after Heysel came immediately into force and would lead to there being no European fixtures, a new competition was introduced. The six teams who would have qualified were included, and it lasted until the end of the 1986–87 season, with Liverpool reaching the final, where they eventually lost to Everton.

In those days, I was friendly with one or two of the first-team squad but not yet with Kenny, so I could watch his progress objectively. People used to say, 'Oh, he's inherited Joe's squad,' but that was nonsense. He was his own man, and his team won the Double in his first season, for goodness' sake! The league *and* the FA Cup! It was another achievement ticked off the club's bucket list!

The big tune of 1985 was Jennifer Rush's ballad 'The Power of Love'.

FA Cup Final – Liverpool v. Everton, Wembley Stadium, 10 May 1986

The 1986 FA Cup final was a rare derby match at Wembley, played between England's two top clubs at the time: a week earlier, Liverpool had won the championship, with Everton finishing runners-up. Liverpool came from behind to win 3–1, completing the Double. As we had already won the league, Everton would have secured a place in the 1986–87 European Cup Winners' Cup, but the ban on English clubs in European competitions meant that they were excluded, as were Liverpool from the European Cup.

The whole week was traumatic in our household. I'd managed, after a lot of hassle, to get tickets for myself and the boys. Kim was still only four, and Liz was quite happy to avoid the traffic chaos we'd had two years previously, so she volunteered to stay at home while we went as a threesome. Two nights before the final, there was a reserve-team match at Anfield, the last of the season. After it was done and dusted, I headed home, ready to chill out and look forward to Wembley. No such luck. When I arrived back, there was no sign of Liz, and my stepmother (looking even glummer than usual) was sitting in my front room. Laurie (then just eleven) had been rushed off to hospital in Ormskirk with suspected appendicitis! My first thought should have been, 'Poor lad!' but was actually, 'There's Saturday messed up!'

Laurie underwent several tests on the Friday. Appendicitis was ruled out, but he was still not well. To this day, we haven't a clue what he had, although we were given a list of things that weren't wrong with him. I went to visit him on the Friday night and found him looking a lot brighter. I went to find the ward sister to ask for a prognosis. She thought he might be fit to come home on the next day. I asked when on Saturday. I tried to explain to her that he had a cup-final ticket, but the significance didn't register. I was told that the doctor would be doing his rounds sometime after 10.30 the following morning. I tried again to get through to her that we should be well on our way down the M6 by then but to no avail. Eventually she twigged but said, quite sensibly, that he wouldn't be fit for a long journey, as he'd hardly eaten for three days! I gave in. I had to go back and tell the poor lad that he wouldn't be going to Wembley.

So it was that I set out with Rob early on Saturday morning, just the two of us. Liz spent the day with Laurie in Ormskirk Hospital, and my stepmother looked after Kim once again. The journey lasted as far as Stafford. Happily heading south, my car started to make some strange noises. Suddenly, it sounded as if someone had dropped a giant bag of spanners from a great height. The big ends had gone. I managed to glide on to the hard shoulder at a point where there was a small piece of banking up which I could push the car out of harm's way. I was wondering (in a flat panic) what to do next when a car pulled over next to us. It was driven by Chris Hassall, who was the Everton club secretary (and later chief executive of Yorkshire Cricket Club) and whose son went to the same school as Rob. After a few seconds weighing up the prospect of finding my car later, I took Chris up on his offer of a lift. He dropped us off at a station at the end of a line heading to Wembley and said he'd pick us up again later if we got back to the station in good time. We did! When we got to the spot on the M6 where I'd left my car, my worst fears were confirmed. The car had been towed away! After a few phone calls on the Sunday, Liz drove me to Stafford and I tracked the car down to the police car pound outside of the town, rang the AA and waited patiently to be towed home.

In July, Ian Rush accepted an offer to join Juventus. He was going to stay with Liverpool on loan for twelve months, but it was still a huge blow.

The Communards' 'Don't Leave Me This Way' was a huge hit in 1986.

1986–87

John Aldridge made his long-awaited debut for the Reds on 21 February 1987. Aldo's route to playing for his boyhood club was a long one. Rejected by Liverpool as a teenager, he played for lowly Newport County and moved to Oxford United before again attracting the attention of the Reds. One of the reasons that he did so was because he had famously scored one of the Oxford goals that had beaten Manchester United in Alex Ferguson's first game as manager.

I've heard John tell the story himself a couple of times but still like to quote it as a great example of what a proper Liverpool player would do. He was told by his manager at Oxford that Liverpool were interested in signing him and was instructed to rendezvous with the club secretary and chairman the following day. Overnight, he took an unsolicited call from a well-known agent who offered to become his representative and extract a better wage than was already on the table. John turned him down flat. He'd dreamt of playing for Liverpool all his life and wanted no obstacles placed in his way now. The following morning, he got to the meeting and cut short the pitch for his services: 'Just give me a pen!' He simply wanted to wear the red shirt. He served the club well and is still revered by Liverpool fans to this day. He is, incidentally, a great bloke. I've had the privilege of sharing several dinner tables and stages with him at fan gatherings in England and Scandinavia, and his love for, and relationship with, the Liverpool supporters is unmatched. If you have seen the video of John and Steve Hunter doing the LFCTV commentary at the famous Barcelona semi-final in 2019, you will have witnessed his euphoria at the final whistle.

There were other new faces at the club, with Peter Beardsley joining Liverpool at the same time as John Barnes, with Beardsley and Aldridge taking over from the hugely successful partnership of Kenny Dalglish and Ian Rush up front.

Cliff Richard's 'Mistletoe and Wine', in spite of some sarcastic responses, was the biggest song of 1987.

1987–88

FA Cup Final – Liverpool v. Wimbledon, Wembley Stadium, 14 May 1988

During the 1987–88 season, Liverpool lost just twice in the league, winning the title with Alan Hansen as skipper. They also reached the FA Cup final but were denied a second Double when they were beaten 1–0 by lowly Wimbledon (whose team was known, for good reason, as the 'Crazy Gang') in one of the competition's biggest ever shocks.

Wimbledon were a club with a small fan base, and the feeling was that a large chunk of their ticket allocation would be unused and, hopefully, put back in the 'pot' before eventually being added to Liverpool's meagre allocation. In the event, there were unexpectedly long queues at the ticket-office windows when Wimbledon put them on sale. There were several stories of Scouse accents in the lines, but whatever the case, they sold out. I had managed to get tickets for myself, Rob and Laurie, but their mutual best friend Jon, who lived opposite, lost out. Early on the morning of the game, I received a call from a friend at a local radio station. Someone in Manchester had just phoned to say that he had two spare tickets and wanted to advertise the fact on the station. Before mentioning them on the air, my friend rang me. Did I want them? Not half. My lads sprinted to Jon's house. He was in – and so was his dad! Unfortunately, it was Wimbledon's day. Lawrie Sanchez scored, John Aldridge had his penalty saved and the drive home was a sombre one.

1988–89

After an unhappy spell in Italy, Ian Rush came home. He had been missed, for sure, and there was a feeling amongst the fans that Liverpool was where he belonged. When I heard of his homecoming on local radio, the first thing I did was put through a call to Bielefeld in Germany where Rob was on a school exchange visit with the Vogel family.

'Rushie's coming back to Anfield!' I said.

'Wow! Great stuff. Hang on a second.'

At this point, he excitedly turned to his hosts and told them the news. He soon realized that they neither knew nor cared about someone called Ian Rush! The wind was taken out of his sails for a moment, but the bottom line was that, come the new season, he would be able to watch Rushie week in, week out. Order had been restored, and Ian's exile was at an end.

In spite of various quotes and misquotes, the bottom line was that Rushie didn't settle in Italy and didn't need much persuading to come home. It of course meant a new song for the Liverpool faithful: 'Rushie is back, Rushie is back'. Although the Liverpool team of 1987–88 had played some outstanding football, such was Rush's stature amongst the Anfield faithful that they were very pleased to see him return to the club.

The song that set Kylie Minogue on the golden road, 'I Should Be So Lucky' was the biggest seller in the UK charts in 1988.

The new year saw Liverpool set on a steady course for the league championship, and the FA Cup trail was even smoother. On 7 January, we won 3–0 away to Carlisle. That was followed at the end of the month by another away win against Millwall at the Den. Very early in my career at Anfield, I read an article in the *Sunday Times* about Millwall that contained a line that stuck in my mind. 'If Liverpool ever play Millwall, there will be a civil war!' There wasn't, fortunately, and we went on to another away win against Hull City before getting our first home draw. Fortunately, it was against an overachieving Brentford, and we duly saw them off by four clear goals. Everton were still in the competition, and we wondered whether we would avoid them in the semi-final. We did.

Next, there was a day out in Sheffield to look forward to. What we got, of course, was the blackest day in the history of Liverpool Football Club, and of English football.

FA Cup Semi-final – Liverpool v. Nottingham Forest, Hillsborough Stadium, 15 April 1989

The Hillsborough Disaster was the worst stadium-related disaster in English sports history. I think that, after all these years, the circumstances surrounding what happened should be well known, but I'm still often appalled by the ignorance of some people I meet and the vicious comments made by online trolls.

South Yorkshire Police blamed Liverpool fans for causing the crush on the Leppings Lane terraces, and it took nearly three decades of tireless effort before an unprecedented second inquest decided that the victims had been unlawfully killed following failures by police and ambulance services.

I hate semi-finals. They are usually tense and nervous affairs. Lose and you've missed out, by the narrowest of margins, on an appearance in a major final. Win and you have a big day out to look forward to. This day was a case in point. Rob was keen to go, and I wasn't. Two of his school friends (Jamie Case and Jon Singleton) also wanted to go, so I somehow managed to get my hands on four tickets and all three went with Jamie's dad at the wheel. I was relaxed about the arrangement. The lads were in safe hands, and I didn't have to put my nervous system through the mangle! If only I'd known what was on the horizon.

I was chilling out in the armchair with the newspaper when Liz returned abruptly from the supermarket. There had, she said, been some sort of incident in Sheffield. We turned on the TV to see what was going on and were horrified by what we saw. Although it looked chaotic, we were still shocked when we heard the words 'possible fatalities'.

Because there were no mobile phones, we were completely out of contact. All we knew was what the TV commentators were telling us. Our immediate assumption was that this was an incidence of hooliganism. That idea was soon dismissed, and it became clear that people had died, although we had no idea of how many. My stepmother rang and was relieved to hear my voice . . . until I told her that Rob was in Sheffield.

All we could do was sit and wait. And wait. And wait. An hour and three quarters later the phone rang. It was Rob. He and his fellow travellers were all safe. They had found an unoccupied phone box some distance from Sheffield. Our relief/joy/gratitude/euphoria was indescribable.

When we'd calmed down, we had things to do. Liz went off to tell her parents the good news. I rang my stepmother and quickly headed to Ormskirk, where Jon Singleton's parents had a stall in the market. I got there as fast as I could and found his mum getting ready to shut up shop for the day. I greeted her with, 'I've just heard from Rob, and they're all safe!' She looked blank. She hadn't heard a word about the disaster. Just as well. Her husband then appeared from an alleyway between the shops. He had been to fetch their van and had heard the news. He was frantic. Thankfully, I could calm his fears.

Those couple of hours or so were the longest of my life. I have no idea how the poor people whose loved ones didn't come home coped. Liz and I were among the lucky ones. Sometime later, Dave Case brought Rob and his pals home safe. We are for ever in his debt.

FA Cup Final – Liverpool v. Everton, Wembley Stadium, 20 May 1989

After Liverpool somehow managed to win the semi-final replay in the wake of the tragedy, the final, played just five weeks after Hillsborough, was another all-Merseyside affair. The usual marks of respect were paid before the game, and Gerry Marsden led the crowd in an incredibly moving rendition of 'You'll Never Walk Alone'. Although Stuart McCall scored twice for the Blues, Liverpool lifted the trophy thanks to a goal from John Aldridge and two from Ian Rush. It was the high point of the season, though, as the Reds were heartbreakingly denied a second Double in four seasons when a late Michael Thomas goal won the title for Arsenal at Anfield six days later.

That was a very emotional night. Arsenal had to beat us by two clear goals to equal our points total and overtake our superior goal difference. In the end, they won 2–0 thanks to goals from Alan Smith and Thomas, who, ironically, later joined the Reds. The Liverpool players looked shattered towards the end of the game, and I think the events of the previous weeks had finally taken their toll.

Off the pitch, there was a technical problem at the end of the game. The TV presenter's microphone was supposed to be fed through my system so that the crowd could hear him simultaneously to the TV audience. It failed, but by then I was completely past caring.

Earlier in the night, I had a shock when my door opened and Tom Watt, in those days better known as Lofty Holloway in *EastEnders*, was pushed through by my steward, Alan Green (aka 'Big Al'). Apparently, Tom couldn't get a ticket and was smuggled in by the TV producer on condition he stood quietly on the TV gantry. When Arsenal scored their first, he lost his cool and could be heard shouting on the TV and radio. We looked after him, and Tom says I saved his life that night! I didn't, but we're still friends thirty years later.

'Ride on Time' by Black Box was the song (and style) of the year.

1989–90

On 28 April 1990, Liverpool clinched the league championship with a 2–1 win over Queens Park Rangers, whose team, incidentally, included stars David Seaman and Ray Wilkins, who both made their names with bigger clubs – Arsenal and Chelsea, respectively. The joy of that day for me was the fact that Aston Villa, our nearest challengers, could only draw, and I got the chance to announce to the crowd that we were champions.

We had looked like we were heading for another Double but somehow managed to lose the FA Cup semi-final 4–3 to the same Crystal Palace team whom we had thrashed 9–0 earlier in the season. That day was one that really sticks in my mind. Rob was booked to run the line at a junior game in south Liverpool, which also coincided with a weekend visit from someone he had met on a school trip. I was chauffeur and minder that afternoon so had to listen to the game on my trusty transistor radio while watching his match. None of us could have possibly imagined what lay ahead for Liverpool. If someone had said that we were in for three whole arduous, heartbreaking decades without a league title, we would have thought they were crazy. There were golden days in the meantime of course – Istanbul, Cardiff, Dortmund – but the league title became the holy grail once again.

PART FOUR

The Nineties

1990–91

L iverpool's ultimately unsuccessful defence of their title began on 25 August 1990 at Bramall Lane, beating newly promoted Sheffield United 3–1. Little did we know that it would be thirty years before we regained the title, when, coincidentally, the top league would again include a newly promoted Sheffield United. Liverpool's unbeaten start to the season lasted fourteen games, but it was to no avail!

> Scorpions' 'Wind of Change', about revolution in Eastern Europe, marked 1990.

I was working on contract in Hyde on my forty-fifth birthday and having a quiet lunch when a business colleague, Vic Groves, rang me. 'What do you think of the news about Mr Dalglish?' he asked. Kenny had just announced to an incredulous press conference that he had resigned as Liverpool manager, even though the Reds were still in contention for another Double, having just earned a hard-fought 4–4 draw with Everton.

Kenny says in his autobiography that the accumulated pressure of the Hillsborough Disaster and its aftermath coupled with that of managing his beloved Liverpool was seriously affecting him mentally and physically, and his family knew he had to have a break. I remember remarking at the time that I was suffering immense pressure running my Under-12 sides, which caused me several sleepless nights. I couldn't begin to imagine how much pressure a caring man like Kenny was under, running a huge club that meant so much to us all. The ever-reliable Ronnie Moran was appointed caretaker manager of the first team until a permanent successor could be found, and a disappointing month ended with Everton finally putting the Reds out of the FA Cup.

Alan Hansen had been injury-plagued for some time. I remember when the players were lining up for their team photograph after the 1990 title win. He was struggling to squat down for the camera. Obviously in pain, he had to stand straight to relieve the discomfort. He didn't play competitively the following season and eventually retired. During the close season, Peter Beardsley made the short trip across Stanley Park and signed for Everton. I was disappointed to see him go, as I had always enjoyed watching him play.

Strangely, the only time I ever spoke to Peter at Anfield was to ask him for a photograph with a friend of one of my sons. Several years later, I met him and Gordon Milne in the departure lounge at Manchester Airport when they were coaching Newcastle youngsters.

During the 1991–92 season, one of my sons was playing for a junior team called Rufford Colts alongside Simon Kendall, son of the great Everton manager Howard Kendall. More or less every Sunday morning, while watching our offspring play, I had the same conversation with him. 'Morning, Howard. Time to stop messing around and send Beardo back to Anfield!' The response was always the same: a broad smile. I had a lot of time for Howard.

1991–92

The 1991–92 season was Souey's first full one as Liverpool manager, and he had made a number of changes to the playing staff over the summer. Peter Beardsley, David Speedie and Gary Gillespie all left, as did young Steve Staunton, and Souness signed striker Dean Saunders and centre-back Mark Wright, both from Derby County. To be fair, Graeme had the foresight to promote youngsters like Steve McManaman and Jamie Redknapp, as well as Rob Jones, whom he had bought from Crewe. All three were soon England internationals.

I still see 'Macca' occasionally. His mum and Liz worked together for the NHS in Liverpool and were good friends. Jamie, of course, was married to the lovely Louise and managed to help me broker an interview with her on Dune FM in Southport when she was performing in the town – did my street cred no harm at all.

Although there was cause to celebrate the six-year European ban coming to an end, with Liverpool in the UEFA Cup, John Barnes sadly picked up an Achilles injury in September and, apart from a brief spell in January, was out for most of the season. John is someone I often still see around Liverpool at various functions and at the Hotel Tia, the Norwegian-owned hotel in Anfield Road. He is a very articulate man and is often the go-to voice for the media on issues of racism. He was, of course, a victim of racism during his career, and there's a famous picture of him backheeling a banana from the pitch in a derby game in 1988. The issue has recently come to the forefront of the national discussion, although I don't think overt racism is as prevalent today. Having said that, I'm not on the receiving end and am not in a position to judge. I hate the word 'racism'. Surely we are all one race – human! Racism is the refuge of the moron and the coward. Better minds than mine are doing everything they can to change things. I hope they succeed.

The biggest seller of 1991, by some distance, was '(Everything I Do) I Do It for You' by Bryan Adams.

FA Cup Final – Liverpool v. Sunderland, Wembley Stadium, 9 May 1992

Graeme Souness underwent major heart surgery in April but managed to be there at Wembley when Liverpool won the FA Cup final in May. However, he was under strict orders from the medics not to overdo it, and it was Ronnie Moran who proudly led the Reds out on the day.

Our opponents were Sunderland. They were in the Second Division, and looking likely to stay there for some time, but had battled their way to the final. They had turned over Leeds United in the 1973 final and were hoping for a repeat performance. Fortunately for us, Ian Rush and Michael Thomas had other ideas, and we won 2–0.

My domestic arrangements for the match were problematic. I told my sons that their mum was going to get priority if my ticket allocation was limited. She had missed out on a couple of trips to Wembley to stay home and look after Kim. As it happened, things weren't as tight as in previous years, and I managed to get four tickets.

The logistics were not straightforward. Rob was at university in Stafford. Laurie was seventeen and in the sixth form but still living at home. He arranged to travel with some of his school friends. So that just left us with the problem of who would take care of Kim. She was ten, and we didn't just want to 'farm her out' for the day. Moreover, she hadn't yet expressed any interest in football. Then I had a brainwave. Rob had a girlfriend in Stafford. The plan was simple. We would take Kim and Rob's girlfriend with us and then, while we were at the FA Cup final, the two girls could do a bit of shopping in London, go sightseeing, have a coffee or whatever else took their fancy.

I rang Rob and asked him whether he thought she'd be amenable. He promised to nip round and see her. Half an hour later he rang back and dropped a bombshell! 'Yes,' he said, 'she'd love to go to the cup final.'

I didn't realize that the young lady in question hailed from the North East! She had a sort of mid-Atlantic accent which came from her childhood spent in different corners of the world. Her parents worked for the United Nations and the World Health Organization respectively. They were basically professional nomads.

I caved in. A fair bit of grovelling ensued, and I managed to get another two tickets for the two girls. Those were the days! Tickets in the twenty-first century are the bane of all our lives at Anfield. So it was that a car packed like a can of sardines arrived at Wembley. Sunderland's optimism was unfounded, and we took that fabulous old trophy back to Anfield!

1992–93

August 1992 saw the birth of the Premier League. In the inaugural season there were twenty-two clubs in the competition: Arsenal, Aston Villa, Blackburn, Chelsea, Coventry, Crystal Palace, Everton, Ipswich, Leeds, Liverpool, Manchester City and Manchester United, Middlesbrough, Norwich, Nottingham Forest, Oldham, QPR, Sheffield United and Sheffield Wednesday, Southampton, Tottenham and Wimbledon. For the record, Manchester United won the title for the first two seasons but were edged out by Blackburn in the third season.

On 16 September 1992, the Chancellor of the Exchequer announced an interest-rate increase from 10 to 12 per cent, followed by another rise later in the day to 15 per cent, in an attempt to prop up the ailing pound and keep it in the European Exchange Rate Mechanism. The move was unsuccessful and the massive trading losses led to the day becoming known as Black Wednesday.

From my perspective, it was another eventful day. I was

working for a finance company in Chester whose operations were spread over two sites. When the first interest-rate hike was announced, I was driving from site B (where I was based) to site A (their older office building). I heard the news on the car radio and stopped to do some mortgage calculations. I came to the conclusion that I would have to take on extra work to pay it in the future. After I'd finished at site A and set off back to my own office, the second rise was announced. Once again, I did some mortgage calculations and this time decided that I would have to rob a bank to pay it! The atmosphere in work was deadly – silence and long faces.

As it happened, I had a match to distract me – Liverpool were playing Apollon Limassol at Anfield that night in a European game unremarkable except for the fact that a young lad I'd watched playing alongside my son Laurie for several years was making his debut. Phil Charnock had joined Liverpool at the age of twelve. That night he became the youngest player ever to play for Liverpool in a European competition. He was just seventeen. He eventually left the club at twenty-two and went on to play for several clubs in the lower leagues before returning to Liverpool's youth academy to coach in 2012. The other item of note from that night was that for the first and only time in my career I had to give a newsflash to the crowd. About forty-five minutes before kick-off, it had been announced that the UK was withdrawing from the Exchange Rate Mechanism and all the day's interest-rate rises had been cancelled!

1992's monster hit was 'I Will Always Love You' by the late, great Whitney Houston.

The Anfield Boot Room was basically a tiny storage space near the changing rooms in which the players' football boots were stashed, but Bill Shankly turned it into an informal meeting room, where he and his coaching staff, including Bob Paisley, Reuben Bennett, Tom Saunders, Joe Fagan and Ronnie Moran, could discuss football. They were joined later by chief scout Geoff Twentyman and reserve-team coach Roy Evans. I had only been in the Boot Room intermittently and infrequently since 1971, but I still felt privileged to have set foot in it at all. It was for a long time the engine room of the club.

On 21 January, I arrived at Anfield for a junior game and was met by several angry and upset club stewards, some of whom had managed to grab some small pieces of memorabilia – without warning, the Boot Room had been gutted. If I'd known what was going on, I would have left work early and grabbed something for myself. This was truly the end of an era.

A small group of assorted locals in Southport (businessmen, BBC presenters, hospital radio DJs) got together early in 1993 and decided that Southport needed its own radio station. They were in an area covered by BBC Radio Merseyside and Radio City, but Southport has its own identity and has never felt like part of the county of Merseyside. In fact, a lot of the locals were outraged when local government boundary changes had 'moved' the town from Lancashire into Merseyside. I knew a couple of the guys socially and was asked along to a meeting, where they asked me if I wanted to be involved. Of course I did. I did, however, have some reservations about the catchment area. Broadcasting from Southport (behind the Southport Theatre on the seafront) meant that half our listeners would be seafarers or gulls! That said, the romantic prospect of a radio station in a seaside town brought back memories of the proliferation of independent radio stations in sixties America which had spawned so much of the music I loved. I was hooked!

Dune FM originally broadcast under two restricted-service (temporary) licences in 1993. The first RSL was broadcast from makeshift studios in a small caravan parked in the car park at the rear of the town's Floral Hall complex, with the transmitter on the roof of the Southport Theatre. The second RSL saw the station move to a new base above the Victoria Health and Leisure Club, with the transmitter at Greenbank High School in the Hillside area of the town. To my amazement, I was offered the breakfast show for the first RSL, which ran through the month of March 1993 and ended at Easter.

My routine was insane: up at the crack of dawn, driving over to Southport with a box of CDs, collecting the morning papers from a newsagent just off Lord Street and into the studio. I had lent a large chunk of my personal CD and vinyl collection to Dune but always had a small selection of music with me. It was a valuable back-up and also made sure that I had enough music to take to Anfield on match days.

I arrived, if I remember rightly, just after 6 a.m. and broadcast from 7 a.m. till 10 a.m. After that it was a coffee and off to work. Luckily, I was working for my friend Ian Fryer, who owned a company near the South Docks in Liverpool and was very happy for me to do the show before heading into the office. I have to say that by the end of the first twenty-eight-day RSL, I was exhausted. I did my final show on the morning of Good Friday 1993 and more or less slept the rest of the weekend!

This was Liverpool Football Club's centenary season, and in the spring we were honoured with a visit from Her Majesty the Queen. I was asked to be in place in my box under the roof of the old Main Stand ready to operate the public address system in case of a possible emergency, such as if the stadium had to be evacuated.

I got to Anfield very early and hung around the reception area while someone went off to find my security pass. While I was waiting, I was amazed to see the number of police officers and people in various other uniforms who were busy around the ground. I was told that the place had undergone a thorough safety check, right down to dismantling fire extinguishers and searching every inch of the place. I was also aware of a few armed snipers heading out to take up their positions around the ground well before Joe Public turned up. There were also lots of 'men in suits' who were part of the Royal Protection Team.

After a while, I got a message to say that nobody had remembered to get me security clearance but that I should just make my way up to my room anyway. 'You're joking!' was my immediate reaction. My route would take me along the car park and up the exposed fire escape on the outside wall of the Main Stand then through the roof space to where there was a ladder down to the TV gantry. I refused to make the trip. There were so many armed personnel hidden about the place I didn't fancy my chances.

Eventually, I negotiated the presence of a minder, and one of the detectives accompanying Her Majesty came with me. He had a big security pass attached to his top pocket, and we went up in tandem – me keeping as close to him as was possible without starting rumours! We must have looked like Morecambe and Wise from a distance. Nevertheless, I made it safely and luckily had nothing to do from then on but watch the events down below me. There were demonstration training and coaching sessions going on all over the pitch, and David Moores, the chairman at the time, guided Her Majesty around.

At the end of the event, I looked up from my desk to see my daughter Kim appear in my room. She had got a lift from school with two schoolmates, driven by their mum. The arrangement had been that I would pick Kim up from outside the players' entrance, but she had made her way up the fire escape, along the catwalk in the roof of the old Main Stand and into my room on her own without any trouble. After my reluctance to make the same trip earlier, I was, to say the least, a bit taken aback!

1993–94

League Cup – Liverpool v. Fulham, Anfield, 5 October 1993

This was the second leg of the tie. Robbie Fowler had scored on his Liverpool debut in the away leg two weeks earlier, which they had won 3–1. In the home leg, however, they put five past Fulham – or should I say, Robbie put five past them! And I didn't see any of them, the reason being that I was listening to the game on my little portable radio in my son Rob's flat in Walthamstow!

I was a freelance analyst/programmer at the time, and the only work I'd been offered for a while was a three-month contract with a mobile phone company in Borehamwood. I detest not being in my own bed at night, but my preferences were overridden by the need to make a living.

As it happened, Rob was doing a year out from Stafford University in the City of London and was sharing a flat with two other guys in the same situation. The flat had a tiny extra room with a settee and table, so I slept in there during the week and came home on Friday nights. My friend Ron

Tierney, who, incidentally, became my official understudy in 2019, stood in for me for the midweek games, so he was the lucky guy who witnessed the 'arrival' of Robbie Fowler. I saw Robbie play for the first team a couple of weeks later when he scored the winner against Oldham Athletic. I'd seen him a couple of times at youth level and once for Liverpool Schools, but he was another of those players who blossomed when in the company of world-class players. He was always good to watch and would give 100 per cent week in, week out.

My long-distance commute got me down after a while. The gearbox in my old car fell to bits quite early on in the contract, and I was stranded more than once. Eventually, I gave up the drive and got the train down to London late on Sunday nights. Even that scheme let me down once or twice. The first time I ended up on the night bus to Seven Sisters which, as you may know if you've tried it, is not a nice place to be. The second time I managed to miss my train to London altogether. Luckily, I managed to get a train to Crewe and then connected with the Glasgow to Euston train. On arrival, I legged it to King's Cross to catch the last Tube train to Blackhorse Road on the Walthamstow line and thought I was safe. Not quite! The train hung around long enough to collect the last few people heading home from the West End. Having done that out of the apparent goodness of his heart, the driver got as far as Finsbury Park and then announced over the Tannoy that he had done his shift and wasn't going any further! Every passenger on board was emptied out into the cold night air.

I really wasn't happy being around there at that time of night. I saw that there were queues of people waiting for night buses, but I didn't know which bus to get or even what direction I should be heading. Out of the corner of my eye, I could see two suspicious-looking characters in the doorway of a pub. I didn't know what they were up to and wasn't going to hang around to find out. At that moment, a police van screeched to a halt nearby and two coppers climbed out: one male, one female. I asked the bloke if he could give me directions. 'Sure thing,' he said. 'But wait till we sort these two out,' gesturing towards the two blokes in the doorway. A couple of minutes later, he and his colleague returned having found that there was no crime in progress. I told them my problem, and the guy smiled.

'You're in luck, mate. We're on our way back to Walthamstow nick. We'll drop you off. Climb in.'

By 'climb in', he didn't mean snuggle up to him and his female companion up front, but instead I was invited to sit on one of the benches in the back, usually reserved for the local hoodlums! Any port in a storm! I climbed in and hauled my luggage after me. The accompanying sound of the rear door being slammed behind me was *very* unnerving. I'm proud to say that I've never had my collar felt by Her Majesty's finest, but at this point it hit me that I was an itinerant Scouser locked in the back of a Black Maria in a ropey part of London in the early hours of the morning. The journey was surreal, but, true to their word, my hosts dropped me off at the bottom of Blackhorse Road, E17, and I walked the rest of the way to Rob's flat.

I survived my unwanted exile and eventually finished the contract on Christmas Eve 1993. I got the last seat on the last train from Euston to Lime Street and often wondered where I would have ended up if I'd missed it. I suspect the Missing Persons Bureau would still be looking for me!

Sadly for my career in local radio, my time in London coincided with the second of Dune FM's temporary broadcast licences, and I was more or less out in the cold, as there was no way I could take any part in what they were doing.

'I'd Do Anything for Love (But I Won't Do That)' by
Meat Loaf topped the sales charts in 1993.

Following a tough start to the new year that saw us knocked
out of the FA Cup by lowly Bristol City after a replay, Graeme
Souness was sacked, and on 28 January Roy Evans was
appointed as his successor.

When I started work at Anfield, Roy was a fringe player at
the club. He was a thoroughly professional full-back whom I
once saw do a good job against the wizard who was George
Best. Bill Shankly recognized that Roy had the makings of a
great coach and persuaded him to take the plunge in the early
seventies. He managed the reserve team to the old Central
League championship no less than nine times over the course
of a dozen seasons.

No one deserved his chance more than Roy. He was imbued
with the 'Liverpool Way'. He won us the League Cup in 1995,
but his career petered out with the arrival of Gérard Houllier.
I regard Roy as a friend. His lad Steve played in the same team
as my son Laurie, and I've watched Steve and his lovely sister
Stacey grow up. Roy would often join me on the old TV gantry
to watch a game if his reserves weren't playing, and it would
be an education listening to him during those ninety minutes.

Liverpool's historic Kop terracing dated back to 1906 when
Ernest Edwards, the sports editor of the local evening
newspaper the *Liverpool Echo*, remarked that the new standing
embankment at Anfield resembled the Spion Kop – the site
of a major battle during the Boer War, which, coincidentally,
involved large numbers of soldiers from the Liverpool area.

Now, in the summer of 1994, it was due to be closed and demolished to comply with the requirements of the Taylor Report, which, in the wake of the Hillsborough Disaster, made all-seater stadiums obligatory in the highest two divisions of English football. A new Spion Kop was built in its place, with 12,390 seats.

Author and broadcaster Mike Nevin wrote a brilliant piece on the *Anfield Wrap* digital magazine about the last day of the standing Kop. With his permission, I've reproduced a large chunk of it here:

Not long after the sacking of Souness, the old Spion Kop was about to be demolished and replaced with a shiny 12,000 capacity all-seater Kop Grandstand. Looking back, at a time when acceptance was a by-product of being usurped by Manchester United, and feeling emotionally overwrought in the wake of Heysel and Hillsborough, I wasn't that bothered.

The old place had been dead for years and I had got used to watching from the stands at the side, still in the newly named Centenary Stand but now back under the shadows of the old Kop roof, with my dad to one side and my sister to the other. The knee-crunching old relic on Kemlyn Road held its own charms, a perverse pleasure taken from wincing in the icy, swirling wind which whipped in from Flag Pole Corner and brought in the Mersey rain and sleet at a peculiarly different angle every week. Hip flasks were traditionally the preserve of old men, but you needed one in that weather, and it went some way towards numbing the pain of watching Paul Stewart. The penultimate game in front of the standing Kop illustrated our decline on and off the pitch. This, a turgid 1–0 win over Ipswich in front of a moribund crowd of 30,485 on Grand National morning, courtesy of a Julian Dicks penalty – probably the only thing he hit straight during a pitiful Liverpool career. If the game served a purpose, it was to lower the Kop performance bar to a level under which only a slug could slither. As I wrote out my bets for Aintree during the second half torpor, I concluded that we could soon mourn the Kop's passing without too many regrets. But there was one game left. Clearly, I hadn't bargained for The Kop's Last Stand – as it was heralded by the club and media in the lead-up to the game. In pre-internet days, 'Flag Day' leaflets – inspired by 'No Seats' campaigner and match-day bon viveur, John Mackin – were doing the rounds in pubs imploring Reds all round the ground to mark the occasion. Get the banners out, belt out the songs, bring the old flags and make the Kop on its last day a fitting tribute to its glorious past. Tickets for the sell-out game were like gold dust – in days when pay on the gate was still the norm. Suitably enthused and engaged by the prospect of a bit of Anfield nostalgia, I went out and got pissed the night before, and lost my mate's ticket for the game. I woke with horror on the morning of the match faced with the prospect of missing out myself – I would have to do the decent thing and let him use my seasie. As a last resort, I rang the ticket office to see if I could get a spare. Remarkably, an old stager at the club, Bryce Morrison, fell for my, admittedly true, sob story and said if I could get to the ground pronto he would leave me one ticket at the window. I was up there like a shot and that was me out for the day early doors. I'd entered into the spirit of the occasion, bearing a 1965 cup final replica shirt, resplendent with oval badge, tucked into a pair of ridiculously high-waisted light blue jeans – it was a dismal era for male fashions. Compounding this, I had a souvenir from a recent UEFA Cup trip to Italy adorning my head – effectively, a plastic bag featuring adverts for Italian pressure-cookers and pictures of star Czech striker Tomáš Skuhravý, which was designed to fend off Genovese rainstorms. Suffice to say, on a bright spring day in L4, I looked a tit.

Unbeknownst to me, when I met my dad at our pre-match watering hole, The King Harry, he had come armed with a video camera to record the occasion for posterity. Not your modern-day slinky camcorder or camera phone; instead, picture a Russian army-issue beast of a machine which would be difficult to smuggle into your own house, never mind a football ground. At least he would be able to capture the scenes outside if the worst came to the worst and it was confiscated by an overzealous turnstile operator. And the scenes outside were spectacular. Walking down Back Rockfield Road, known lovingly to us as 'Dog Shit Alley', towards the ground, anyone who was anyone seemed to be bearing snazzy flags, well-worn scarves, historic banners, even Genovese rain-cheaters. The Kop was going out in a blaze of glory.

My dad's opening footage captures the jutting angles of the Kop's unique exterior at the corner of the Main Stand, the crumbling masonry tarted up in red and cream paint, probably administered by Shankly himself on one of his two days a year off. The growing din from inside the ground was already audible. Waltzing down the alleyway to the side of The Albert and turning left, the full extent of the splendour loomed into view. A magnificent crimson banner outside The Park pub lamented the death of the 'Spion Kop 1906–94. R.I.P. Reds in Power'. Holding court near the turnstiles on Walton Breck Road we encountered Lenny Campbell, aka the colourful 'Dr Fun' and his puppet, 'Liverpool Charlie'. The worse for at least a few lagers, my dad – camera in hand – decided to conduct a brief interview with one of the Kop's finest and unique Liverpudlians, a chat which comprises some extremely bad Huytonian ventriloquism, several utterances of the word 'sound', and the revelation that the good doctor and his sidekick were 'disappointed' at the Kop's demise. RIP Lenny.

It was time to go in. As we climbed the gangway and made our way to our seats, close to the pitch in row ten and in line with the eighteen-yard box, it was evident the Kop had pulled out all the stops. The famous old terrace was festooned with scarves and banners – the chequered flags of Rome '77 interspersed with those of AS Roma and Juventus, tokens of our two most-recent European Cup finals, which of course, ended in the most contrasting emotions. The greatest banner of all, a tribute to the cult-hero Joey Jones's part in the epic path to that first European Cup triumph at the Stadio Olimpico – 'Joey ate the Frogs' legs, made the Swiss roll, now he's Munching Gladbach' – had been restored to its former glory and was making its way down the Kop from the far corner that used to house the infamous Boys Pen. A vast surfer flag, adorned with that iconic image of Shankly, arms outstretched, bore the sentiment 'All Round the Ground, the Kop Spirit Survives' and fluttered on the breeze, while the patrons hummed along to a *Dam Busters* theme that was the soundtrack to many of those fabled European nights. All the while, my dad dutifully captured the sounds and scenes with his weighty piece of kit. Another blast from the past came with a high-pitched rendition of 'She Loves You', with PA man supreme, George Sephton, as always, finely in tune with the Kop vibe, before The Beatles gave way to a trademark interpretation of 'Scouser Tommy', performed by the Anfield diehards with an almost military precision. Shankly's 'professional supporters' were well and truly at work as the decibels were elevated to a new plane. It was only twenty past two, with the crowd practically oblivious to the players warming up on the pitch – the great Ian Rush and John Barnes in the twilight of their careers, the emergent local talents, Robbie Fowler and Steve McManaman, and the Souness flotsam – Dicks, Ruddock and Clough. I've always detested any form of pre-match entertainment but at this juncture the club were ready to play a blinder. With the crowd in ferment, former player and head of PR Brian Hall stepped into the centre circle to introduce a selection of the men who had inspired and been driven on by those watching from the Kop over five decades. First up was old Albert Stubbins (he of *Sergeant Pepper* album-cover fame), then legendary Billy Liddell of 'Liddellpool' – belying his seventy-two years with a spritely jog to the acclaim of many who never saw him kick a ball. The 'Anfield Iron', Tommy Smith, managed similar jauntiness – with the DSS no doubt looking on aghast – followed by rapturous ovations for the indestructible Ian Callaghan, 'Supersub' David Fairclough, striker David Johnson, flying winger Steve Heighway, Aussie whirlwind Craig Johnston and actual Kopite Phil Thompson. To a man, they wore terrible garish jackets. We didn't care. The best was still to come. Even Brian Hall's dour Lancastrian diction couldn't dampen the crowd's anticipation of the next arrival. As soon as a career spanning 1977–91 was mentioned by

Hall, a collective, momentary gasp gave way to an ear-splitting roar, as the unparalleled Kenny Dalglish strode to the turf. A thousand flags waved as a jubilant Kop piped up a lovestruck recital of 'I'd Walk a Million Miles for One of Your Goals'. For many, it was no idle claim on such an evocative afternoon. No supporters in football laud their managers like we do. The last guests to arrive at the Kop's colossal party were the ever-popular Treble winner Joe Fagan, flanked by the wives of the godly Shankly and Paisley. Of course, no one embraced the infatuation of the Kop like Shanks, and as the elderly trio made their way to greet the ex-players in the middle of Anfield, a perfect, mournful chorus of 'Shank-ly' to the tune of his favourite song, 'Amazing Grace', filled the air. How the hell did Kopites hold those notes? It was hard to fight back the tears, but this was no lament; instead, a celebration of the Holy Trinity Shankly spoke of – the communion of players, manager and supporters that made Liverpool unique and great.

In the blink of an eye, Gerry Marsden had been smuggled on to the pitch, his identity further masked by the smoke billowing from a Kop now burning with flares. Marsden's failing voice tuned up to serenade the ground with one last performance of the song that gave him a number-one record but more importantly and enduringly provided the Kop with its signature hymn. The fans helped old Gerry out and let him sing along with them rather than the other way round. As was the case when I was a boy, viewed from the calm of the stands, the fluid, smoky Kop was still a raw, passionate, inspiring, even moving sight as it belted out football's most famous anthem for the last time. After all that, anticlimax was never more inevitable. The occasion got to Liverpool – or maybe they just weren't very good – and the last-ever goal scored in front of the Kop was lashed in during the first half by Jeremy Goss of Norwich City. This sad statistic was corrected (sort of) after the final whistle, when Kop stalwart John Garner broke free of the stewards to invade the playing area, capping a mazy dribble with an emphatic low finish into the red netting at the Kop end. Perhaps Garner could see the future and a fifth European Cup in Turkey? He was wearing a fez. Otherwise, after a rather hollow show of thanks from the playing class of '94 and a brief half-hour resistance against the stewards, everyone tootled off home, perhaps disbelieving they would never set foot on the Kop again. By August, the lower reaches of the new Kop Grandstand were in place on the old Kop's footprint, and it steadily grew in size and stature over the course of 1994–95.

So, was the banner correct? Did the 'Kop Spirit Survive' all round the ground? Ask anyone who was at the Champions League semi-final against Chelsea in 2005, when less than half the Kop's original number made a noise to compare with Inter Milan and St Etienne, and the answer would be yes. Equally, listening to boos that greeted Liverpool's ascent to the top of the league in November 2008 made you wonder. It feels like the vocal, standing Blocks 305 and 306 at the back of the 'new' Kop, the Reclaim the Kop movement and laudable organizations like Spirit of Shankly are fighting a losing battle. Times have changed. So has Anfield, along with Liverpool's crowd in the sanitized arena that is the modern Premier League. The old Kop was a great spot to spend your formative years – a dirty, stinking, noisy, occasionally dangerous place, always funny but raw in the extreme. In many ways, you really did get your education from the Kop. Its like will not be seen again, and it was never in better form than on its last day.

My dad stood on the Kop at every opportunity from the early twenties until the end of the fifties. I did my time up there for ten years after that, and my lads took over when they were old enough. It was inevitable, therefore, that the last match in front of the standing Kop would be a sad occasion for us and so many other Liverpool supporters. We Kopites didn't want to lose it, but the law said that we had to say goodbye. Rob and one of his uni friends came home for the weekend, and I'm ashamed to say that, try as I might, I just couldn't get tickets for them to stand on the Kop one last time. I did manage to get them stand tickets, thankfully, but it wasn't the same.

1994–95

Not long before the start of the 1994–95 season, I got a postcard through my letter box one morning instructing me to attend the annual pre-season stewards meeting. I was surprised. I wasn't a steward, and I'd never been summoned to one of these meetings previously. Apparently, the clerk who had handwritten all the postcards hadn't noticed that my name, although it was on his file, wasn't included on the actual list of stewards.

Intrigued, I thought I might as well go to the meeting anyway. When I arrived, a succession of people told me that it was all a big mistake. The head steward suggested I go home, but my attitude was that, having driven to Anfield and left my comfy chair in front of the TV, I might as well stay and watch the comings and goings. It was, to say the least, an eye-opener. I was appalled to hear the way the stewards were spoken to. What most upset me, though, was the fate of the guys on the turnstiles. Some of them had been doing the job for decades. For years, week in and week out, they had gone through the same routine, taking the gate money, cashing up, bringing the takings round to the cash office deep underneath the stands, and then finding a place on the fringes of the Kop and watching the game. One of the gate men asked what they would do now that the stadium was turning all-seater. He was told in no uncertain terms that if he didn't have a ticket, he had better go home, otherwise he would be thrown out of the ground. Nice! No one appeared to have thought about these guys. Or, if they had, they didn't care. During the rest of the meeting, various other questions from the floor were met with the same sort of response.

I had my complimentary cuppa and sandwich and went home. At that time, my daughter Kim was going to the match on a regular basis. I would get hold of a ticket whenever and wherever there was one available, and she always enjoyed the whole experience. Liz asked me if I thought it might be a good idea to enquire about getting her a job as a steward. Kim is the sort of person who will stand up for herself and was just about old enough to do the job. The prospect of her working at Anfield had its attractions. She would get in every week and get paid for being there, thus saving me from having to buy her a ticket for every home game. But I refused point-blank on the grounds that if anyone spoke to my daughter the same way they talked to all the other stewards, I'd be inclined to get *very* angry. I still get invited to the stewards meetings, and I think it's fair to say that things have changed for the better.

The Kop Stand wasn't completely ready for the start of the new season. The delay was apparently caused by the incredible and unexpected amount of soil that had to be removed from underneath the old Kop, which overwhelmed the proposed dumping sites. In the end, only 4,000 seats were available at the start of the new season, and the stand wasn't up to its full capacity until the new year in 1995.

The year 1994 was also notable for an interview I did. Eddie Cotton of the Liverpool-based *Xtra Time* magazine interviewed me at length, and when the piece was published, it carried the headline 'The Real Man Behind the Voice of Anfield'. Somehow the handle stuck, and to this day I'm still known as the 'Voice of Anfield'.

'Love Is All Around' by Wet Wet Wet sold nearly two million copies in 1994, followed closely by the queen of the one-hit wonders, Whigfield. If you look back at the 1994 charts, there are a few songs you could call 'reggae light', upbeat, summery music which might make you feel as if you were at a beach party in the West Indies: Aswad, Big Mountain, Chaka Demus, Bitty McLean and Pato Banton. A young duo from Newcastle made an appearance, too. The previous year I had been waiting for a train at Borehamwood Station one Friday night when I noticed a couple of young lads with a group of admiring teenage girls round them. The next morning at home they appeared on my TV! I asked who they were and Kim told me their names – Anthony McPartland and Declan Donnelly!

League Cup Final – Liverpool v. Bolton Wanderers, Wembley Stadium, 2 April 1995

In the run-up to this game, I got a call from the guys organizing the pre-match on-pitch events. They wanted me there to say a few words and promised to look after me on the day. I'd got tickets for my sons and had arranged to pick Rob up from Stafford on the way. Laurie made his own way with some of his pals. Rob and I got to London ridiculously early after a rare trouble-free trip. So early, in fact, that we had time to park up for an hour and watch the London Marathon from Tower Bridge. At Wembley, I went to the Coca-Cola hospitality set-up, and Rob headed off to meet his brother. After a cuppa and a bite to eat, we discussed what the pre-match format would be. For me, it would involve wandering into the centre circle to be asked a couple of questions by Jon Hammond that would be broadcast over the PA.

After a brief run-through and sound check, I went to sit in the dugout to await my turn. It was another one of those surreal 'what the hell am I doing here?' moments. I was sitting in the Wembley dugout on the benches where later Roy Evans, his coaching staff and the Liverpool substitutes would sit. The same place where countless managers, coaches and world-famous players had sat since the stadium had been built in the twenties.

When it was my turn to do my bit, Jon Hammond and I went out to the centre circle and had a brief chat. Jon has had a long and varied career in the media. Of all the things I thought I might do in life, being interviewed in the centre circle at Wembley was definitely not one of them. My abiding memory of that moment was the size of the place and the number of people watching and listening – just over 75,500. Unreal!

One of the questions was about Roy Evans. What I said is as true now as it was then. 'Nobody,' I said, 'deserved the honour of leading Liverpool out at Wembley more than Roy.' He is, as I've said earlier, one of the nicest guys in football, and, to be honest, that may have eventually been his downfall.

Bolton controlled the game until the thirty-seventh minute when Steve McManaman scored, and he got another one midway through the second half before Wanderers pulled a goal back. Thankfully, we held on and brought home the League Cup yet again, our fifth success in the competition. Steve was named man of the match and was reported to have impressed Sir Tom Finney, who was watching from the stands.

Liverpool v. Blackburn Rovers, Anfield, 14 May 1995

Blackburn were poised to win the Premier League, and only Manchester United, who were away to West Ham, could stop them. If Blackburn didn't lose at Anfield, they'd be OK. It was such a weird game to be a Liverpool fan. First, of course, Blackburn's manager was Kenny Dalglish – 'King Kenny'! Second, I don't think there was a single soul inside Anfield who wanted United to win the league. And third, although we were all on Kenny's side, we could hardly start hoping that the Reds would lose!

I was sitting alongside John Bennison that afternoon. John had retired from the coaching staff at Anfield and occasionally came to spend an afternoon in my room to watch a game. He was an ex-member of Bill Shankly's 'Boot Room Boys' and a very knowledgeable man. I asked him before kick-off about Liverpool's attitude to the match. I confessed that I wouldn't have it in me to send out a team with the prospect of winning the title for United. John, as usual, spoke a lot of sense. Liverpool would be professional and play to win: 'Kenny would do the same to us if it was the other way round!'

So it was that a very nervous afternoon kicked off. The game was 1–1 going into injury time when Robbie Fowler was felled outside of the penalty box, and Jamie Redknapp took a tremendous free-kick that whistled into the top corner of Blackburn's net. We were stunned. Jamie looked downcast. It was like watching a car crash unfold. Then I looked down at Kenny standing in the players' tunnel and suddenly realized that he was grinning from ear to ear. The match at Upton Park had finished before ours and United could only draw. Blackburn were champions! Kenny was ecstatic, and so were we.

1995–96

During the summer of 1995, Roy Evans paid a British record fee for Nottingham Forest striker Stan Collymore. Then, early in the 1995–96 season, he bought Jason McAteer on the back of his impressive performance in the League Cup final. Jason was signing for his boyhood club, and he became part of a group of Liverpool players, including David James, Jamie Redknapp, Robbie Fowler and Steve McManaman, who were labelled the 'Spice Boys' by the media. I think it was a misleading title, although the notorious white suits they wore to Wembley in 1995 were a bit flash and didn't help their cause. All this, of course, was fodder for the tabloids, and a couple of the guys were actually friends with the Spice Girls. When Kim and I were at the Brit Awards in 1997, I had time for a chat with Steve, who was with Robbie at the Spice Girls' table! During his time at Anfield, Jason also filled in at right-back at times, despite primarily being a central midfielder. He broke his leg whilst playing against Blackburn Rovers at Anfield in 1998. It was one of those freak injuries, and it happened right in my eyeline.

A revival of 'Unchained Melody' by Robson and Jerome topped the pile in 1995.

Early in the 1995–96 season, Liverpool looked like contenders, but the title race ended up being a two-horse race between Newcastle United and Manchester United. The latter eventually won, and we had to settle for third place in the league. We did reach the FA Cup final but lost 1–0 to a late Eric Cantona goal for Manchester United. With Man United having won the league, we qualified for the Cup Winners' Cup.

Euro 96 took place in England in June 1996. It was the first European Championship to feature sixteen finalists, and games were staged in eight cities. Germany ended up lifting the trophy, beating the Czech Republic 2–1 in the final with a golden goal during extra time, the first time a major competition had been decided using this method. It was also Germany's first major title since reunification, following the fall of the Berlin Wall.

I'd been looking forward to the tournament ever since UEFA had named England the host country. Anfield was obviously a prime candidate for inclusion as one of the stadiums to be used in the competition, and I was excited when it was duly chosen. Thereafter things got a bit complicated. The North West Euro 96 organizer was Jim Greenwood. He'd retired as chief executive of Everton in 1994 and embarked on a two-year project to ensure that this corner of the world would have a smooth-running tournament. The problem I had was that he decided to bring Alan Jackson with him. Alan was the stadium announcer at Goodison Park and one of my predecessors at

Anfield. I was miffed. I had nothing personal against Alan, but I was being elbowed out of my chair without so much as a please or thank you. It was a situation that would happen more than once over the years. I was reduced to the level of deputy announcer, although I was, thankfully, still in charge of the music!

We were given strict instructions by UEFA as to the sequence of events at each game. We were also given a CD of 'approved' music, although we were given special dispensation to play 'You'll Never Walk Alone' at Anfield. One of the stipulations was that, once the UEFA chief at each stadium had given the go-ahead, the 'countdown' sequence would commence and nothing (up to and including World War Three!) would stop it.

Of course, things did go wrong, and the first game at Anfield (Italy v. Russia) nearly came to grief. Thirty minutes or so before it was due to start, we heard that many Italian fans were in a long queue of traffic a couple of miles from Anfield. They had completely miscalculated the time needed to get from the motorway to the ground and find somewhere to park. There was talk of delaying the kick-off, but no decision had been made by the time it came to start the countdown, so I went ahead and started the sequence of messages and music. Not long after that, we got a message to say that UEFA were still thinking about what to do. My answer was, 'Tough – it's too late!' Luckily for me, the decision was eventually taken to kick off on time.

At the third game (Russia v. the Czech Republic), the preamble on the pitch got a bit behind, and I ended up shouting down my two-way radio 'Time for "You'll Never Walk Alone"' about three times before killing the pitch mic and banging on the music. Serious complaints were made, but I was exonerated as, once again, I was the only one sticking to the rules!

After the three group games, we were the venue for the quarter-final between France and the Netherlands. The Dutch fans in particular were a joy to behold. Wherever the Dutch national team play, their fans turn up in vast numbers. They're loud and colourful and generate an atmosphere at every game.

As I said in the introduction, I'm old enough to have seen the World Cup games that were played in Liverpool in 1966. I never for one moment, though, thought that I'd play a small part in the proceedings of another major international tournament thirty years later!

1996–97

Liverpool v. Charlton Athletic,
Anfield, 13 November 1996

Charlton Athletic are a London club with a long history. In November 1996, they were in the second tier of English football and not having a good time. We drew with them away in the League Cup, and the replay was played at Anfield a couple of weeks later. We got past them comfortably (4–1) with goals from Mark Wright, Jamie Redknapp and a brace by Robbie Fowler. At half-time, Stan Boardman appeared on the pitch with a mic in hand and did a few minutes of stand-up. Stan is a lovely fella, a proper Scouser and a genuine, natural comedian. One gag that night, however, went down like the proverbial lead balloon with the massive following that Charlton had brought with them to Anfield. He cracked that Lord Lucan had been found in Athletic's trophy room. You have to be of a certain age to understand the joke, but basically Lord Lucan had gone missing in 1974 after the murder of the family nanny and had apparently disappeared into thin air. There was a chorus of booing from the terraces holding the

Charlton fans, who were already unhappy at being 3–0 down by half-time. The atmosphere continued to take a turn for the worse in the second half, so at the end of the game I tried to placate the travelling Londoners. I can't remember exactly what I said, but it was something along the lines of, 'Well done for coming all this way to support your team. We hope you have a safe journey home, and we look forward to seeing you here in the Premier League next year!'

The match commander came to find me after the game to congratulate me. 'You just avoided a riot,' he said. Nice to be of use for once!

The R&B cover of 'Killing Me Softly' by the Fugees sold big time in 1996.

I have a soft spot for the romance of the Grand National. Although I haven't actually attended the race in person for a few years, in 1997 it was a regular event in our household. That particular year it was just Kim and I who went, and it turned out to be an eventful day. An IRA bomb threat meant that 60,000 racegoers had to be evacuated from Aintree, and approximately 20,000 people were left stranded in Liverpool when their transport was trapped inside the racecourse. With most of the city's hotels full, the locals pulled together and made sure that none of the visitors went cold or hungry.

Kim and I were lucky. I heard the phrase 'Commence Operation Aintree' over the racecourse's public address system and realized that they were implementing the safety procedure which we still test at Anfield to this day. I looked at Kim and said, 'Let's go!' She thought I was crazy, but I explained that this was not a practice and that there was trouble brewing. We headed for the nearest exit only to be halted temporarily while the horses in the parade ring were led back to the stables. You couldn't make it up! We went home, and the race was run the following Monday.

The 1996–97 season was the closest Roy came to winning the Premier League. He bought Czech midfielder Patrik Berger, who had impressed at Euro 96, but the star of the show was a promising seventeen-year-old striker called Michael Owen. Stan Collymore moved to Aston Villa in the close season, and in came ex-Manchester United hero Paul Ince and legendary German striker Karl-Heinz Riedle.

1997–98

Going into the 1997–98 season, many people pegged Liverpool as title contenders, mainly thanks to their exciting strike force of Robbie Fowler and Michael Owen. Michael scored eighteen goals in thirty-six Premier League games, but an injury to Robbie kept him out for most of the season. It was a hammer blow. We can only imagine what those two would have done if they had been given a clear run at the league. In the end, the Reds had to settle for third place and entry to the UEFA Cup. For the record, I have no axe to grind with Michael, in complete contrast to some of the people who abused him for his career choices after leaving Liverpool.

There was a youthful look about the squad: Robbie Fowler, Steve McManaman, Michael Owen, Jason McAteer, Rob Jones and Jamie Redknapp. These were the days when I used to chat to the guys before matches, and I can testify that they are some of the nicest men in the game.

Rick Parry, a Liverpool fan, arrived at Anfield in the middle of 1997, and he was made CEO the following July by chairman

David Moores. Parry was best known for helping to set up the Premier League in 1992, when he negotiated a TV deal worth £304 million.

I got a message from Rick's PA that he wanted to meet up, and I arranged to call in to his office in the old Main Stand on 28 November 1997. He basically wanted to make contact and touch base. When he'd arrived at Anfield, he had met with most people but said it seemed that I didn't 'belong' to any one manager or department. This was true at that time, although these days the staffing computer system has me listed as a 'Casual Match-day Steward'! I heard someone from UEFA once say, 'Oh yes, you're the guy who turns up when he's supposed to, does what he has to do and goes home again!' I'm a great believer in not complicating things. I arrive at Anfield with my music, follow the running order, pack up and go home. My mantra is 'everything in its place' and 'if it ain't broke, don't fix it!' If I were a child today, someone would be assessing me for Asperger's syndrome.

It was an interesting afternoon. It was the day when the application for American goalkeeper Brad Friedel's work permit had been denied, and there was an air of mild panic about the place. During our chat, various people popped in and out with faxes and emails to worry about. I was an inadvertent fly on the wall.

In the few dealings I had with him, Rick Parry was one of those people in whose company I couldn't relax. I remember remarking to Liz that he would make a terrific poker player. His facial expression rarely changed. I was, however, aware that he was a football man, a Liverpool fan ('This is my dream job,' he said) and that he had dealt successfully with big hitters like BSkyB. We were in good hands. Of course, the same couldn't be said when he left.

Elton John's 'Candle in the Wind' tribute to
HRH Princess Diana was the nation's favourite in 1997.

FC Twente of Enschede are a Dutch club who play their home
games at the De Grolsch Veste stadium. It had previously
been known as the Arke Stadion when it was built in the late
nineties, and Liz and I were invited to the closing ceremony
of the old Diekman stadium in April 1998. FC Twente fans
sang (and still sing) 'You'll Never Walk Alone' before every
home game. They were hoping to get Gerry Marsden over to
sing the anthem before their last game in the old place, but he
was unavailable, so I got the trip!

We were picked up at Schiphol Airport in Amsterdam and
driven to Enschede, where we were guests at a civic banquet.
After that, we were treated to a guided tour of the new site. In the
evening, it was off to the Diekman stadium, where FC Twente
were playing Heerenveen in the Dutch Eredivisie. I made a
little speech on the pitch beforehand (live on Dutch TV!) and
then said to the guy looking after me, 'Better get back to my
seat. It's nearly kick-off time.' Just as we approached the main
stand, the entire crowd got to their feet and started cheering. I
turned around to look at the players' tunnel, expecting to see
the two teams emerging. My guide laughed and said, 'No, no.
They are cheering you.' Blimey. What an experience! I slowed
down slightly and milked the situation for all it was worth!

After the final whistle, we headed to a smart nightspot in
downtown Enschede. The guy who had driven us from the
airport owned a hotel in the city centre and was our host for the
night. We happened to be sitting with a guy called Theo Snelders,
who was Aberdeen's goalkeeper at the time, but he had started
out with FC Twente and had popped home for the ceremonies.

He spoke perfect English and greeted us with 'Bloody Scousers!' All this with a smile on his face, I hasten to add. A guy called Willy van de Kerkhof, who had been in the Dutch 1974 and 1978 World Cup squads alongside his twin brother René, was also in the nightclub. I couldn't resist returning to my football-fan roots and got Willy's autograph on my programme.

Around midnight, the long day of travelling suddenly hit us and I told our host that Liz and I were going to have to make our way back to the hotel. Within two minutes, a guy in a chauffeur's uniform (complete with flat hat under his left arm) arrived at the door. 'Mister Sephton?' The idea of a discreet exit had gone. The entire FC Twente board of directors lined up to shake our hands, thank us for coming and wish us a safe journey home the following day. It was a weird but welcome feeling to be treated so well, and I was more than proud to represent Liverpool Football Club on FC Twente's big day.

Five years after Dune FM had originally broadcast on a temporary basis, the Radio Authority, as it was then known, advertised a small-scale local licence for the towns of Southport and Ormskirk and the Merseyside borough of Sefton, which attracted three bids, including the winning Dune FM consortium. I was a bit annoyed by the fact that I heard the news of Dune FM's success in the bidding process from a third party. A few weeks later, I received a message from the station head asking me to pop over one night to speak to him. He was doing an oldies programme on Sunday nights and wanted me to do a regular spot in the programme with my favourite vinyl tracks. 'Oh,' I said. 'I'm back in the fold then?'

He looked shocked. 'You were never out of the fold, George.' He could have fooled me, but I was keen to contribute to the station's output and accepted the short Sunday slot. Not long afterwards, a permanent long-term schedule was agreed, and I heard on the grapevine that some of the guys who had been in the mix from the start were being asked to pitch for what they thought were already their own programmes. I didn't waste time and decided to play the game. I knew there was a sixties programme in the schedule and sent a formal application to take it over to the station controller, Jonathan Dean. I was invited to pop in for a chat and was pleased to be given my own show. Jonathan then threw me a curveball, however, when he told me I was earmarked for the rock 'n' roll programme and not the sixties one, which was already spoken for. I was slightly taken aback but then realized that the rock 'n' roll era was just as much mine as was the sixties.

In July of that year, Mark Lamarr started a rock 'n' roll programme on Radio 2 called 'Shake, Rattle and Roll'. My programme, on the other hand, was eventually pulled on the grounds that 'no one was interested in that sort of music any more', even though 'Shake, Rattle and Roll' went on to receive a national radio award – such was the popularity of his music! At the same time, Suzi Quatro was presenting yet another late-night programme of rock 'n' roll music. Unpopular? I don't think so, but such is life.

One legacy of my time with Dune FM is that I qualified for an Equity card! I was now a member of the actors' union, which was a long-held ambition fulfilled.

In 2012, Dune FM was wound up in the Liverpool District Registry. As I write, two radio stations are operating in Southport: Sandgrounder and Mighty. Good luck to all concerned!

The Roy Castle International Centre for Lung Cancer Research was opened by his friend Sir Cliff Richard in May 1998. Sadly, Roy had died of the disease in 1994. Following the official opening, the VIP party departed for a celebration lunch at Anfield, as Liverpool Football Club had been a staunch supporter of the project. The previous Sunday had seen a charity game at Anfield to raise funds for the centre. At the end of the game, I'd collared the charity's press officer and, using the fact that I was presenting the rock 'n' roll programme on Dune FM, had wangled an invitation and a press pass for the Anfield lunch. I'd also been told that Sir Cliff would be doing interviews afterwards. In the event, the speeches and the food came and went, and Cliff suddenly vanished. I managed to find the press officer, who then told me that there were not going to be any interviews after all. I was fuming. 'Where's Sir Cliff?' I asked. He told me that he was in one of the private rooms upstairs. I was turning all the colours of the rainbow by now. 'I was promised an interview.'

'Well, he'll be leaving soon – you'll have to grab him!'

'I can't grab Sir Cliff Richard,' I said. Then I thought, 'Sod it! Yes, I can!' and made my way upstairs. The lunch was held in what was then the Centenary Stand but is now the Sir Kenny Dalglish Stand. This is basically my place of work, and I know it intimately. I'm also well known to the security staff. I made my way up to the third floor and was greeted by a steward.

'Where's Cliff?' I said. He knew where Sir Cliff was being entertained, and I headed in. It was packed. I basically just used my weight and barged through to the great man: 'Can you spare me five minutes for a radio piece, please?'

'Of course,' he said. 'But can we do it somewhere a bit quieter?' He followed me down the corridor, and he was as good as his word. Forty years after wangling my way into the Liverpool Empire to see him, I was having a one-to-one conversation with the guy in the back corridors of Anfield. Who would have thought it.

I explained that the interview was for my evening rock 'n' roll show and that the plan was to play wall-to-wall Cliff Richard and the Shadows for a night. That tickled him. It also occurred to me that The Shadows had only just changed their name from The Drifters when I saw them back then, but he was about to appear with the American originals who had necessitated the name change in the first place. At this point I think he decided I knew what I was on about, and we had a good chat. He told me he still loved the old-style rock 'n' roll when he was chilling out on his travels. 'But,' he said to my astonishment, 'it's all rock 'n' roll really, isn't it? All the way through to the Spice Girls.' Blimey!

With the interview in the can, we shook hands and went our separate ways. He has, alongside Peter Crouch, one of the strongest handshakes I've ever encountered – a real bone-cruncher. What a day!

After leaving Anfield, I went to the diabetic clinic for a check-up. I was slightly late, so I ran up the path to the clinic, arriving red-faced and breathless. 'Sorry I'm late,' I said. 'I just had lunch with Cliff Richard!' The nurse looked at me quizzically and was thinking about calling the proverbial men in white coats until I explained about my encounter with a living legend.

1998–99

In July 1998, Gérard Houllier was brought in as the joint manager of Liverpool, alongside Roy Evans, but the arrangement didn't work out and Roy resigned in November. Once Roy had departed, Houllier set about restoring discipline to the squad and rebuilding the team, a project that he said would take five years.

In the summer of 1998, the World Cup produced a new England star, a young lad whom Reds fans had been admiring since he'd been part of the FA Youth Cup success a couple of years earlier: Michael Owen. We, of course, knew what he was capable of and, after that magical goal against Argentina, so did the whole world. Later that year, Liz, Kim and I went over to Dublin to see Liverpool's pre-season friendly against Inter Milan at Lansdowne Road and were lucky to see Michael score one of the goals in a 2–0 win.

Liverpool v. Blackburn, Anfield, 29 November 1998

The final whistle was fast approaching when I was alerted to the fourth official raising his board on the far touchline in front of the dugout. Gérard Houllier had his arm round the shoulder of one of the academy kids. The numbers went up above the fourth official's head, and I announced the substitution: 'Leaving the field, number fourteen, Vegard Heggem' – pause – 'And coming on for the Reds . . . number twenty-eight, Steven Gerrard!'

Everyone was pleased to see a youth player getting his chance, but very few in the ground that night could have predicted the impact this fresh-faced young Scouser was going to have on us all.

'Believe' was a comeback smash for Cher in 1998.

We finished a miserable seventh in the league in 1998–99. Being so off the pace was unacceptable to the likes of us old enough to remember Shankly's maxim that 'second is nowhere'. Goodness knows what he would have made of seventh. The fans of approximately eighty-five other clubs would tell you how much they would love to finish seventh in the Premier League, but, to coin a phrase, 'We are Liverpool'. We did, however, have some decent players in the squad and many reasons for optimism.

Gérard was putting a great team together. Robbie Fowler and Michael Owen were up front, and we had classy young midfielders Jamie Redknapp, Steve McManaman, Stevie Gerrard and Patrik Berger in the middle of the park. Behind them was the rock that was Jamie Carragher. In addition, Liverpool Football Club appeared to be running their own transfer market in 1999. In came Sami Hyypiä from Willem II in May, followed in June by Titi Camara from Marseille, Stéphane Henchoz from Blackburn Rovers and Sander Westerveld from

Vitesse. July saw the arrival of Vladimír Šmicer from Lens, Erik Meijer from Bayer Leverkusen, and 'The Kaiser', aka Dietmar (Didi) Hamann, from Newcastle. Out went David James to Aston Villa, Steve McManaman to Real Madrid, Steve Harkness to Benfica, Jean-Michel Ferri to Sochaux, Tony Warner to Millwall, Jamie Cassidy to Cambridge, Sean Dundee to Stuttgart, Paul Ince to Middlesbrough, Øyvind Leonhardsen to Spurs, Bjørn Tore Kvarme to Saint-Étienne and Karl-Heinz Riedle to Fulham. I was sad to see Steve go, and Jamie Cassidy too. I still see Steve quite often and Jamie's family are neighbours of mine.

In the greater scheme of things, it looked as if Gérard Houllier was implementing his five-year plan. We Liverpool fans were in unfamiliar territory as far as foreign managers were concerned. We hoped he knew what he was doing and, of course, he did.

I knew that I was due to be moved from my little room suspended from the roof of the Main Stand as a result of the Taylor Inquiry into the Hillsborough tragedy. One of its recommendations was that the stadium announcer should be in direct visual contact with the match control staff. For twenty-eight years, I'd been in phone contact with the police room at Anfield, but that was it. It made sense that the guys in charge of crowd safety should be able to see me. If I wasn't there, for whatever reason, they needed to know. Any important message for the crowd has to be delivered immediately. If I'd passed out, nipped to the gents or dropped dead in my chair, they would need to bypass my involvement.

I was told that I would be sitting in a new DJ room in the corner of Anfield between the Kop Stand and the Main Stand. I assumed, foolishly, that the room would be at an angle of forty-five degrees to the stands so that I could still see the entire pitch. But when the match-day control room people had a pre-season look around their new home, I tagged along and was horrified when I sat behind my new desk and discovered that I couldn't actually see the goal at the Anfield Road end of the ground. After some thought, the maintenance guys created a mirror to go on the left-hand side of the column containing my window. It was less than useless. So it was that I started the new season dodging around my new room to keep track of the ball. Things have improved since, of course, as I now have a monitor and can normally see everything that happens out on the pitch in high definition. This, however, led to another minor problem for me to overcome: the TV cameras are on the Main Stand side of the ground so that if the ball travels from the Kop end to the Anfield Road end, it moves from right to left, whereas in my line of vision it's actually travelling from left to right. In the early days, I'd often watch an attack break down in the Kop goal area and then see the ball disappear out of my view, heading towards the Anfield Road goal. At that point, I'd turn to the TV screen and watch the ball apparently change direction. It was *very* disorientating, but my old brain got used to it and adapted to the change.

There was yet another unexpected problem after my first game in the new room. At the end of the match, I announced the scores from the other Premier League games – in those days there were still a few games at 3 p.m. on a Saturday afternoon. I told the crowd that Arsenal had drawn 1–1 at home to Leicester City. Unbeknownst to me, however, that match had kicked off fifteen minutes late due to crowd congestion around the ground. After we'd finished up at Anfield, Dennis Bergkamp had scored a late winner for the Gunners. Early the following week, I received a phone call at work from an irate club secretary called Bryce Morrison. He had been inundated with complaints about my misinformation. I explained to him that I had been blissfully unaware of the late kick-off at Highbury, because the glass windows in my new position were so thick that I could only just about get a signal on the little transistor radio I always had with me. 'What? A transistor radio? I thought you got the scores from a teleprinter.'

'Er, no, Bryce. I've had this little radio for years.' He thought I was winding him up. I wasn't. To be fair to Bryce, who was a decent bloke, he went over to the match control office during the week to see for himself. When I arrived for the next home game, I had a TV screen in there with Ceefax, a primitive information service but one that showed football scores if you asked it nicely. Sometime later, *Soccer Saturday* started up on Sky, and nowadays, of course, the scores from all over Europe are available on my phone.

My long career as a freelancer in IT was faltering. My field was programming in the RPG language on IBM AS/400 machines. The industry as a whole was moving away from the 'traditional' set-ups and everything was downsizing. The term 'personal computer' was unthinkable when I started in IT in 1968, but now people's horizons were changing. I had managed to get my hands on a list of AS/400 installations in the north-west of England. An IBM engineer had wandered off after a hardware repair at an office I was working in and left his address book behind. I phoned him to let him know but made sure I'd photocopied the contents before I did so. Having sat on this information for a while, I now put it to good use. The agencies were no longer calling me with offers of work, so I turned proactive. I sent an up-to-date CV to everyone in the address book. Bingo! I got a phone call from Stuart Keating, an ex-colleague from my Preston days fifteen years earlier, who was now in charge of the IT department of ROMEC, the Royal Mail's in-house engineering department in Stockport. He had some work for me. After having sat at home jobless for a while, I was really happy to be back in the harness.

I am well used to speaking to crowds of people in excess of 50,000 and the greatest number of people I've actually spoken in front of was at Wembley before the 1995 League Cup final. While I was working at ROMEC in Stockport, one of the girls in the office asked me if I could help out her husband. They had recently moved north and settled in Rochdale. He had joined the local Rotary Club and had somehow found himself elected as the new speakers secretary. He knew very few people in the area, so his ears pricked up when his wife told him that she was working alongside me. He said, 'I bet that guy's got some stories to tell! Do you think he'd come to one of our dinners and tell some of them?'

I accepted the challenge. It wasn't a paying gig, as they were a charity, but there was a free dinner involved. How could I refuse? I cobbled together a few lines and headed for Rochdale on the appointed night. There were twenty-one people around the table. They didn't like football, and they didn't like Scousers! After about five or ten minutes, my best jokes had come and gone without so much as a titter! I was a bit taken aback. More than that, though, I was angry. Rochdale is a drive you don't want to make after a day's work, especially when you're not getting paid for the privilege. Adrenalin kicked in. I threw away my notes and did forty-five minutes off the cuff. Shortly before my trip to Rochdale, I'd been the subject of a trivia question on the radio station talkSPORT. The question, set by my actor-friend Tom Watt, was, 'Who was it who had a loaded gun pointed at him at three successive European finals?' The answer, of course, was me. I pounced on it as the basis of my impromptu talk. Suffice to say that my colleague's husband received a letter to say I was the best speaker they'd ever had at one of their dinners!

1999–2000

Ex-Spice Girl Melanie C released *Northern Star*, her first solo album, on 18 October 1999. Always on the lookout for a freebie, I phoned the PR department at Melanie's record company and pitched to them that because Mel regarded having the Spice Girls' first single played at Anfield as 'the greatest day of my life', it would be nice if the debut of her first solo CD was at Anfield too. They agreed, but on one condition. They were promoting a new girl band who were all Scousers. If I would plug them as well, I was very welcome to Mel's CD. Enter Atomic Kitten.

Formed in Liverpool in 1998 by founder members Natasha Hamilton, Kerry Katona and Liz McClarnon, the group's debut single 'Right Now' was released in December 1999, and they made a live half-time appearance at Anfield to promote it. They gave it everything. After the final whistle, I met up with the girls and their manager Martin O'Shea in the Main Stand reception, and I still have the demo single they signed for me. Not only that, I was privileged to be there when the news came through that their single had cracked the Top 10. Their joy was a sight to behold. They made some good records over a period of time, and Liz in particular has carved out a career for herself. However, she's a dyed-in-the-wool Everton fan and felt a bit out of place at Anfield.

In 1999, Britney Spears burst on to the world scene with 'Baby One More Time'.

My contract at ROMEC turned out to be the last of a long freelance career in IT. My (Blue) friend Stuart Keating had been good to me and even extended my contract past the Christmas period, which was always a bad time for freelancers, and into the new year. After that, however, there was absolutely nothing in the way of work coming my way. Believe me, I tried! I was a very experienced IT professional but had one major drawback: I was way too old to be working at the forefront of technology. Well, at least in the eyes of the HR professionals and agency staff I dealt with on a daily basis. I sat back, took a deep breath, tidied up my CV and set out to find a job.

I turned fifty-four in February 2000, and I was still in the market for work. My daily routine was repetitive and tedious. Liz was still working, so I was disinclined to lie around all day. Every morning, I was up, showered and breakfasted for 9 a.m. at the latest, stopping only for a cup of coffee and to catch up on the breakfast news. I'd be sitting in front of my PC when the emails started arriving from all the recruitment agencies I was registered with, and believe me, there were very few I didn't sign up to! I'd work my way through them, note the jobs that might suit me and email my CV to the relevant consultants. Then I'd trawl the websites that didn't email me automatically with job listings. More often than not, that took up most of the morning. By the time I'd covered all the bases, it was usually time for lunch. The drawback with the routine was that when Liz went off to work, I was perched in front of the TV with a coffee, and when she came home for lunch, I was in the same spot, looking for all the world as if I hadn't moved all morning!

Eventually, after four months, when I was very nearly at the end of my tether, I was offered two promising job interviews on consecutive days. One was at an agency in Manchester for a six-month contract in Dublin. The second was about two miles from home at the IT department of Sayers bakery in Norris Green. There were pros and cons to both jobs. Sayers was close to home, although the job was basically an operator's role, whereas the Dublin post was for an analyst/programmer. Sayers meant I could go to work every morning from the comfort of my own home. Dublin would mean living away and, of course, it would kill my career at Anfield.

I was eventually offered both jobs! You wouldn't credit it, would you – no work for months and then two job offers simultaneously. I plumped for Sayers. The Dublin role offered much more money but was only temporary, and the travelling and living expenses would have taken a big chunk out of my salary anyway. One thing people know about me: I like my own bed at night! I was never a good traveller. So it was that on 2 June 2000 I arrived at the factory and offices of Sayers bakery on Lorenzo Drive in Norris Green. My hours were a bit odd and included Saturday mornings, so there were a few hairy moments when I ended up driving at great speed from Norris Green to Anfield around lunchtime on a Saturday. But it was good to be back at work!

My mum and dad's wedding day in 1934   Me with my dad, circa 1950

Liverpool manager Bill Shankly shocks the football world by announcing his retirement, 12 July 1974

Kevin Keegan emerges from the players' tunnel for the first time,
14 August 1971

Liverpool manager Bob Paisley, surrounded by his players, holds the First
Divison Championship trophy, prior to their match against Aston Villa at
Anfield, 7 May 1983

Rushie celebrates Phil Neal's goal in the European Cup Final, 30 May 1984

European Cup Final, Brussels, 29 May 1985: Liverpool 0 v Juventus 1 –
chaos around the collapsed wall on the Juventus terrace

Above: In the days after the Hillsborough tragedy, floral tributes cover the pitch, April 1989

Left: Kenny Dalglish salutes the crowd at his testimonial match, 14 August 1990

Below: The last day of the standing Kop, 30 April 1994

Left: Recording 'You'll Never Walk Alone' with Chris De Burgh and assorted Kopites

Below: The Miracle of Istanbul: Steven Gerrard celebrates with the trophy following victory in the UEFA Champions League final between Liverpool and AC Milan, 25 May 2005

Above: Me with 'Saint' –
Ian St John

Right: My fortieth
anniversary at Anfield,
13 August 2011

Above: My three offspring
at the Boot Room in
2013. Kim and Laurie at
the back and Rob seated
front.

Above: Me and my wife Liz

My favourite Spice Girl: Melanie Chisholm

My treasured seventieth birthday present from the club

Above: At the controls, 2019

Right: Champions of the World, 2019

Jordan Henderson lifts the Premier League trophy at last, 22 July 2020

Jurgen Klopp leads the team in a rendition of 'You'll Never Walk Alone' as they celebrate winning the League during the presentation, 22 July 2020

PART FIVE

The 2000s

2000–01

Liverpool v. Bradford City,
Anfield, 19 August 2000

This was quite a day. Liverpool were playing Bradford City in
the first Premier League game of the new season. A business
partner and I had been running some record collectors' fairs
around the area, and we'd scheduled one for that day in a
church hall in Aigburth. I went there during the morning
and helped everyone to get set up, and he was happy to run
the show after that until I was finished at Anfield. Little did I
know what I was in for.

I got to the ground at my usual time and headed up to my
room. No sooner had I got set up and unpacked my bag of
CDs than the door opened and in wandered Phil Easton with
a guy who turned out to be his sound engineer. Back in 1975,
Radio City employed a then unheard of – at least by us – DJ
by the name of Phil Easton. He hosted an evening radio show
at 6.30 p.m. each weekday called 'The Great Easton Express'.
On the programme, he featured all the news and sounds
in rock music, and it soon became essential listening each

evening. Every music fan in the city looked up to Phil. He was DJ royalty. 'The Great Easton Express' ran for twelve years, culminating each year with a battle-of-the-bands competition at the Empire Theatre. In 1988, with the popularity of rock music in decline, he moved on to other things and finally ended up presenting the 'City Talk Breakfast Show' every day. But on 19 August 2000, he was suddenly, unexpectedly and unannounced, striding into my room at Anfield.

We looked at each other and, more or less simultaneously, asked the same question: 'Hello, what are you doing here?' To which we both replied, 'I was about to ask you the same question!' It turns out that I had been replaced. I knew that Radio City had wanted for years to get one of their guys into my job at Anfield but had always been rebuffed. Now the club had acceded to their request. There was one minor problem: no one had bothered to mention the fact to me! I was told a while later that someone in the know had been aware that no one had told me what was going on but had concluded that when I found Phil in my room, I would walk away in a huff. I didn't. I wouldn't. Why should I?

I was more or less edged out that afternoon, but the club got so many messages about the apparent change that they had to think again. Before the following home game, I got a call from Brian Hall to say that the plan was for me to carry on as usual but to hand over to Phil twenty minutes before kick-off. I wasn't happy with that, as you can imagine, but at least I hadn't been pushed out completely. This arrangement carried on until February 2009 when Phil died suddenly at home the day after a game at Anfield.

People used to think I hated Phil because of the situation at Anfield. Nothing could be further from the truth. Phil and I got on like a house on fire. I had the utmost respect for him and thought the world of him. We did several dinners together, and he used to invite me to his 'Evening With' events, which were an absolute treat. The arrangement was that a big singing star would entertain an invitation-only audience in a small but classy venue. There was always a Q and A session, and I was usually a 'plant' in the audience. I did several of these with Phil's good friend Chris de Burgh, one with Hayley Westenra and one with Russell Watson. The resultant programmes were broadcast across the entire Magic network.

The big seller of 2000 was a novelty children's song, 'Can We Fix It?' by Bob the Builder.

A note for the amateur football historians and keyboard warriors: 2001 was the year Liverpool won five major trophies. *Five trophies!* The first three were a cup Treble during the 2000–01 season: the League Cup, FA Cup and UEFA Cup. Steven Gerrard was voted PFA Young Player of the Year, and the efforts of local stars Michael Owen, Robbie Fowler and Jamie Carragher were matched by new signings Gary McAllister and Emile Heskey in an increasingly Continental side that included new captain Sami Hyypiä, Sander Westerveld, Jari Litmanen and Dietmar Hamann. Sami was a rock, the Virgil van Dijk of his day. Gary McAllister was very classy and highly experienced.

UEFA Cup Fourth Round – Liverpool v. AS Roma, Anfield, 22 February 2001

We had our backs against the wall in this UEFA Cup fourth-round tie against Roma, surviving an Italian fightback to reach the quarter-finals. We had beaten them 2–0 away, and were favourites to complete the task in the second leg at Anfield, but we were under the cosh for much of the match and, despite some dogged defending, couldn't keep out a second-half goal that offered the visitors a lifeline. Referee Jose Maria-Garcia-Aranda then awarded Roma a penalty for a handball by Markus Babbel before controversially changing his mind! To this day, I don't know why he reversed his decision, but, if I'm honest, I don't really care.

A couple of weeks before the game, someone at Radio Merseyside had suggested to me that the tune 'Arrivederci Roma' would be an appropriate one to play on the night of the game. If you've ever listened to the words, they basically say, 'We look forward to seeing your beautiful city again soon.' So I played it at the end of the game. The Kop, to a man, fell about laughing. The Italians were irate, Fabio Capello, the Roma manager, was furious and Gérard Houllier was embarrassed. Apparently, a journalist asked him if he thought the song was funny. Houllier said, 'I only pick the team – not the music!' I was in trouble.

I phoned up the manager's office at the club's Melwood training ground the following morning to apologize – not for playing the song, but for the fact that he'd become involved. There was no malice on my part. I thought that would do the trick. Far from it! I sat next to a guy in my office at Sayers whose dad was the person responsible for signing the safety certificate that allowed Liverpool to play their games at Anfield, and he was not happy. It seems I had nearly started a riot! I phoned the match commander at Lower Lane Police Station, where he was based. He denied any knowledge of trouble after the game and said he'd remarked to the stadium manager what a nice piece of music it was. OK, so the police and the manager were sorted. Panic over. But that wasn't the end of it! Rob had a bank of screens above his desk. One of them was connected to Reuters news agency. Suddenly, he was seeing headlines like 'Italian Fury!' Then Radio Merseyside rang. Would I like to do an interview on *Drive Time*? I welcomed the opportunity to explain myself.

A couple of weeks earlier, my GP had changed my blood-pressure medication to something called Zestril. She was going off on maternity leave, and I was the last patient she saw before she left. When she was writing up my notes after I'd gone home, she discovered that Zestril should not be prescribed to patients with angioedema, as it could prove fatal! She left a note for the doctor who was taking over her caseload to get in touch with me sharpish and stop me from taking the medication, as I suffered from the condition. The note was overlooked.

A trigger is needed to bring about a bad reaction to Zestril. One of the possible triggers is stress, and believe me there's nothing quite as stressful as upsetting two internationally acclaimed managers, the English press and the Roman mafia! Twenty-four hours after getting home from the Roma game, I was sitting in my armchair with my face puffing up slightly and my tongue swelling like an inflating balloon. Thank God Liz was a nurse. She didn't hang around but drove me straight to A & E at Aintree Hospital, which is no more than half a mile from our house. There I was pumped full of intravenous adrenalin, and, thankfully, my tongue stopped swelling just before it would have choked me. I was told later that my wife's quick thinking had saved my life.

After a night in hospital, I was as right as rain and had a full twenty-four hours to recover before Kim and I set off for Cardiff and the League Cup final. It would take more than a brush with death to stop me from going to the big game.

League Cup Final – Liverpool v. Birmingham City, Millennium Stadium, 25 February 2001

I was attending at the invitation of the organizers to talk to the crowd pre-match again. I'd been told to use the park-and-ride car park at Cardiff City's stadium, but that turned out to be a park-and-walk facility, so Kim and I arrived exhausted but just in the nick of time, and she was able to follow me through the bowels of the stadium and sit pitchside while I did what I had to do. When I'd finished, we set off to find our seats, which were at the opposite corner of the ground. All the way round, we met Liverpool fans coming the other way who burst into their own rendition of 'Arrivederci Roma' when they saw me.

We won 5–4 on penalties after ninety minutes of normal time and thirty nervous minutes of extra time. Robbie Fowler had scored midway through the first half, and we seemed to be heading for a win inside regulation time until Birmingham equalized in injury time. It was the first time a major English domestic cup final had been decided by a penalty shoot-out. In theory, we should have seen off Birmingham City easily but, sadly, football isn't played in theory. This was one of several games over the decades when we asked ourselves, 'Why do we put ourselves through this?' I still get wound up during penalty shoot-outs to this day – even when they don't involve my team!

FA Cup Final – Liverpool v. Arsenal, Millennium Stadium, 12 May 2001

After the park-and-ride antics in February, I took advice from seasoned travellers and drove to Bridgend Railway Station. Friends had done this previously and had found that the return fare from Bridgend to Cardiff was well worth it. No parking worries, no sitting in traffic jams after the game – it was straight on to the train and a comfortable journey back to your car. That was the theory anyway. On the day, I parked easily enough at Bridgend, bought two return tickets to Cardiff and then realized I'd left our precious cup-final tickets in my glovebox. I legged it back to the car and then returned to Kim via a shortcut across the tracks. At this point, I was collared by a member of British Transport Police. He wasn't happy. I had trespassed on railway property. I was about to be arrested! I thought about passing our tickets to Kim just in case I was detained in Bridgend, but in the end I was allowed to leave with just a flea in my ear, and we headed for Cardiff. Phew!

Freddie Ljungberg put Arsenal ahead twenty minutes from time, but, in typical fashion, Michael Owen ran rings round the Arsenal defence in the last ten minutes, scoring two goals. Ecstasy! Liverpool's victory marked the second part of their unique Treble. The League and FA Cups were in the bag, and now the team were flying off to Germany to attempt the third leg. Followed, it should be said, by hordes of happy Scousers.

Kim and I had to queue in the hot sun for quite some time after the game for a train back to Bridgend, where I'd parked my car. For several weeks beforehand, I'd been repeatedly reading out a message at Anfield from the Welsh authorities, pleading with us all to use public transport and not drive to Cardiff. This was all very well, except no one appeared to have worked out that the hordes arriving in Cardiff by train would probably also want to go home by train after the game. Luckily, the Arsenal fans were magnanimous in defeat, but things could easily have kicked off, with both sets of fans being forced to hang around like that.

UEFA Cup Final – Liverpool v. Alavés, Westfalenstadion, 16 May 2001

In their first European final following the Heysel Stadium disaster and subsequent ban, and the team's first UEFA Cup final since 1976, Liverpool took on Alavés, who were appearing in their first European final.

I was delighted to be asked to go to Dortmund to act as the official English announcer. I was told that I'd be flying out on my own on the day before the game and was booked into a hotel. Rob was working in America at the time and was obviously not going to get back for the game, and Liz and Kim both wanted to be there but couldn't take more than a day off work, so they booked on to one of the available day trips. Laurie had only recently graduated from university and was, naturally, skint. As was I, so I hatched a plot. I put it to Bryce Morrison, the club secretary, that the club would be paying for my hotel room and another body in there wouldn't cost them anything extra, as the charge was for the room and not for the number of occupants, so would it be OK if my son bunked in with me. He agreed, and Laurie had somewhere to stay in Dortmund. I then took a deep breath and suggested that as Liverpool FC were booking airline seats galore, perhaps he could ask for another seat, which would be a lot cheaper than a regular fare. Once more, God bless him, he agreed, and Laurie had a flight to Dortmund with his old dad. I hasten to add that I paid for the flight; it was just a lot more affordable. After all that, getting him a ticket was comparatively easy. So it was that we both headed for Manchester Airport the day before the big game. Excited or what!

We were booked on a scheduled flight to Düsseldorf and would have to make our own way from there to Dortmund. In the envelope with our tickets to Germany were two more tickets for British Airways first class from Düsseldorf to Manchester the day after the final. I was gobsmacked! After a bit of confusion getting the right train from Düsseldorf to Dortmund, we made it to our hotel in the suburbs and checked in. I got a message to say that I was needed at a UEFA meeting at the team's hotel (which was much further out of town) that afternoon. I suggested to Laurie that he should come with me, as he'd only be hanging around at our hotel, and if he came with me, he'd be hanging around at a much more interesting hotel! That proved to be the case, and he was fascinated by the comings and goings around the press lounge up there. I'm a great people watcher myself, but Laurie got the better part of the deal that afternoon. He was ideally placed to watch Gérard Houllier and Phil Thompson heading through the gaggle of press guys. He was amazed to see how big and imposing Sami Hyypiä was and was quietly tickled to see how many of the media people stopped to say hello to me.

I went upstairs to the UEFA meeting to be greeted with, 'Why weren't you here this morning?' There had been a meeting that morning in the same room at the same hotel that I was supposed to attend but (a) I didn't even know there was a meeting, and (b) I was in the air somewhere over France when the meeting took place! And I didn't choose my flight time! This is typical of communication levels in the wonderful world of football and applies to all sorts of organizations, from FIFA all the way down to local junior leagues. I was taken aback, but, as usual, my explanation didn't cut any ice with the men in suits, and I was in the doghouse even though I wasn't at fault. I'm the sort of person who will hold my hands up if I make a boo-boo, but I get really angry when I'm accused of doing something that is clearly someone else's mistake. Anyway, having boxed my ears, the UEFA guys continued with the meeting. It was basically to go through the running order for the following night's final. The 'running order' on this occasion was more akin to *War and Peace* than anything else. There would be a performance by the German equivalent of the Three Tenors, who had gone down so well at Italia 90. Prior to that, there would be a demonstration by the Danish Super Kids, a troupe of young acrobats from Copenhagen. In the middle of all this, the stadium DJ would be playing some tunes selected by me and my opposite number from Alavés, and I was pleased to see that 'You'll Never Walk Alone' was in the schedule. Pleased, that is, until I noticed the allocated time – a quarter past seven. Considering that this was a full ninety minutes before kick-off, I suggested that there would be very few people in the stadium to sing along. This observation was pooh-poohed, of course. After all, what did I know?

Laurie and I went back to our hotel, and it was just as well that he'd come with me, as we had a stack of 'goodies' to take back with us for some of the sponsors' guests. Laurie and I then spent the evening with some of his friends in the town square before heading back to catch up on our sleep. That night out was a unique opportunity for me. I rarely if ever get to away games, and when I do it's usually a case of getting there in time to do what I have to do and going home again straight afterwards. It was a happy couple of hours.

On the day of the game, I had to be at the stadium for what UEFA call a 'technical rehearsal' around lunchtime, so I left Laurie to his own devices and headed off in the very upmarket, chauffeur-driven car that UEFA had supplied. This was a new experience, but one I could quite happily get used to. At the stadium, I was introduced to my opposite number from Alavés, who was looking very nervous. He didn't speak much English, but I speak a little Spanish, so we got by. I asked him (knowing the answer full well), 'Is this your first big final?'

'*Si*,' he squeaked.

I explained that this was my fifth and put my arm round his shoulder. I then pointed at the huge running-order document and told him not to worry about its contents. 'It will never happen,' I told him.

The run-through went well. The German tenors did a full sound check, entering the field from the opposite side of the pitch to the players tunnel where I and my counterpart were stationed. They walked in formation (and perfect harmony) to the centre circle, and I have to say they were impressive, even to my ill-educated ears. Once the organizers were satisfied, I headed back to my chauffeur. There was a fan party in the Market Square, and I was due there. My limo had sat-nav, a recent innovation in 2001. But my driver didn't look happy with the new technology and eventually dropped me on the wrong side of the square. I found myself trying to fight my way through a crowd of several thousand Spaniards. When I got to the back of the stage, the officials seemed surprised to see me. A Liverpool musician friend of mine, George Windsor, who had just released an album of songs about Liverpool, had arrived a little earlier, and I think the officials must have thought that he was the George they were expecting. George was having a whale of a time, and the Reds fans in front of the stage were enjoying themselves. I eventually got hold of the mic and spoke to the crowd, but I really don't think they listened to a word I said, so I handed back to George and he carried on. At that moment, Liz rang. She and Kim had just arrived from the airport and were wondering where I was. I decided to abandon the fan party and went to meet them. I wasn't missed! At that moment the heavens opened, so we grabbed a taxi and headed back to my hotel. They dried out and freshened up before we went and had something to eat.

The time was coming for me to head back to the Westfalenstadion ready for the pre-match entertainment. We decided Liz and Kim would come with me, as there was an underground station just outside the ground that would take them into town to do a bit of shopping before heading back for kick-off. The only problem was that the station was inside the ring of security around the stadium. I purloined the UEFA car again and didn't even try to explain to the driver why I now had two women with me. We were dropped off as near to the stadium as was possible and walked over the footbridge. A policeman at the other end of the bridge asked for our tickets. I had a UEFA pass, so I was through. Kim fished her ticket out of her pocket, and she was waved through too. Liz tried to explain to the policeman she wasn't going inside the stadium yet. After an impasse, Kim and I simultaneously pointed at the guy's flat hat with 'Polizei' on it and said, 'Just show him your ticket!' Thankfully, that did the trick. They headed for the train back into town, and I went off to do what I had to do.

When it got to 7.15 p.m., ninety minutes before kick-off, the allotted time for playing 'You'll Never Walk Alone', the powers that be looked around the stadium and saw that (surprise, surprise) there were very few people in there, just as I had prophesied at the previous day's meeting. Suddenly there was a mild panic. Someone from UEFA came running down to the edge of the pitch where I was standing and told me there had been a change of plan. Our anthem had been postponed. Now he collared the poor guy behind me who was in charge of the Danish Super Kids. They were to go on next, in five minutes' time. Their leader protested that it would take him at least fifteen minutes to get their apparatus assembled. More panic. In the event, I think it took him around ten minutes to get organized, and his troupe did their routine.

Before the German tenors arrived, the stadium DJ was playing the tunes that I and my new friend from Alavés had selected. The DJ was English and had taken it upon himself to bring a couple more tunes that got the Reds fans singing along. This, of course, upset the Alavés announcer, whose English suddenly stretched to, 'Why you have more tunes than me?' He was in a bit of a state. His top crowd back home was in the region of 8,000, whereas I was used to numbers north of 40,000 and had worked at Wembley in front of nearly 80,000 people. He eventually calmed down and we moved on to the tenors. What none of us had realized was that soon after the technical rehearsal at lunchtime, the small team of guys responsible for building the podium on which the trophy would be presented later had decided to bring all the separate pieces of it inside the stadium and stack them in a convenient place ready for later on, rather than leave them outside where they'd been stored. All well and good except that they had stowed them neatly on top of the cables attached to the tenors' microphones. So, the three singers, in full evening dress, strolling in formation (and still in harmony) to the centre circle, were abruptly stopped halfway across the grass when their microphone cables suddenly jammed underneath various chunks of podium. Like the troupers they were, they carried on – albeit nowhere near the spot they should have been for the TV cameras.

A few minutes later, my Spanish friend and I stood in the centre circle to announce the two teams. It was only then that I discovered that the Westfalenstadion had its own in-house TV. As I started to read, I was suddenly aware that I was on the giant screen above my head. Very off-putting, as was the fact that the images of the Liverpool team were flashed up in a completely different sequence to the team sheet I'd been given. Liz, Kim and Laurie had arrived shortly before this and were in the front row of the upper tier of the stand on my side of the ground. The ladies were trying to pretend that they didn't know the giant on the big screen, and Laurie was still chuckling to himself, as he'd popped into a bar next door to the stadium and was halfway through his pint before he realized it was a theatre and that he was mingling with the audience having a pre-show drink.

As for the match itself, 48,050 crammed into the home ground of Borussia Dortmund. Markus Babbel scored for Liverpool in the fourth minute, and Steven Gerrard doubled our lead less than fifteen minutes later. This was the classic 'end to end' football much loved by the TV companies. Alonso pulled a goal back for Alavés, but Gary McAllister made it 3–1 before half-time with a penalty. Within a few minutes of the second half kicking off, Moreno scored twice for Alavés to level the match at 3–3. Robbie Fowler then put Liverpool in front yet again, but just as we thought we were home and dry, Jordi Cruyff (son of the great Johan) equalized to send the game into extra time.

At this point, I had to grab the mic and explain to the crowd that the golden-goal rule was in operation, which meant that we would play thirty minutes of extra time unless one team scored. In that case, the game would end with victory for the team who had just scored. After announcing all this, I turned to go back to my seat near the front of the main stand. I couldn't get there. While I was out on the pitch, the local police had taken up positions all the way around the perimeter of the playing surface. I went and stood behind the Liverpool dugout, but my knees had gone to jelly by now, so I was actually clinging on to the roof. From close quarters, I could see Gérard Houllier's expression. His face was grey – not white but grey – and he was pacing up and down. Directly in front of me, in the centre of the dugout, was the club doctor, Mark Waller. I remember thinking that one of us would need Mark's services at some stage. In the event, it was Gérard, although not until a few months later.

With extra time running out and a penalty shoot-out looming, Deflí Geli headed into his own net, and Liverpool had won thanks to the golden-goal rule. The cup Treble was ours! I stood in the centre circle to announce the man of the match and was privileged to be on hand as the trophy was presented. I scooped up two fistfuls of the ticker tape that had been liberally dumped on the winning team. When the dust had settled, I phoned Rob in California, who was as ecstatic as I was. I then phoned Liz. She and Kim were on their coach on the way to Dortmund Airport for the flight home. Laurie was back in our hotel room, watching the replay of the game on TV and availing himself of the minibar.

I set off up Westfalenstrasse looking for a taxi when my phone rang. It was Bryce Morrison. 'Where are you?' he asked. I explained what I was up to, but he said, 'You're supposed to be here!' 'Here' was the plane chartered for LFC staff at Dortmund Airport. I was taken aback. I reminded him that I had tickets for the following morning and, in spite of his protestations, assured him that I still had a hotel room because my son was already tucked up in bed there. As it happened, Laurie and I were lucky, because there were long delays at Dortmund Airport, which sounded really uncomfortable. The following morning, we headed off to Düsseldorf Airport armed with our first-class tickets and made the most of the VIP lounge and the company of several famous faces. What a trip!

Gérard Houllier had steered Liverpool to three major trophies in the season and, just to put the icing on the cake, we had qualified for the UEFA Champions League for the first time. It was time to enjoy our summer holiday and bask in the warm glow of the Reds' success.

However, there was sad news after the season's end when

Joe Fagan died on 30 June, followed by the great Billy Liddell on 3 July and Boot Room Boy Tom Saunders on 8 July. Liddell had spent his whole career at Liverpool, scoring an incredible 228 goals in 534 appearances. Billy was, incidentally, the subject of my first celebrity photo. In the summer of 1956, he opened our local church fete, and he and his wife Phyllis posed while I (a ten-year-old) took their picture with my little Kodak Brownie camera. Not only that but I sent him a copy care of the club and got a handwritten thank-you letter, with his home address at the top, in return. Can you imagine any of the current squad doing that now!

2001–02

UEFA Super Cup – Liverpool v. Bayern Munich, Stade Louis II, 24 August 2001

The August bank holiday weekend in 2001 found me on the Liverpool team plane on my way to Monaco. It was another schoolboy dream come true. The Stade Louis in Monaco was the regular venue at that time for the annual early season game between the winners of the UEFA Champions League and the winners of the UEFA Cup. Bayern Munich had won the 2001 Champions League and Liverpool, of course, were still glowing from the golden-goal victory against Alavés in Dortmund. I'd been told to report to Liverpool Airport the morning before the game and arrived fully expecting to be on an aeroplane full of office staff and suchlike, but I was directed to a quiet room and told that I was on the same plane as the first-team squad – blimey!

After landing in Nice, we hung around waiting for transport to our various hotels. I wandered over to where the players were and collared Gary McAllister. A friend of my son's was about to become a father and had said that the baby's middle name would be McAllister, regardless of his or her sex. I told Gary the story and asked him if he'd mind signing a card for the child when the time came. Gary said of course he would. He was a real gentleman. Just then the team's bus arrived, so I said my goodbyes, wished them luck and turned to go back to the pick-up point. As I turned, I accidentally trod on the foot of a guy standing behind me. 'Sorry, mate!' says I glibly. Then I looked him in the face and realized what I'd done. It was Michael Caine! I tried to strike up a conversation but failed miserably and gave up. He had a face like thunder. When I stood back, I could see his wife at the far side of the baggage hall. She had a scowl on her face too. They'd obviously had a row on the plane from London.

The minibus to take me and one or two LFC staff to our accommodation arrived shortly after the Liverpool squad had left for their upmarket hotel in the suburbs. Having said that, our hotel, The Columbus in Monaco Town, was a palace. I checked in and was sorely tempted to hang around all night to admire the view but decided against it. I'd never been to Monaco before and would probably never go again. It would be a shame to miss the opportunity to take in the sights. First things first, though, I needed to get my bearings and find the Stade Louis so I'd know where to go the following morning for the technical rehearsal. I had one of those pocket maps to hand, and the stadium didn't seem to be too far away, but I walked round the block where I thought the stadium was and then walked round again. At the end of the second circuit, I bumped into a couple of familiar faces. Ged Poynton, Anfield's stadium manager, was accompanied by Inspector Bernie Swift, who at that time was the match commander at Anfield for Merseyside Police.

I asked them if they knew where the stadium was, and they simultaneously looked to the skies and pointed upwards. The

Stade Louis, I discovered, is like no other stadium on planet Earth. It's actually on the roof of a three-storey building. The Monaco Club offices are on the ground floor, there is a car park on the second and the stadium is on the third. Once you find your way up there, you are confronted with a beautiful piece of architecture in a ground that is very small in comparison with some of the huge arenas common in world football but that is a pleasure to be in.

Afterwards, I took a bus to Monte Carlo. I'd been told by an ex-boss that I couldn't go to Monaco without a visit to the casino – not to spend my hard-earned money but instead to do some serious people watching. I stood by the fountains in the square outside the casino for a while watching the comings and goings. Every couple of minutes, a top-of-the-range car would pull up and the driver would casually climb out before disappearing into the casino. Within seconds, one of the casino staff would emerge with the car's keys in hand and drive it away to the car park. After a while watching these antics, I wandered inside. At the front desk, you are asked for your passport and have to surrender your mobile phone. The passport is checked against some sort of list of undesirables and you're in.

It's quite an experience just setting foot in that famous old building, the setting of a few James Bond scenes and many more movies besides. I left only to discover that the last bus back to my hotel had already gone. The sun was still shining, which was just as well, because I decided to walk back along the seafront to my hotel.

On the match day, some bright spark at UEFA had decided to have the technical rehearsal at noon. The Stade Louis resembles nothing more than an upturned wok in shape. The midday Mediterranean sun was at its peak, and my German counterpart and I were uncomfortably hot! Everything went off smoothly, however, and I scuttled back to The Columbus to cool down. Lying in my room with the curtains drawn was less than useless, so I decamped to the bar where I'd spent the previous evening, where I knew there would be a cool corner in an air-conditioned atmosphere with no natural light and where I could indulge in a pint of heavily iced, good-quality orange squash.

I sat quietly and read through the match programme and running order for the evening when Kenny Dalglish wandered past with a friend and sat at the next table. We exchanged pleasantries and went back to what we were both doing. A while later, my mobile phone rang. It was a recruitment agency in London, one of the agencies that had studiously ignored my calls when I was desperate for a job eighteen months earlier. He greeted me like a long-lost brother. They always do when they need something. I let him ramble on for a while then explained to him that I was settled in my new job, which was no more than a couple of miles from home. He tried to persuade me that the 'opportunity' he had for me would be well worth giving up my safe job, leaving my family and relocating to the south coast for six months! I turned him down flat. He suddenly realized that the sound quality of the phone call was a bit odd and asked me where I was. 'Monaco,' I said, trying to sound like I went there weekly.

My caller was taking stock: 'I've just realized where you are and what you're doing there! You jammy bugger!' Just then Kenny and his friend got up from their table, and I asked my caller to excuse me for a moment. Kenny leaned over and said, 'See you later,' or something similar.

'Cheers, Kenny,' I said. 'Enjoy the game!' He smiled and left, and I picked up the phone again.

'Please tell me that wasn't who I think it was,' the consultant said. He could almost hear the smug smile on my face.

'Yes,' I said. 'It was Kenny Dalglish.' The conversation ended shortly after that. I think he was in tears.

I got to the stadium in good time after a 'meal' at the Monaco branch of McDonald's, which was packed, wall to wall, with Liverpool fans. It was by far the cheapest place to eat. We then saw off Bayern Munich 3–2, and there were five trophies in the bag for the year, as we'd beaten Manchester United a couple of weeks earlier in the FA Charity Shield at the Millennium Stadium in Cardiff. Silver polish was in short supply on Merseyside that year.

UEFA Champions League Group B – Liverpool v. Boavista, Anfield, 11 September 2001

Liverpool's first Champions League game ended in a 1–1 draw with Portugal's Boavista. Michael Owen rescued a point for Gérard Houllier's side when he scored a marvellous goal, curling a shot into the top corner.

Never was a game of football less relevant, important or meaningful. The world was changed for ever that day, after the series of coordinated attacks by the Islamic terrorist group al-Qaeda that killed almost 3,000 people and injured 6,000. I had taken a half-day off work so that I could chill out before the big game at Anfield, but as soon as I settled down in my front room for lunch, I started to receive texts that all said much the same thing: 'Turn on the TV news.' Horrific images unfolded before our eyes. First, we were told of an awful 'accident' involving a passenger plane crashing into one of the Twin Towers in New York. News coverage of the resultant fire meant there were cameras galore in position to witnesses the second collision – another jetliner crashing straight into the second tower. Elsewhere, there were stories of plane hijackings, and it soon became clear that this was a man-made disaster. Another plane crashed into the Pentagon, and the fourth crashed in Pennsylvania, apparently brought down by an act of selfless heroism by passengers and crew.

As all this became clear, I wondered if we could possibly go ahead with a football match that night. Closer to home, Kim was worried that her close friend Laura Godfrey might be caught up in the attack. Laura had been working in Boston all summer and was heading into Boston Airport that very morning to catch a flight home. I phoned her father Barry to check she was OK. He was a worried man. He couldn't make contact with her, but he knew for a fact that she was in the area when the hijackings took place. We thought that the hijacked planes were internal flights within the USA, but we couldn't be sure she was safe. Rob was in Tampa and Laurie had flown out to visit him on a holiday with a work colleague called Colin Hogg. They changed planes at Washington Airport on 10 September, the day before 9/11. He was safe in Tampa. And Kim was booked to fly to Tampa on 12 September, the day after. Someone up there was looking after my family that day.

It was up to UEFA whether or not our game would go ahead. In the end, they made the decision to play the match, preceded by a minute's silence. The afternoon was spent staring aghast at the TV. When the time came to leave for Anfield, I asked Kim what she wanted to do. Normally she would travel to the match with me, but I gave her the option of catching a taxi later, in the hope that she would have heard some good news about Laura. It would also give her the option to forget about going to Anfield altogether, given the circumstances. But she decided to come with me on the grounds that she would have something else to occupy her mind if she was at the match. Thankfully, we got a phone call from Laura's dad just after I'd parked my car. She was safe! She and her travelling companion had indeed been heading for Boston Airport when the attacks took place. When they arrived, the airport was closed by the authorities and they were turned away, so they made their way back to their digs. It took several days before they could get a flight back to the UK. Laurie and Colin, meanwhile, were stuck in Tampa for almost a fortnight before they found a flight home. We discovered sometime later that Laura and her friend had a free day between finishing their contracts in Boston and returning home. That day was 10 September, and they decided to go into New York and do the tourist bit. The highlight of their day was a guided tour of the Twin Towers! Twenty-four hours later and they would have been among the victims!

I received a message on 13 October to go into Radio Merseyside's studio to do an interview with Adrian Chiles for his Saturday morning programme on BBC Radio 5. Liverpool were playing Leeds United in a lunchtime kick-off at Anfield, so I was on a tight schedule to get there on time. Luckily, the BBC sent a car for me, which made life a lot easier. On the way into Liverpool, I got chatting with the driver about football in general, and I was telling him about the frantic extra time in Dortmund and explaining my worries about Gérard Houllier's health. After half-time during the Leeds match, Gérard disappeared from view, and it transpired later that he had been rushed off to the cardiothoracic unit at Broadgreen Hospital. It's not too far from Anfield, especially if you're in an ambulance with its sirens blaring and blue lights flashing. I found that out for myself eight years later. It's also the best place in England to be if you have heart problems. Gérard was also lucky in that the club doctor realized very quickly what was wrong and called for immediate help. I remember thinking that the driver of my BBC car must have heard the news later in the day and decided that I was psychic!

Phil Thompson took over as caretaker manager and did such a good job that he actually got a Manager of the Month award during his time in charge. Liverpool were fourth in the league at the end of October, and top at the end of November, two points ahead of Leeds with a game in hand, but they dropped back to fourth by the end of December, two points behind leaders Arsenal, although they did have a game in hand. That run also saw Robbie Fowler move to Leeds in November, and Nicolas Anelka was brought in as his replacement, signed on loan from Paris Saint-Germain until the end of the season. Anelka's arrival was a real bolt from the blue. I remember ringing Kim late at night to tell her. We were both in shock.

Top of the pops in 2001 was the unmemorable 'It Wasn't Me' by Shaggy.

Liverpool remained near the top of the league during the first couple of months of the new year, during which time they beat new league leaders Manchester United 1–0 at Old Trafford. Then Gérard Houllier returned to the dugout in March following his medical problems. It was just before kick-off in the Champions League game against AS Roma on 19 March when he unexpectedly appeared from the players' tunnel to be greeted by a rapturous reception from the Anfield crowd and a bear hug from Roma manager Fabio Capello. Fabio and Gérard had a great deal of mutual respect for one another, and it shone through that night. For the record, we beat them 2–0, although the result was much less important than the manager's health in the grand scheme of things. We ended up exiting the competition at the quarter-final stage in our first season in the Champions League and capped off a decent but ultimately unsuccessful campaign by finishing second in the Premier League, with Michael Owen again top scorer, netting twenty-eight in all competitions.

Instead of signing Anelka on a permanent basis, Gérard spent a king's ransom on Senegalese striker El Hadji Diouf, following the latter's role in Senegal's 2002 World Cup campaign. The least said about El Hadji Diouf the better. His stay at Anfield was not a happy one. Apart from anything else, he had a propensity for spitting that didn't go down well with either the opposition or, more importantly, the Reds fans.

Pop Idol winner Will Young had the big song of 2002 with 'Evergreen'.

2002–03

When Bolton came to Anfield on 8 March 2003, we hadn't won a home league game in four months. Thankfully, our form picked up after that 2–0 win, and we were looking good for European qualification until we lost the last two games of the season, to Manchester City and Chelsea. We did, however, beat Manchester United 2–0 in the League Cup final on 2 March, which was easily the brightest moment of an otherwise disappointing season.

On 3 July, I was in London visiting the offices of Maison Blanc, the upmarket branch of Lyndale Foods, the owners of Sayers bakery in Liverpool. When I was driving back to my hotel, the local evening news announced that an unknown Russian businessman had agreed to buy Chelsea. His name was Roman Abramovich, and although we didn't know it at the time, his acquisition would help transform the footballing landscape in England. Money rules the waves in 2020, and I think Chelsea's takeover was the starting point.

In 2020, Liverpool FC is in the hands of the perfect owners. The club is successful on and off the pitch. The downside is that the traditional working-class fan base has, by and large, been priced out of the game. I naively thought that the new Main Stand in 2016 would mean there was room for some cheaper seats, but such is the worldwide popularity of the club that supply and demand has dictated otherwise. My poor dad wouldn't recognize the old place nowadays. He used to cycle to Anfield every Saturday, park his bike in the backyard of one of the rows of two-up two-down terraced houses and pay his shilling to get on to the Kop. Simpler times!

The Black Eyed Peas hit the jackpot in 2003 with 'Where Is the Love?'.

2003–04

In 2004, I was still working full-time in the IT department at Sayers bakery. When there was a midweek game, I used to fill my case with a selection of CDs in the morning and go straight from work to Anfield. On the day we were due to play Manchester City, a week before the Brit Awards in London, I went home for lunch and found my copy of *Brit Awards 2004* had arrived with the postman. I didn't have time to listen to it, but I took it back to work and threw it, still shrink-wrapped, into my case.

When I arrived at Anfield, I went to my room, took the CD from my case and put it on one of the CD decks while I was getting myself organized. Side one, track one was number one in the singles chart at the time: 'Leave Right Now' by Will Young. Unbeknownst to me, over in Manchester, the regular football talk show was under way on Century FM. In the background, they had a live mic at Anfield ready for reporting on the game later on. They had been discussing Gérard Houllier's future at Liverpool in the light of the discontented rumblings of some fans. When 'Leave Right Now' started up, their ears pricked up and someone commented, 'Even old George over at Anfield is joining in!' I was, of course, doing no such thing, although quite a few people thought I was!

More than once during my time at Anfield people have put two and two together and made five! Gérard left during the close season that year, but I can honestly say that I played no part in his departure.

Back in 1962, I was a big fan of a young English singer called Louise Cordet. I mentioned in the prologue to this book that I got to see her in the flesh just once, supporting The Beatles on tour in 1963. In 2004, the internet led me to her via her brother, who told me that she had been in Greece since 1965. Two days later, I got an email from her – wow! The following day, I was walking round HMV in Liverpool when I bumped into Spencer Leigh of Radio Merseyside. Spencer is a walking encyclopaedia about all things music related, especially The Beatles era. I told him about the email, and his eyes lit up. He said he was in the middle of updating his book about The Beatles tours and would love to talk to her about it. I asked Louise if it was OK to give him her email address, and she said, in typical fashion, that she didn't know why anyone would want to talk to her but yes. Two weeks later and I was in Radio Merseyside and talking to her on Spencer's programme. Louise and I are still in touch via email today. I also put her back in touch with Gerry Marsden. One of her hits was a Gerry Marsden song called 'Don't Let the Sun Catch You Crying', but she confessed she'd lost touch with him over the years, and they were both chuffed to have a long phone call after a break of more than forty years.

In the wake of Gérard Houllier's departure, the Reds pulled off a master stroke by recruiting Rafael Benítez. The Spaniard had worked wonders with Valencia in Spain, propelling them up that country's pecking order, and Liverpool fans were justifiably optimistic about the club's immediate future.

It must be said that Gérard didn't leave under a cloud. He'd revolutionized Liverpool FC and brought us into the twenty-first century. The outpouring of grief and tributes when he passed away in December 2020 confirmed that. He was revered and loved by Liverpool players, staff and fans alike and his legacy is clear to see; not least in the array of trophies on the wall of the corridor leading from the dressing rooms to the pitch at Anfield. He was, moreover, a true gentleman in every sense of the word. My overriding memory of him is the seemingly permanent twinkle in his eye. As a commentator remarked after his passing, 'He was a man about whom you only heard good things.'

2004–05

John Peel, who was idolized by generations of music fans, was on a working holiday in Peru when he died suddenly from a heart attack on 25 October 2004. He was responsible for launching the careers of many musicians, and throughout his time on radio stuck religiously to his eclectic musical choices. I met him at the Picket Venue in Liverpool in the mid nineties and then a couple of times at Anfield. One of my treasured possessions is a handwritten Christmas card and a note from him saying that mine was the only other job he'd ever wanted. He'd actually invited me to his house in East Anglia not long before he died – an invitation I sadly never got to take up.

> The remake of Band Aid's 'Do They Know It's Christmas?' outsold the competition in 2004.

League Cup Final – Liverpool v. Chelsea, Millennium Stadium, 27 February 2005

The League Cup was a competition I always used to look forward to, and it's sad that it's no longer treated with respect, as I can point to several happy experiences connected to that particular trophy, 2005 being a good example. Once again, the organizers had invited the stadium announcers from both teams to be at the final to talk to their respective supporters. There was going to be a light-hearted competition to decide which club had the louder supporters.

When I turned up, I was directed into the back corridors of the stadium and asked to wait around. I could see (and hear!) Katherine Jenkins out on the pitch rehearsing the national anthem. She finished and headed towards me. I was thinking that I must say hello but was dragged into a production meeting, which was basically just a rundown of the pre-match antics on the pitch. When that finished, I emerged into the corridor to find the lovely Ms Jenkins standing there. Before I had a chance to say hello, however, a minder escorted her to her dressing room.

My counterpart from Stamford Bridge went on to the pitch and tried to persuade his crowd to sing their club song as loud as they could. They did their best but came nowhere close to our 'You'll Never Walk Alone' after I'd wound the Liverpool fans up. When I'd collected my microphone, I'd noticed that there were three numbered mics on the bench in front of me. Number three was Chelsea's, number two was mine and number one was Katherine's. After I finished my bit, I decided to hang around at the bench, rather than go back to my seat, but just as KJ emerged to sing the national anthem I was asked (told!) to go and sit down and didn't get the chance to speak to the lady. My luck changed exactly a month later when I turned up at Anfield for a charity game to raise funds for the victims of the Boxing Day tsunami to find her doing a sound check directly in front of the dugout. This time I was on home turf and no one was going to stop me. She took time out to chat with me, as well as hanging around long enough for a picture.

One postscript to the match in Cardiff: our seats were very near the front of the lower stand behind the dugouts. When Chelsea equalized John Arne Riise's opener, José Mourinho stood, faced the crowd behind him and put his finger to his lips in a 'shush' gesture. He later told the press this was for the benefit of the reporters who had been criticizing him. That just isn't true. Our section was all red, and he was definitely looking at us when he did it. Thankfully, Liverpool exacted their revenge later in the season, dumping Chelsea out of the Champions League at the semi-final stage.

UEFA Champions League Quarter-final – Liverpool v. Juventus, Anfield, 5 April 2005

Football has a habit of throwing up strange coincidences, and this was one of those. Twenty years since the horrors of Heysel Stadium, Liverpool and Juventus were drawn together in the Champions League quarter-final. Our visitors still bore a grudge against the Reds fans, and there was the potential for trouble, so the powers that be went into overdrive to try and make sure the tie went off smoothly. Civic dinners were organized, and the pre-match events on the pitch were expanded to incorporate ex-players and local youngsters parading banners round the pitch, displaying messages of friendship. There was also an exchange of pennants to be carried out.

The half hour before European games is always nerve-racking for me. Everything is timed to the second and must be strictly adhered to. When I saw the running order, I took a sharp intake of breath. This night was going to be exceptionally tight. To complicate things, Pope John Paul II had died on the Saturday prior to the game, and I was told that we would also have to squeeze a minute's silence into the running order which, in my humble opinion, was already full.

I arrived, very nervous, at Anfield on the night of the game and was taken to see the UEFA delegate. He had in his hand a copy of the usual UEFA welcome message, which was always read out in the run-up to a UEFA game. He gave me the English version but was making alterations to the Italian copy. He amended it several times before handing it to me. He was satisfied that the wording was now suitable for the unique occasion.

I took both messages over to my room in the far corner of the ground. My first job was to get the welcome message to the interpreter who was waiting for me. Every time there's a European game at Anfield, an interpreter turns up to make important announcements in the mother tongue of the visitors. Over the years, we've had some characters. By and large, the interpreters are multilingual, helpful and slot easily into the running order. But on this night, of all nights, we had a real turkey. I was introduced to the guy concerned and said, 'Pleased to meet you!'

His response was a surprising, 'Ulloh,' in an accent which was definitely not Italian. I asked where he was from. This response was even more surprising: 'Wigan.' At this point, one of the civilian police personnel who was helping out in the match day control room was standing behind the guy and quietly pointed out an Italian dictionary on his desk. She mouthed the worrying phrase, 'He doesn't speak much Italian!'

I spent some time making minor (unauthorized) changes to the running order to cut out as much of the Italian language bits as I could get away with then noticed my new friend scribbling away on the welcome message. I asked him what he was doing, and he replied that there were grammatical errors on the piece of paper I'd given him. I explained to him that the UEFA delegate had written it, and on that basis alone he should not alter it.

In 2005, all Champions League fixtures (except for some of those in the Eastern bloc) kicked off at 7.45 p.m. exactly. Not one second before or after. On this night, of course, the pre-match running order was packed solid, with not a second to spare. My script said that the players' warm-up on the pitch would finish at 7.30, but it came and went. A couple of minutes later, I was on my two-way radio shouting at a senior UEFA representative for the second time in my life: 'Get them off the pitch! Now!'

Someone down below must have suddenly realized what was happening, and the players were ushered off the pitch at speed. The parade of banners went off smoothly, the welcome messages were read out, and I announced both line-ups at speed, omitting the substitutes for the one and only time in my career. When the game finally kicked off, I looked at my watch and we'd started ten seconds behind time. Under normal circumstances that would have been the subject of a major inquiry, but given that we'd started the preamble three minutes late, it was a triumph. I slumped back into my chair – nerves shredded – and got a terse message on my radio: 'Thank you!'

'That's OK,' I replied, 'but please don't do that to me again!'

As for the match itself, Liverpool beat a fabulous Juventus team 2–1. Sami Hyypiä and Luis García scored our goals. The Italians got a consolation via Fabio Cannavaro. It's strange to remember that Juventus included the likes of Zlatan Ibrahimović, Pavel Nedvěd, Alessandro Del Piero and

Gianluigi Buffon in their ranks, but we outplayed them. Scott Carson was in our goal, with the eventual Istanbul hero Jerzy Dudek on the bench. We then clinched the tie when we drew the away leg 0–0 and headed into a semi-final against José Mourinho's Chelsea.

UEFA Champions League Semi-final – Liverpool v. Chelsea, Anfield, 3 May 2005

After the nerve-racking night against Juventus the previous month, the prospect of facing Chelsea at Anfield in the Champions League semi-final after a goalless draw in the first leg at Stamford Bridge was a daunting prospect.

I had never been so nervous. To alleviate the symptoms, I did something that night that I have never done before or since. I took a small amount of alcohol with me. It said 'Evian Water' on the label, but it was actually gin and tonic. I'm not a drinker, but I thought it would calm me down – and so it did. On the night, Luis García (again!) scored the only goal. It was disputed by the Chelsea crew, but there was no goalline technology then, and the referee awarded the goal. One-nil was enough to take us through, but all Chelsea had to do was sneak a single goal to go through themselves on the away goals rule.

Approaching full time, we were under siege. As the ninetieth minute arrived, the fourth official came to the touchline and held up his board to show how much added time was to be played. We were shocked to see the number six on display. To this day, I have never understood where those six minutes came from.

After a couple of seconds' delay (while I focused my disbelieving eyes), I announced the added time. Rafa and José both looked shocked, the latter waving his team forward. People say that Chelsea threw everything but the kitchen sink at Liverpool during those six minutes. I'd dispute that. I'm almost certain I saw a kitchen sink flying through the air at one point. Those six minutes seemed like six hours. Liverpool, however, held out, and we were back on the biggest stage! Back in the big time, our rightful place.

I put on 'You'll Never Walk Alone' at full volume and then launched into an adrenalin-fuelled rant about the atmosphere being the best I'd experienced in forty-five years of watching Liverpool at Anfield. This was actually true, but I'd lost the plot by then.

UEFA Champions League Final – Liverpool v. AC Milan, Atatürk Olympic Stadium, 25 May 2005

After Liverpool got through to the final, I, like everyone else involved with the club, was looking forward to going to it. However, a couple of weeks before the big day, I received an email from club secretary Bryce Morrison. UEFA had apparently decided that they no longer required the presence of the finalists' stadium announcers. 'I know you'll be disappointed,' he said. Understatement doesn't even come close. My three children were all grown up by now. Rob had been living in Crawley for ten years, but Laurie and Kim both had season tickets and qualified for a trip to Istanbul. I knew that the club had chartered a plane for staff, and I assumed that I'd get a seat on that, but there was nothing I could do for Rob. About a week before the final, I emailed the assistant secretary (who was organizing the staff plane) and pleaded with him: 'If you have a spare seat at the last minute, please bear me in mind.' He said he would, but two days before the event he rang to say the plane was full.

On the day, I took my son and daughter to Liverpool John Lennon Airport to catch their flight to Istanbul. It was an emotional experience for all of us. They were both excited to be going but sad to be leaving me behind. I was in bits. Just in case of a last-minute change of heart or someone failing to show up, I had a small shoulder bag with me, containing my passport, water, biscuits and some cash. I dropped my kids off and had a coffee in the airport lounge. Several people went past and said, with a smile, 'I thought you weren't going?' They all got the same reply, through gritted teeth: 'I'm not!'

On my way back to the car, I passed the assistant secretary, and he looked surprised to see me. I explained that I was just dropping my family off and then went to work. In the subsequent weeks, I heard two stories that shocked me. Several people said that there were empty seats on the plane. I was told that one staff member who was going through family problems got as far as the check-in gate and suddenly shrieked, 'I can't face it!' and promptly went home. Worse still, a young girl who had started work in the club store warehouse a fortnight before the game was now on the staff so she suddenly qualified for a free trip to Istanbul! At the time, I had just completed thirty-four seasons working for the club. I have never found out whose decision it was to omit me from the list of employees on that plane, but, whoever it was, I will never get over it. To this day, people look aghast when they ask about Istanbul and discover I wasn't there. For the record, I watched it from my armchair with Liz!

The story of the match is well known. We were 3–0 down at half-time – 'Game over', to quote pundit Andy Gray at the time. Then came the spontaneous and inspirational 'You'll Never Walk Alone' during the break, which the team could hear, followed by the greatest comeback in football history. Following an exhausting extra time, which included some incredible saves from Jerzy Dudek, the match went to a penalty shoot-out. Jerzy, of course, saved the final penalty from a guy he himself described as the 'greatest striker in the world': Andriy Shevchenko. I still watch the video of that match occasionally for the sheer joy of the ending. The Liverpool squad sprinting across the pitch to hug Jerzy gets me every time!

The postscript for me was that I'd told Kim to text me when she and Laurie were boarding the plane home so that I'd know when to collect them from John Lennon Airport. She did. It was 4 a.m., and I was just nodding off to sleep. Nevertheless, I was there to collect them. Luckily, I still had my shoulder bag in the car that I'd taken with me the previous day. The water and biscuits went down very well with my two exhausted children. I don't think the catering on the plane home was up to the usual standard. They were hot, thirsty and hungry . . . but *very* happy!

2005–06

Liverpool v. Wigan,
Anfield, 3 December 2005

Peter Crouch had been waiting and waiting to chalk up his first Liverpool goal, and it had reached the point that it had seemingly developed into some sort of psychological barrier for him. But it's a situation in which strikers often find themselves – it's nothing new. When Wigan arrived at Anfield on 3 December, the crowd were living in hope. Nineteen minutes in, they thought the wait was over. Crouchie shot from twenty yards out, and the ball looped over Leighton Baines and hit keeper Mike Pollitt. The radio commentators swore it was an own goal, and when I poked my head into the match-day control room next door, at least three different people told me the same thing. On my way back to the microphone, however, I saw on my TV monitor the joyful scene on the pitch, with every Liverpool outfield player clustered around Peter, who was grinning like the Cheshire Cat. At that point, I made a decision – I announced him as the scorer. There was relief in the stadium, the Kop were delirious and Peter was through the barrier.

Later that season, I went through the same rigmarole when Steven Gerrard scored a goal at the Kop end. The TV commentators muttered that I'd 'got that one wrong'! In the event, the Dubious Goals Committee eventually did award the goals to the two men, and I had a smug smile on my face. The icing on the cake as far as Crouchie was concerned was that he doubled his tally against Wigan, and a very large weight was lifted from his shoulders. Peter Crouch always wears a smile and looks pleased to see you. He's also got the firmest handshake I've ever encountered!

Tony Christie's lively '(Is This the Way to) Amarillo' cleaned up this year thanks to Peter Kay's reissue for Comic Relief.

Liverpool v. Birmingham City, Anfield, 1 February 2006

This should have been a run-of-the-mill Premier League game. The 1–1 scoreline was a bit unexpected, but as far as I was concerned this was still a great day – Robbie Fowler was back! I'd heard all sorts of stories about the reasons he left in the first place, but I didn't know the truth. All I knew was that he was back in the fold!

On the night, I had some unusual tracks on my playlist. 'Welcome Home' and 'Going Back to My Roots' were on there, but the *pièce de résistance* was the 'Hallelujah Chorus'! There was a running joke on Sky's *Soccer Saturday* whereby they played a brief snatch of it every time Robbie was on. So it was that when Robbie ran out to warm up, Handel's masterpiece was blasting out over the PA. The roar when Robbie finally joined the fray after sixty-five minutes was wonderful to hear. A rousing climax was cut short when a linesman's flag ruled out Robbie's injury-time goal.

FA Cup Final – Liverpool v. West Ham United, Millennium Stadium, 13 May 2006

The 2006 FA Cup final against West Ham was quite an occasion. I made the trip because I was now listed on the club's IT system as a steward. The allocation of tickets was even worse than usual, so the names of the casual staff making the trip were based on attendance records for the season. Guess who came out on top! I had 100 per cent attendance. Who's a good boy, then.

The final itself was one of the greats. Kim, her husband Mike and I travelled together to Cardiff with me at the wheel. The Hammers were 2–0 up when Djibril Cissé got one back before the break. Stevie G equalized early in the second half, but Paul Konchesky put the Londoners ahead, and all looked lost until a late, late thunderbolt from Steven Gerrard took us into extra time and an eventual penalty-shoot-out win. My eldest grandson is named in honour of Steven, which gives me a great sense of satisfaction. It's nothing short of tragic that Stevie left Anfield without a league champions medal. He was an inspirational, classy player with the heart of a lion. He's up there in the upper echelons of Liverpool's most legendary players. Maybe he'll be back one day to follow in Jürgen Klopp's footsteps. Who knows?

In July, I got a call from an ex-neighbour of mine whose Norwegian friend was involved in organizing a visit to Norway by the Liverpool 'Legends' team. My name had apparently come up in conversation, and I was invited to join the tour alongside a team of ex-players plus Gerry and the Pacemakers. The deal was that the Reds Legends would play a local team, and Gerry would sing 'You'll Never Walk Alone' live before the game and then do a concert in the town later in the evening.

It was a real treat for me. We flew from John Lennon Airport to Ålesund, a beautiful port on the west coast of Norway, and checked into a very nice hotel. The following morning at breakfast, I had the sensation of being in the middle of a living, breathing Panini sticker album. Phil Neal, David Johnson, Jimmy Case, Ronnie Whelan, Jan Mølby, Bruce Grobbelaar and David Fairclough: I was the only guy there I'd never heard of! It was another schoolboy dream come true! That night we were all bussed to the town's football stadium, the home of Norwegian First Division side Aalesunds FK. The arena was then only a year old and very impressive. My travelling companions played a game against the Aalesunds Legends. I was interviewed on the pitch before kick-off and watched the match in the company of my opposite number there. Gerry Marsden sang 'You'll Never Walk Alone' when the teams lined up and later did a concert in the town square. I was oblivious to the famous Scandinavian daylight hours and during the gig suddenly realized that it was one o'clock in the morning – I was *very* tired!

After a couple of days in Ålesund, we flew to Florø, the home town of Tage Herstad, to play a game against the local footballing legends. Nowadays, Tage is well known to several generations of Liverpool players and fans. He's the part-owner of the magnificent Hotel Tia in Anfield Road and the driving force behind the large numbers of Scandinavian visitors to Liverpool who are now commonplace at every home game. The weather was more Mediterranean than Norwegian, and I had the time of my life. Once again, Gerry sang 'You'll Never Walk Alone' live before the game and did an open-air concert later that evening. I was on the public address systems at both stadiums and got to attend both of Gerry's concerts, as well as doing the technical side of running the backing tracks for his live rendering of 'YNWA'.

Socializing with the guys was incredible, albeit exhausting! The organizers of the trip made sure we were always entertained, and the town of Florø welcomed us all with open arms. The short trip was a flurry of boat trips, barbecues and sportsman's dinners. There was a surreal moment when I texted one of my sons who was on holiday with his wife in Italy. I said, 'I'm in a community hall in the wilds of Norway. I'm eating reindeer. And these are the people round my table.' I listed Ronnie Whelan, Bruce Grobbelaar, David Fairclough, Phil Neal, Alan Kennedy and more. Within seconds, I received a terse reply: 'Dad – have you been drinking?'

When it was all over, I flew to Bergen in a private plane alongside Gerry Marsden and Ian Rush. I'd never been on a private plane before and probably never will again. We had lunch in Bergen Airport and then took a scheduled flight to Manchester. I was on one side of the aisle next to Gerry and his tour manager. On the opposite side of the aisle, Rushie sat next to two English guys who were on their way home from a business trip. When Gerry nodded off, one of the Englishmen turned to Rushie and said, 'Is that Gerry Marsden?' It was only when Ian turned to confirm the fact that the guy realized whom *he* was sitting next to. I can see his face now. Priceless!

The super-catchy 'Crazy' by Gnarls Barkley was the big song of 2006.

2006–07

Following the arrival of billionaire Roman Abramovich at Chelsea in 2003, Liverpool were in danger of being cast adrift from their big-spending rivals. David Moores was convinced that in order to compete the club needed a new ground, and unable to fund it himself he decided to sell up in 2004. Chief executive Rick Parry and Moores embarked on a painstaking process that finally appeared to be reaching a conclusion in December 2006 when the club announced an exclusivity agreement had been struck with Dubai International Capital (DIC). In Dubai ruler Sheikh Mohammed bin Rashid Al Maktoum, it looked like Liverpool had found the perfect sugar daddy.

That deal, for whatever reason, came to nothing, and on 6 February 2007 we were instead sold to two American businessmen, George Gillett and Tom Hicks, who were 'not coming over here to make a quick buck'! By chance, I had taken a day's holiday from work and was on my knees next to the TV all day while installing a new fireplace. I received a message to say that Liverpool's new owners would be holding a live press conference at lunchtime, so I duly switched over to LFCTV to listen to what our new American owners had to say. They said all the right things, although I blanched when Gillett said that his son played 'soccer' and his position was 'goaltender'! They promised to respect the club's tradition, build the new stadium in time for the 2009–10 season and invest in the playing squad. 'We're not here to milk the fans,' Gillett insisted, and he vowed that the ground would be broken in Stanley Park, the proposed site of the new stadium, inside sixty days. 'Give us a little time and we are going to have some fun together.'

Hicks added, 'This is not a takeover like the Glazer deal at Manchester United. There is no debt involved. We believe that as custodians of this wonderful, storied club we have a duty of care to the tradition and legacies of Liverpool.' It seemed too good to be true. However, many people were worried that they were leveraged-buyout specialists – buying on the cheap with borrowed money and then selling high at a massive profit. Liverpool had been underperforming commercially, and it seemed to me that they saw the chance to make a quick buck thanks to the club's global fan base.

Within months of their arrival, the club was riddled with debt and disunity. Gillett and Hicks swiftly fell out with each other and left a trail of broken promises in their wake. 'It soon became clear that they had very different philosophies on how the club should be run,' Rick Parry said. 'One was hands off, the other hands on; one courted publicity, the other didn't.'

Liverpool was, according to managing director Christian Purslow, one day away from administration before later being sold to the Fenway Sports Group in 2010. Money was spent on big-name signings, but it was the bank's money, and as the world recession wrecked any hopes of borrowing more to build a new stadium and £30 million per year went on paying interest on debts, the cash dried up and Benítez's calls across the Atlantic went unanswered.

Washing the club's dirty linen in public became a regular occurrence, and for me there was nothing more sickening than Hicks's PR stunt at home in Dallas with a Sky TV crew. Clutching his Liverpool mug, watching the side in action on a big screen with his kids around him in club merchandise, he demanded the resignation of chief executive Rick Parry.

On the back of the takeover, incidentally, I had a shock of my own. In March, I was at my annual school reunion dinner at Anfield, standing in the queue for the bar. Someone tapped me on the shoulder and said, 'There's someone here wants a word with you!' I turned around to find George Gillett smiling up at me.

I was speechless for a moment but quickly composed myself and got as far as, 'Hello, Mr Gillett,' before the other guys standing behind him burst into fits of laughter. This wasn't George Gillett at all but his doppelgänger – Albert Connolly, another dinner guest who had attended Liverpool Institute before me. He told me later that he was a season-ticket holder in the Main Stand at Anfield and was currently being treated like royalty by the stewards and catering staff who had made the same mistake that I had and thought he was their new boss! Some months later, of course, when Hicks and Gillett became, shall we say, less than popular with the fans, he worried for his personal safety every time he attended a game.

I only met the real George Gillett once and that was after the 2007 Champions League semi-final against Chelsea. I was standing in the Main Stand reception when he collared me, shook my hand vigorously and told me what a great job I'd done getting the atmosphere going that night.

My friend Ian Fryer and I had a great and surreal day out thanks to Laurie and Ian's younger son Matt, who had won a charity auction in which the prize was a day out at BBC Television Centre to watch *Match of the Day* being broadcast. In the end, we negotiated a swap for *Football Focus* – the lunchtime football programme – so that we could get there and back in one day. It was fabulous. We were picked up at Euston, driven to BBC Television Centre, given a guided tour of the building (including the *Blue Peter* garden) and then visited the *Football Focus* studio, which was actually the same one used for *Match of the Day*. The presenter, Manish Bhasin, was very welcoming, and we sat on the famous couch while the camera crew were setting up the shots ready for the live broadcast. I stood in for Lee Sharpe, and Ian pretended to be Mark Lawrenson. During the live broadcast, we sat silently in the gallery watching the production crew. The gallery is like the flight deck of an airliner but with lots more screens! It was a unique experience.

One of the items on the programme that day was a piece about Brentford FC's longest-serving supporter. At the end of the film, the guy doing the voiceover revealed himself to be the stadium announcer at Griffin Park, Peter Gilham, and he said he was the longest-serving announcer in England. I was gobsmacked! He had one more year under his belt than I did! After the programme, I suggested to Manish that someone was taking the mickey, but it turned out that the timing of the Brentford clip was an absolute coincidence.

UEFA Champions League Final – Liverpool v. AC Milan, Olympic Stadium, 25 May 2007

After the shenanigans in 2005, I didn't even ask about tickets for Athens. I knew I would only be humiliated again, so Rob and I decided to make our own way. After a really arduous trip (Liverpool–Crawley–Sofia–Athens), the match itself was disappointing to say the least, with AC Milan exacting their revenge for 2005 with a 2–1 win. More to the point, the venue was a shambles. Rob and I got in early but had to push our way through chaotic crowds while clinging on tight to our tickets. Laurie caught the last flight out of Liverpool on the day of the match and was promptly tear-gassed by the local police for no apparent reason. I've still never found out where he was for the first half. All I know is that he couldn't see anything for the first hour or so he was there. There were loads of stories about forged tickets. A guy whom we met at our hotel back in Sofia the day after the final was with his two young sons. They all got in with forged tickets. The whole ethos of the Greek authorities was 'take the money but accept no responsibility'!

Another reality TV stunner 'Bleeding Love' by Leona Lewis won out in 2007.

2007–08

The Ray of Hope Appeal was launched on 21 January 2008. The aim was to raise enough funds to buy essential equipment and services for Ray Kennedy, who suffers from Parkinson's disease. The illness has deprived him not only of his health but of his livelihood, robbing him of the chance to make a living through the media or coaching, a shame given that he has won everything in the game and probably knows more than a few people in those roles today. But Ray is essentially a private man who would never complain about his condition or the turn his life has made since his diagnosis. Liverpool and Arsenal fans who know him would not be surprised by this, as Ray's demeanour has always been that of a dignified and stoical man.

The Ray of Hope Appeal saw its first official event on 23 February 2008 at the Paisley Suite at Anfield. Many people came along in support, including celebrities and past players. The night raised a staggering £10,000, a figure that would not have been possible without the help of John Mackin, Kevin Sampson and Bob from the memorabilia dealers Retro Reds. I was glad to be involved in a small way. I compered some of the auction and then got to introduce Liz McLarnon on to the stage. She did a couple of Atomic Kitten songs, and I was really impressed with the way she carried on a cappella and in perfect time after her backing track died.

I'd been running the IT system at Sayers since June 2000. In 2008, I was sixty-two and had no reason to believe it wouldn't see me through to retirement. Wrong again. In spite of having been told that all our jobs were perfectly safe, things fell apart rapidly. I came back from lunch one afternoon to find the head of HR waiting for me in my boss's office. I was told that I was now on gardening leave – I cleared my desk and was escorted from the building. I was, as it turned out, the first out of the door. Two days before payday, the people still in work were told to go home. I believe some people weren't even allowed to collect their coats. It was cruel. I lost a month's salary. There were many families who had worked for Sayers for years. Quite a few married couples lost both their livelihoods. All in all, 450 jobs were axed and forty shops shut.

Tage Herstad and his crew saved my bacon again by inviting me on another Legends tour. This time we started off in Odense in Denmark, the birthplace of Hans Christian Andersen. I was invited to go on the players' golf day, but I don't play golf, so I did the tourist bit and wandered round the Andersen Museum, which is quite a place. Odense is a lovely old town and was the site of a famous match between the local team and Liverpool in 1983, when the home supporters were thrilled to have narrowly lost to the only goal of the game! After that, it was on to Stavanger and Florø in Norway. Great times. I've grown to love Scandinavia over the years, and these trips were a real treat. By now, I was part of the gang! To this day, however, I can't believe the copious amounts of alcohol the guys who were once professional athletes manage to put away!

Back home and it was back to reality. Here I was, sixty-two and out of work. People think I'm on the staff at Anfield, but I'm not – never have been. I'm part-time and classed as a casual employee. So, I needed a job. Having been told eight years earlier that I was far too old to be working in IT, this time round I didn't even try to find a job that matched my skills. I was up for anything that would pay the bills. It eventually took more than a year before I was gainfully employed again on a nine-to-five basis.

2008–09

Merseyrail had decided to name a new three-carriage train the 'John Peel', and it got its official launch at South Parkway on 23 October 2008. John's widow Sheila did the traditional smashing of a champagne bottle on its side, before the guests travelled back into the city centre on the new service. One of John's favourite songs was Amsterdam's 'Does This Train Stop on Merseyside?', which the band's frontman Ian Prowse performed at the event – and on the train. Ian also invited me to the launch and the get-together at Radio Merseyside later. Sheila said John would have been thrilled and emotional to have a train named after him in Liverpool. I suspect he would have also been more than a little amused!

It was a memorable year for the city in 2008, with Liverpool named the European Capital of Culture. Theatres, music venues, museums, galleries and the media all had a field day. The musical highlight was the Liverpool Sound concert on 1 June at Anfield with Paul McCartney, The Kaiser Chiefs and

The Zutons. I wasn't needed to work the event but was allowed to sit near my normal seat and just watch. I got in early to make sure I could park and timed it nicely, as I got to hear Macca's sound check right through! The night was fabulous. All three bands were on top form, and Paul was even joined by his mate Dave Grohl of the Foo Fighters for a couple of numbers later on. The encores went on and on, and we only just got in the fireworks display before the 11 p.m. cut-off time!

Earlier that year, in January, I had the rare privilege of playing Ringo Starr's new song 'Liverpool 8' before any other outlet. We had a midweek home game a couple of nights prior to the release date. He sang it from the roof of St George's Hall during the opening ceremony of the Capital of Culture celebrations. That was a magic moment. What wasn't so magical was the way he made some sarcastic remarks about his home town on TV the following week. I got rid of the CD and never played it again. I couldn't believe what I'd heard.

The icing on the cake for me in 2008 was at the Tate Gallery on the Albert Dock. I'd long held an ambition to visit Vienna to see the Gustav Klimt permanent exhibitions, and in the summer an exhibition of his work came to Liverpool. Result!

Alexandra Burke's cover of Leonard Cohen's classic 'Hallelujah' kept Simon Cowell's grip on the charts.

Phil Easton and I had been working as a team since August 2000, me up in my little room and him pitchside. As I said earlier, Phil and I got to be friends and did several events away from Anfield together.

After home games, Phil would do his post-match phone-in on Radio City from the press box, whereas I would usually go straight home. On Sunday, 1 February Liverpool played Chelsea. Afterwards, I had arranged to meet a Swedish journalist. We had a long chat, and when we'd finished, I headed to my car. Phil and Steve were parked next to me, so we had a rare chance to spend five minutes reflecting on the game we'd just witnessed. In fact, I think it was possibly the only time we did. Sadly, it also proved to be the last. We'd beaten Chelsea 2–0 with two goals from Fernando Torres, the first of which had come in the eighty-ninth minute!

The next morning, I listened to Phil's breakfast show as usual and went to work. That night at about 7 p.m., I went upstairs to use my laptop, leaving Liz to watch the Monday evening soaps. I'd no sooner sat at my desk than my phone rang. It was Steve, in sombre mood. He told me that Phil had passed away. It didn't seem possible. He'd been in good form on the Sunday and sounded like his usual self on the radio that morning. It transpired that he had actually left Radio City Tower early, saying he didn't feel too good. His poor wife had come home from work that afternoon and found him dead in a chair.

I was devastated. Everyone who heard the news was equally shocked. Before the next home game, against Manchester City, Steve put together a list of Phil's favourite music, and my entire playlist consisted of Phil's best-loved tunes, including ones by Chris de Burgh, U2, Electric Light Orchestra, Supertramp, Bruce Springsteen and Thin Lizzy.

It was my birthday that day, but I was quoted in the local paper as saying, 'I'll be really glad when it's over, as I don't know how I'll feel on the day. Phil knew some very A-list people, he was very friendly with Bono, and I remember him shaking before interviewing David Bowie as he was looking forward to it so much. Phil Lynott from Thin Lizzy was a good friend and once the two of them swapped roles on the radio with Phil Lynott asking the questions and Phil answering.'

My first trip to Ireland for a while was a very pleasant one. John Barnes, Phil Neal and I were to be the special guests at a local supporters' club dinner in Waterford on 28 February 2009. I was told to report to John Lennon Airport on the morning of the do and meet up with John Barnes. Phil had flown straight to Waterford the previous day, but John and I were flying to Cork and being collected by the organizer, Kieran Power.

Getting on the plane was the hard part. I got to the airport in good time, because I'd heard some horror stories about queues at the security checks. It turned out that getting there early was no use whatsoever. The trick was to pay the £3 fee to go through the fast-track gate. John did that, and although he'd arrived at the airport some time after I had, I saw him walking serenely through the barriers, while I was still battling my way through a scrum of people on their way to the Spanish sunshine. It ended with me running to the departure gate while my name was being called over the airport public address system, carrying my belt and holding my trousers up with the other hand. I made it by the skin of my teeth and slumped into my seat next to a very relaxed John Barnes.

Having some one-to-one time with someone like John is a treat and an education. This was around the time that he was managing the Jamaica national team, and he had lots of tales to tell. Jack Warner, the erstwhile vice-president of FIFA and president of CONCACAF until his suspension and eventual resignation from these roles in 2011, wasn't, to say the least, making his life easy at that time. Kieran was waiting for us at Cork Airport and looked like a child on Christmas morning when John appeared.

We were put up in a lovely hotel, treated to a tour of the Waterford Crystal factory, which was about to be closed, and then ferried back to the hotel to watch Liverpool's away match at Middlesbrough. This turned out to put a dampener on the whole weekend. Liverpool had beaten Real Madrid away in midweek and could reasonably have hoped to give lowly Middlesbrough the same treatment. We didn't. We lost 2–0 and threw away three valuable points in our pursuit of the title. The galling thing was that we were in the middle of a purple patch. During the following couple of weeks, we hammered Manchester United 4–1 away and put four past Real Madrid at Anfield without reply.

The dinner that evening was a joyous affair, full of Irish hospitality washed down with copious amounts of happy juice. After dinner, the compere turned out to be the guy who had given us the tour round the crystal factory that afternoon. More pertinent was the fact that he worked as a comic in the local pubs in his spare time. I was a bit worried about having to follow him, but I am proud to say I got the crowd laughing too.

After a comfy night and a wonderful full Irish breakfast, Phil, John and I were taken to Waterford Airport, and we flew back to Liverpool John Lennon together. The flight was barely half full, and we basically had two seats each. Sitting nearby to us was a young woman with a bored toddler. We all three took turns to play the fool with the little one, and when we landed in Liverpool, I was slower getting off than the other guys. The lady asked me, 'Did they play for Liverpool? Was that John Barnes?' I confirmed her suspicions, and her eyes lit up. 'Wait till I tell my husband!' After a brief pause, her expression changed. 'Did you play for Liverpool too?' I explained that I still played for Liverpool, but the music not the football!

Football heroes gathered at Liverpool Cathedral to pay their respects to club secretary Bryce Morrison on 2 April 2009. Rafa Benítez, Sami Hyypiä, Jamie Carragher and Kenny Dalglish joined family and friends to honour the devoted club man. More than 750 chairs were needed for the many supporters also wishing to attend the event. Bryce had literally given his life to Liverpool FC. He'd been headhunted by the club and worked his socks off, day in and day out. He could have a gruff exterior but was as straight as a die. There were many stories of his PA finding him asleep in his chair when she arrived for work some mornings.

We shouldn't have been surprised, but we were. The twentieth anniversary of Hillsborough was on 15 April 2009, and Anfield was to be the scene of the annual memorial service. Normally, only the Kop Stand was opened for those wishing to attend, but this year three sides of the ground were roped off and stewarded. It was thought that this particular milestone might attract more people to the event, but no one was prepared for the vast crowd that arrived. The people came in waves, and the rope barriers kept getting moved back. I heard one of the senior stewards shouting that he hadn't got enough stewards. Someone retorted, 'You don't need stewards today!'

My friend Glenn Palmer came up from London for the afternoon event. We'd planned to have a quick lunch before going to the stadium, but lunch turned into a hurried bag of chips when we realized that we didn't have time to hang around, such were the size of the queues to get in. I managed to guide him into the corner of the Kop by telling a steward he was with me, and I climbed my tower to the third floor of what was then the Centenary Stand. There were still people trying to get in when the service started, but it soon settled into its regular dignified routine: the prayers, the reading of the ninety-six names, the silence at six minutes past three. I was watching from my room above the Kop. My overriding feeling all these years is simply 'There but for the grace of God go I!' An officer from the West Midlands force who came to our house to interview Rob as a witness described him as a 'lucky boy!' So he was, and thank God he and his travelling companions are still here to tell the tale.

Andy Burnham, the Secretary of State for Culture, Media and Sport, was not listed in the official programme but strode to the microphone to address the crowd. Almost as soon as he began to speak, the boos started from the stands. Eventually, the crowd took up the chant of 'Justice for the ninety-six'. Andy didn't deserve that. He was, and still is, on our side. He's a dyed-in-the-wool Everton fan and, coincidentally, had been at the other semi-final in 1989. Afterwards, I sought him out and apologized for the reception he'd received, but he told me not to worry. I got the feeling he was very angry. Not at us but at his bosses in Westminster who had basically hung him out to dry.

Later that evening, I was interviewed by Eleanor Oldroyd on BBC Radio 5 outside the stadium. My slot was put back five minutes to accommodate an interview that she'd recorded with Andy earlier in which he basically said he would go back to Westminster and kick-start the Hillsborough inquiry. When that was finished, she asked me for my reaction to what he'd said. My response was quite straightforward: 'If the minister does what he said he was going to do, then things might make progress at last!' He did. And they did!

Liverpool v. Arsenal, Anfield, 21 April 2009

Liverpool went into this game still smarting from a painful exit from the Champions League by way of a 4–4 draw with

Chelsea at Stamford Bridge. We were also second in the league by a single point behind Manchester United, although they had a game in hand. A win would have put us on top, if only for a short while, but it turned out, incredibly, to be yet another 4–4 draw! It was a great game for the neutrals watching on TV! Those games are, however, nightmares for the dedicated supporters of the respective clubs. End to end doesn't come close.

Arsenal went ahead and still led by that single goal at half-time. The second half was crazy. Fernando Torres then Yossi Benayoun put us ahead. Arsenal retook the lead, Torres equalized, Arsenal's Andrey Arshavin scored his (and Arsenal's) fourth goal in the ninetieth minute and then Yossi Benayoun equalized in the fifth minute of added time. Phew! Liverpool were top of the league on goal difference, but we had basically thrown away two valuable points. Our prospects of being champions had all but gone. Within the space of a week, we had scored four goals each against two of the big London clubs, but a few defensive lapses meant that it was all for nothing!

July saw another of the most surreal and unexpected experiences of my adult life. Chris de Burgh is a long-standing and dedicated Liverpool fan. He loves the team and the city. He was also a close friend of the late Phil Easton. At the end of Phil's memorial service earlier in the year, Chris had sung an emotional version of 'You'll Never Walk Alone'.

He had then sung it again later in concert, and it had gone down so well that someone suggested he should record it. His management rounded up some members of the Kop Choir, and they were summonsed to Elevator Studios. I received an invitation to join them, and although I think I was originally meant to be an interested onlooker, I suddenly found myself with the Kopites on a small stage at the end of the studio. The outcome was a very spirited rendition of 'YNWA' that was released on two different CDs later in the year. Whatever happens to me for the rest of my life, I can always tell my grandchildren that I was once Chris de Burgh's backing singer!

2009–10

Like seemingly every other suddenly unemployed man in Liverpool, I came to the conclusion that a quick and easy route back into work was to get a taxi driver's licence. To anyone thinking along these lines, here's my advice: don't!

I thought it would be easy-peasy. I had a five-seater Toyota Avensis. I'd lived in Liverpool for sixty-three years and knew my way around. I had a clean driving licence. So, I cobbled together the money for the fees and turned up at Municipal Buildings with my documents and filled in all the forms. At this point, I was told that they needed to see the paper copy of my licence, but I only had with me the licence I carried round at all times – the little credit-card-size one that everyone else (including the police) are happy with. I had to go home, take my desk to bits (well almost), dig out the paper licence, head back again to the council building, and submit all the bits and bobs they needed.

A couple of weeks later, I received a message to go and collect my documents and apply for a test at the council offices. The equivalent exam in London is called 'the Knowledge'. Frankly,

I've never understood how any human being could remember every single nook and cranny of London, but I was quite happy that I knew my way around my home town. I failed miserably, mainly because most of the questions involved pubs, and I'm not a drinker. I was then given an evening appointment to come back and try again, but I turned it down on the grounds that Liverpool had a home game that night. They said they'd find me another date and let me know.

A couple of days after the second proposed test date had come and gone, I got a letter from the council to say that I'd not turned up as arranged and therefore owed them a fee. I phoned up and played hell. There was, I said, no way that I would have agreed to come while Liverpool were playing and that was what I'd told them. To be honest, I couldn't afford the extra fee, and I was glad when they eventually backed down. I went for the retest, and this time I passed. The guy before me in the queue failed miserably, and it transpired that he'd failed the previous week but then memorized all the answers, not realizing that the questions would be different when he tried again. I, however, was now the proud holder of a licence which would allow me to ply for hire. What no one had mentioned was the fact that my car would now have to go through a similar vetting process. It got to the stage that the modifications needed would have bankrupted me and I gave up.

Just before Christmas 2009, Kim and Mike came round and told Liz and me that she'd had a scan and they knew that her firstborn (due in May 2010) would be a boy. They had also decided on a name: Stephen George. I was sitting there thinking how nice it was that my first grandson would carry my name. Then it dawned on me – the lad was being named after Steven George Gerrard! Ah well.

As it happened, Stevie G turned up at the supporters' club dinner the following weekend, and I told him the tale. He was quietly tickled. In fact, he laughed like the proverbial drain. Late in 2010, he signed the back of a Liverpool shirt for young Stevie and got the rest of the squad to sign the front for him.

The wonderful Lady Gaga swept the board with 'Poker Face' in 2009.

UEFA Europa League – Liverpool v. Lille, Anfield, 18 March 2010

I've been lucky enough to see many of the world's greatest footballers playing live over the years. Diego Maradona was one omission from the list, but on this particular night I got to see him in the flesh. Liverpool were playing Lille, and Diego was a guest of the club. I think he was managing Argentina at the time so was on a scouting mission.

Hanging around in the Main Stand reception after the game, I suddenly became aware of a hubbub. Diego and Fernando Torres (who had scored twice in a 3–0 win) had stopped to chat behind me. I was stuck behind a couple of onlookers so pulled my camera from my pocket and held it high to get a quick snap. When my camera's flash went off, one of the great man's minders turned around suddenly with a look of thunder on his face. Luckily for me, the guy in front of me was raising his camera above head height just as I brought mine down. I avoided the wrath of the minder and the guy in front of me suddenly decided he didn't really need a picture of Diego Maradona after all!

I was invited to an 'In Conversation with Janice Long' event at Liverpool's magnificent Anglican Cathedral on 25 March. I was lucky enough to attend several of these in 2010, and I took part in one with Jamie Carragher at St George's Hall a few years later. The format was simple. The interviewee was quizzed about their life and career, and the interview was punctuated by half a dozen of their favourite pieces of music, performed by local musicians. Last up was an unknown name – Ragz Nordset. Everyone else on the bill was a well-known act, but Ragz turned out to be a wonderful young Norwegian graduate of my alma mater, which was, coincidentally, just over the road from the cathedral. I was gobsmacked. She did a gentle version of the Rolling Stones' 'You Can't Always Get What You Want'. I was hooked. Here was a pure voice up there with the best of them. There aren't many that spring to mind, but I'm thinking of the likes of Karen Carpenter, k.d. lang, Emmylou Harris. You get the drift.

In the green room after the show, I collared Ragz, who was having a drink with her manager. Her English was perfect, as was her manager's. After a couple of minutes speaking slowly and carefully to him, it turned out that his name was Dave and he was from Leeds! I followed the pair of them round after that and was lucky enough to MC a few of her gigs. That in turn opened up a whole new world of music venues in Liverpool I'd never otherwise have set foot in. I'm proud to say that we're still friends to this day.

The experienced Roy Hodgson was appointed as Liverpool manager on 1 July 2010, with a remit 'to steady the ship'. I was initially pleased when Roy arrived and was prepared to see what he was made of. He appeared to be a nice guy, but then that was probably not what we needed.

People say that when people arrive at Anfield, they either get it or they don't. I don't think Roy got it. He didn't endear himself to the fans when he declared his friendship with Alex Ferguson, and his signings didn't impress us either. My personal observation was that he more usually set out not to lose games rather than to go out and win them. Not the Liverpool way!

Another one off the bucket list – I took part in the TV quiz *Eggheads* on 19 July. I joined a team called the 'Lawn Arrangers' that had got together to publicize the Lawnmower Museum in Southport. I only discovered this after the auditions at Radio Merseyside. They were one short, and Liz's friend Lorraine (a friend of the Lawnmower Museum's curator) asked me if I wanted to fill the space. I was put forward on the grounds that I was a good quizzer. This is a vicious rumour based on a couple of lucky Trivial Pursuit wins the previous Christmas. I was good at pop music quizzes once upon a time, but no longer. Old age is creeping up on me.

Shortly after the auditions, we were invited to the BBC studios in Glasgow to record an episode of the programme. I was a regular viewer, so sitting in the studio with the eggheads was weird to say the least. I took the notorious CJ to sudden death, but in the end he beat me, and we came away without the £11,000 prize. I still treasure the souvenir photo we were given.

The postscript to our afternoon's work was that after the programme we dashed to Glasgow Central Station to catch the train home. Missing it by a couple of minutes, we went for a decent meal and caught the next train south. In our rush to get home, we'd left the studio in a hurry, and it was only when I climbed into my car at Preston Station and looked in my rear-view mirror that I realized I'd had a restaurant meal and travelled all that way on a packed train in full make-up!

PART SIX

The 2010s

2010–11

The club had been officially put up for sale in April of that year, following the club's bank insisting on the appointment of an independent chairman in return for a six-month loan extension. In came British Airways chairman Martin Broughton, and on 15 October 2010, after an acrimonious legal battle, he arranged for the sale of the club to John Henry and the Fenway Sports Group, the owners of the Boston Red Sox. 'Every Liverpool fan knows that the most nerve-racking way to win a football match is in a penalty shoot-out,' Broughton said. 'But as long as you get the right result, it's worth the wait. We've always known that we were in the right and now we've got justice.'

Henry said he was 'proud and humbled' to be the new owner of Liverpool Football Club. 'We have a lot of work to do and I can't tell you how happy I am that we've finally got to this point.'

Tom Werner was subsequently appointed chairman. We all hoped that the new owners would be an improvement on the previous motley crew. They were. In spades!

> Eminem's 'Love the Way You Lie' featuring Rihanna
> was somehow the top seller in 2010.

John Henry had publicly backed Roy Hodgson, but in the end the manager departed by mutual consent on the morning of 8 January 2011. I was at Anfield for a youth-team game that morning, and someone in the match-day control room next door had a contact at Melwood who was texting him a blow-by-blow account of events over there. The respective messages were 'Nothing happening' then 'He's gone!' then 'Kenny's back!!!' This last piece of news was greeted with great joy by everyone inside the stadium. Kenny was, and still is, revered by the people of Anfield. In typical fashion, he refused to be triumphalist, telling reporters, 'A good man has lost his job.'

Fernando Torres was a world-class striker, there's no doubt about that, but the way he behaved towards the end of the January transfer window left a nasty taste in the mouth. I'm not privy to who was ultimately to blame for his sudden departure, be it club or agent or Fernando himself. The fact was that his unexpected transfer to arch-rivals Chelsea nearly left Liverpool in the lurch.

I'd been put off the man when he and Pepe Reina had turned up to a supporters' club event a couple of years earlier. Les Lawson introduced me as the stadium announcer. This was greeted with a sneer from Fernando and a dismissive 'So'. Pepe, I hasten to add, was the exact opposite. He stopped to shake hands and chat. His first words were, 'You've been here a few years, haven't you!'

On 31 January, the arrival of two other strikers very late in the day steadied the ship: Andy Carroll from Newcastle for an eye-watering £35 million and Luis Suárez for £13 million less. Neither of them were available for immediate selection. Andy was injured, and Luis was still serving a ban for biting an opponent. Comment would be superfluous!

When I was a teenager, everyone my age thought pensioners were a blot on the landscape. But here I was, turning sixty-five and eligible for the state pension. I'm so glad it's not called the 'Old Age Pension' nowadays.

I had a really nice family day. My wife and kids were as generous as always. In the evening, Liz and I went for a meal with Kim, her husband Mike and little Stevie G, who was only nine months old. During the meal, my phone was very active, with a lot of texts coming in. I was trying to be polite and ignore them, but the sheer volume was beginning to get to me. I was chuffed to get so many 'Happy Birthday' messages, but then I also started to receive a few texts along the lines of 'Wasn't it great what Kenny said on LFCTV?' I was blissfully unaware of what Kenny had said and didn't think for a moment it would have anything to do with me. However, when we eventually got home, I went to my laptop to investigate.

Kenny did a weekly interview with Claire Rourke on LFCTV. After finishing her usual questions (injury news, last weekend's game, next weekend's game, etc., etc.), she said, 'Finally, have you a message for George Sephton, who turns sixty-five today?'

His reply stunned me: 'George is part of the history and traditions of Liverpool Football Club, and it would be more relevant if he left than if I left!'

I watched it through a couple more times to make sure I hadn't misheard him. I hadn't. Head spinning, I called Liz to come and watch the clip. The expression 'shoot me now' springs to mind. Life doesn't get any better than that. I idolize Kenny, and I was a big admirer of Claire. She's always at the top of her game and has been a priceless asset to LFCTV since arriving from a similar role with Real Madrid. I am forever in her debt.

Liverpool v. Manchester United, Anfield, 6 March 2011

Liverpool gave Manchester United what can only be described as a good hiding. Luis Suárez played (and starred!), and Andy Carroll made his long-awaited debut as a substitute, but it was Dirk Kuyt who stole the headlines with a hat-trick in a 3–1 win against our arch-rivals from the other end of the East Lancashire Road. United were destined to be champions that season, and Kenny, magnanimous as ever, said that they were 'still the benchmark for everyone else'. Sir Alex, however, chose to boycott the media scrum after the game.

Towards the end of the game, the crowd were, unsurprisingly, in party mood and made sure that Kenny had their best wishes for his sixtieth birthday, which was a couple of days before.

By early 2011, I was at my wits' end looking for work. I had just turned sixty-five, and my days in IT were a distant memory. I was discovering for myself what the job market was like for people 'of a certain age'. A friend of my wife's mentioned that her husband, a retired engineer, was working for DHL delivering parcels locally. It sounded like a very uncomplicated routine. A van would bring a few sacks full of small parcels every morning along with a list of addresses. You piled the parcels into the back of your own car and delivered them. The pay wasn't good, but it was better than nothing.

It turned out that DHL were looking for drivers in the Merseyside area, so I applied. Training was at their depot near Warrington, and before I knew it, I was out on the road. It was tedious most of the time, but occasionally you would find a customer who would appear grateful for his or her delivery, and the odd smile brightened up my day. The lady who trained the guys on my intake said that a good delivery man would deliver ten parcels an hour. I enquired one day if the driver concerned was called Usain Bolt! Initially, I was covering quite a wide area around North Liverpool, but later on DHL became Yodel, and they got the contract for Amazon, which meant that they had to recruit more drivers and the area each driver covered was much smaller. There were hiccups once in a while. When the new Apple phone came out, I had a few hairy moments thinking that my car was going to get broken into and that my physical well-being was in great danger! For a few hours each day, I was carrying several thousand quids' worth of mobile phones in my boot.

One or two people caused more than their fair share of hassle. One lady in particular complained that the parcel I was delivering was late after she'd opted for 'next day delivery' at an extra cost to her.

'When did you order it?' I enquired.

'Yesterday.'

'Well this is the next day.'

'Yes, but I was expecting it this morning.' (This was about 1.30 in the afternoon.)

'But it's still the next day!'

She wouldn't have it, and I believe she complained. To this day, I can't understand her logic.

In the week of the Grand National, BBC Radio broadcast a lot of programmes from the city. A couple of the sports programmes were recorded at small venues around Liverpool, including the Friday night football programme, which was broadcast from the Neptune Theatre (now the Epstein) in Hanover Street. I got an email from one of the production team asking me if I would like to attend the Saturday morning edition of Colin Murray's *Fighting Talk*, his very clever and very funny 'points for banter' panel game. Colin's a lifelong Liverpool fan who once defended me live on another Radio 5 programme when the presenter, Danny Baker, declared that 'all stadium announcers are idiots'. Colin was in the adjacent studio getting ready for his show but poked his head into Danny's to argue the point, mentioning me by name. Anyway, I replied to say that I'd love to come along and watch. Not much later, I got another email saying that they wanted me to play a small part in the programme! Not as a panellist but to do something else. What the 'something else' was remained a mystery.

I got the train into town early to avoid the race-day traffic and headed for the Neptune Theatre. It was locked up with no sign of life! Luckily, I had the producer's number on my phone, so I rang him. What nobody had mentioned was that this programme was being recorded at the Liverpool Empire. So it was that I stood on that famous old stage in front of a full house to do the intro to that week's episode. When I finished, I sat in the front row watching the rest of the show, reflecting on the people who had been on that stage before me: Frank Sinatra, Judy Garland, Bing Crosby, Mae West, Laurel and Hardy, Johnny Mathis, The Carpenters, Neil Sedaka, The Osmonds, Tommy Steele, Adam Faith, Bruce Forsyth, Victoria Wood, Morecambe and Wise, Ken Dodd, Shirley Bassey, Kylie Minogue, Kate Bush, Elton John, Cilla

Black and The Beatles, to name just a few. Short of actually topping the bill at the Empire, this was as good as it gets. Just to set foot on that stage was a memorable experience, and one I shall never forget.

The day in May when the new Liverpool kit was issued was horrendous. I was given about three times the normal number of parcels to deliver by Yodel. Everybody who had paid for their new kit on the promise of delivery on the first day of sale appeared to be waiting behind their front doors, ready to pounce. Eventually, I ran out of daylight and found about five or six parcels left over, but I decided to knock off, as I was due at the supporters' club awards dinner at Anfield with Liz that night.

The dinner was terrific. The food was great, the company was great and the icing on the cake came when the actual award presentations started. When it came to the Tom Saunders Memorial Award, my hero Ian St John stood up and started to speak. He said that the recipient of that year's award was someone who had been at the club for forty years but whose face was not well known, a loyal servant who worked behind the scenes. As his speech went on, I turned to Liz and whispered, 'He's talking about me!'

'Of course he is!' she said, laughing. We were at a table with Mike Lepic of Jamie Carragher's 23 Foundation, and he told me later that my expression was priceless. Never in a million years did I expect an award of any description for just doing my job. I was almost speechless! I recovered my composure long enough to make a brief acceptance speech. Ian Ayre and Damien Comolli (managing director and director of football respectively) were sitting at the top table. What I said still holds true: 'With respect to you two gentlemen, this award is from the people who are the heart of the club. Liverpool fans. It's an honour to get this trophy, especially from the Saint, so all I can say is thank you!'

The next morning, I was out early. My first drop-off was to a lady who blamed me for the fact that her young son had cried himself to sleep the previous night after dashing home from school to see his new kit. While I was apologizing to her, I got an irate phone call from my second customer, who had been given my phone number by Yodel. He was good and mad! It was so bad that I phoned Liz while I was on my way to his house and warned her that I thought I was about to get assaulted! I asked her to sue the hell out of Yodel if I came to any harm. Apparently, they had told the guy that I had called at his house the previous day but found no one at home. That was a lie but shifted the blame from the company to me. Luckily, he recognized me when I arrived and accepted my explanation.

Out of the blue, I received an invitation to attend the graduation ceremony for my old school. By this point, the Liverpool Institute High School for Boys was the Liverpool Institute for Performing Arts, aka Paul McCartney's Fame School.

What an occasion. The atmosphere in the hall is akin to a huge carnival. The students are all heading for the entertainment industry, far removed from your run-of-the-mill jobs. Apart from anything else, the honorary degrees are awarded to some of the greatest names in the biz. I've been to several of the events, and it's still the best free entertainment in the world. Sir Paul always turns up, no matter where he happens to be. One year he was mid-tour. He played in Canada, jumped on a plane and made it to Liverpool. Having shaken hands with every graduate and made his speech, he drove to the airport and flew to the next leg of his tour in New York.

2011–12

Forty years after I made my first nervous appearance on the PA at Anfield, I was presented with a commemorative silver salver on the pitch by managing director Ian Ayre during the half-time break in the game against Sunderland on 13 August. There are no words to describe how proud I felt that day.

Liverpool v. Manchester United, Anfield, 15 October 2011

The match itself was not particularly noteworthy, finishing 1–1, but the aftermath was devastating. Patrice Evra had been shown a yellow card following a prolonged argument with Luis Suárez, and just over a month later, Suárez was charged with racism by the FA and was subsequently banned for eight games.

Order was restored in 2011 when the top-selling song was 'Someone Like You' by Adele.

After a thankless year delivering parcels, I was still hoping to get one more desk job before packing it all in. In February, I saw an ad for an admin clerk at Winners in Aintree, not very far from home. Winners are two companies in one – window cleaners and suppliers of cherry pickers. Due to the high demand for cherry pickers, the job turned out to be quite stressful, but it was indoors and paid regularly. I could fulfil my commitments at Anfield and pay the bills. What more could I ask for? In short, an understanding boss! Gary Winn is a die-hard Evertonian whose professional football career had been cut short by a horrendous injury when playing for Oldham. He did, however, realize my commitment to Liverpool and made sure I could meet my obligations at Anfield.

League Cup Final – Liverpool v. Cardiff City, Wembley Stadium, 26 February 2012

This was another nerve-racking final, ending with Kenny's first trophy in his second spell as manager. The score was 1–1 at full time, and there was one goal for each side in extra time, followed by a penalty shoot-out that Liverpool won 3–2 to lift the League Cup for a record eighth time.

All well and good, you might think, but I didn't enjoy the game as much as most Liverpool fans because I was compelled to watch it at home on the TV in my front room. The way things had been going at Anfield, I hadn't been very optimistic about getting a ticket but then I got an email from the guys organizing the pre-match entertainment to ask me if I would like to take part. There was (or rather had been) a tradition in the League Cup final of inviting the stadium announcers from the competing clubs to take part. I, of course, had been involved at Wembley in 1995 and then at Cardiff's Millennium Stadium in 2001 and 2005. I said that I'd love to take part. I was asked if I wanted a car park pass, and of course I said, 'Yes, please!' Then came the small print. The club would have to provide a ticket for the game! I spent some time chasing the relevant people at Anfield and was completely ignored. Calls and emails went unanswered, and eventually I had to tell the organizers I couldn't come.

The night before the game, I got a message from one of my Twitter followers: 'How are you looking forward to the final tomorrow?'

'I'm not,' was my terse reply.

'Why not?'

My answer didn't really relay my mood: 'Because I'm not going.'

The follow-up question was the one that finished me: 'Why aren't you going?'

'BECAUSE I HAVEN'T GOT A BLOODY TICKET!!!' I didn't add the extra text that was implied; i.e., 'Why else wouldn't I be going, you idiot!'

Before long, my distress was going viral. As I went to bed, I checked my laptop again and was amazed to see the response. People were genuinely amazed that I wasn't going. People were messaging everybody they could think of to see if they could get me a ticket: players, ex-players, Kenny, John Henry, Mrs Henry, journalists, TV presenters and (my favourite) Gary Barlow! I was touched but no further forward and went to sleep.

The following morning, I awoke at 8.45 and discovered an email from the ticket office. This was all a big mistake, misunderstanding or whatever. There was a ticket waiting for me at the Wembley box office (great!), but I had to collect it by noon at the latest (not great!). If anyone could have explained to me how I was supposed to get to the Wembley box office in three hours, I would have gone, but, short of owning a helicopter, I was stuffed! John Henry's wife Linda Pizzuti, bless her, messaged me to make sure I'd been 'sorted out'. I explained that I had, sort of, but had no chance of getting there. I thanked her for her concern.

FA Cup Final – Liverpool v. Chelsea, Wembley Stadium, 5 May 2012

After missing out on tickets for the League Cup final, I held out no hope of getting tickets for the FA Cup final, which has a much smaller allocation for the competing teams. As it happened, I was asked to attend an event organized by the club's sponsors on the day of the final – a bike ride in aid of Standard Chartered's 'Seeing Is Believing' charity, which had been due to travel from Anfield to London, but because of the club's involvement in the final had been switched to the other way round. So it was that Jan Mølby and I found ourselves standing in the old Main Stand car park welcoming the tired but happy cyclists 'home'.

When they were all accounted for and had taken lots of pictures with the 'Great Dane', they all disappeared into one of the lounges to watch the game. I went home in time to watch it from my usual 'spec' in my living room. Sadly, we lost 2–1. Enough said!

On 9 May, I came home from work for lunch to find an unexpected parcel waiting for me. I was curious because it was too big to be a CD, and I didn't have any mail-order stuff outstanding. When I got the thing unwrapped, it was an A4-size hardback book called *A Fulhamish Tale*. It was the autobiography of David Hamilton, a star BBC Radio DJ whom I used to listen to religiously back in the day. He was a regular presenter on *Top of the Pops* and a big name on radio. My only previous contact with him had come in 2011 when I'd turned up at Anfield for the Premier League game against Fulham. One of the stewards had greeted me with, 'Nice picture of you in the programme today!' Sure enough, there I was, next to an article headed 'The Two Best Announcers in the League'. The two turned out to be me and David. Exalted company indeed.

I'd heard that David was my opposite number at Craven Cottage, but I'd not thought to get in touch. This had given me an excuse. I'd guessed that no one would have thought to send him a copy of the programme, so I'd sent one to him care of Fulham FC with a covering letter. To my amazement, he'd replied with a handwritten letter from his home address in Sussex and followed it up with a phone call! Now, a year later, here I was holding a complimentary copy of his autobiography. I said to Liz, 'I hope he's signed it!' He had. And underneath the signature was a note that read 'look at page 129'. I did and was even more stunned. In fact, I was speechless. And that doesn't happen very often, believe me. There was a whole chapter headed 'The Voice of Anfield'!

The simple announcement 'Kenny Dalglish is no longer the manager of Liverpool' took the wind out of my sails! My first thought was, 'We won a cup not a couple of months ago, didn't we?' Followed by, 'We got to the FA Cup final too, didn't we?' Not to mention, 'You can't sack a king!' He was replaced by Brendan Rodgers the following month.

2012–13

The Hillsborough Independent Panel issued its report on the morning of 12 September. First, it held a private meeting with the families of the ninety-six and then a press conference at the Liverpool Anglican Cathedral. As it happened, I was in Runcorn, speaking to the local Probus (Professional Retired Business People) Club. When I finished speaking, I threw the floor open for questions. The first few questions were the usual stuff – who's my favourite player? How did I get the job? Etc. – but the last one came from someone who wanted to know what I hoped for from the report's findings. I said I hoped that the truth would finally emerge, but I feared that there would be a lot of redacted items in there. I was wrong!

I climbed back into my car for the journey home just in time to hear David Cameron rise to his feet in the House of Commons and apologize to the people of Liverpool and the families of the victims. I was on the M57 at the time and had to pull over before I ran my car off the road. I was shaking, laughing and crying simultaneously and really shouldn't have been driving. Eventually, I recovered my composure and went home. The report said that the police and emergency services had been far too slow to react; they'd assumed they were dealing with crowd trouble; and when they'd realized what was actually happening, their response had been less than useless. And just to add insult to injury, they'd lied, blaming the fans! It completely exonerated the victims of any blame. Publicly. Officially. Finally.

Being Liverpool was a fly-on-the-wall documentary series about Liverpool Football Club on Fox Soccer in America, Canada, the UK and other parts of the world. It followed the team behind the scenes on their pre-season tour to North America in July 2012 and the build-up to the new season. The documentary was narrated by actor Clive Owen, a lifelong Liverpool fan. I was asked if I'd like to take part and, being the big ham that I am, agreed instantly. It was, to say the least, an interesting experience! I was in two of the six episodes, which were broadcast on Channel 5 in the UK, but I was told the potential worldwide audience was over 300 million!

The first interview I did for the programme was filmed in my room in the corner of the Kop Stand at its junction with the Sir Kenny Dalglish Stand. When I was asked to go in for the filming, I was taken aback, as my little room was sacrosanct, and the stadium security was such that visitors were not allowed in there. The difference now was that Fox Sports News were making the documentary, and John Henry's people had made it clear that they would have carte blanche.

After the initial session, the producer asked if they could film me at home. I was OK with that, although Liz wasn't too chuffed and made herself scarce when they were due, leaving me with a rather confused dog who, fortunately, sat quietly on the couch all afternoon. I had been expecting a cameraman and possibly a man with a mic. In the end, two people carriers with two full TV crews turned up on my doorstep. After a long filming session, they asked if they could do another the following day when we were due to play Manchester City at Anfield. I was getting into all this by now, so I agreed. I was expecting a few words in my room pre-match. No chance!

When I parked up opposite the stadium, I was greeted by a complete crew (only one this time!) who followed me all the way through the old Main Stand car park, in through reception, down the players' tunnel and right around the pitch to the gate into my tower. There were a couple of minor hitches, of course. Going through the car park, several groups of people coming in the opposite direction stopped to watch and wonder what was going on. And no one had thought to warn the stewards on the entrance to the Main Stand reception, so they pounced on the TV guys as soon as they saw them. Eventually, they were persuaded that the TV people were there officially and let us go. I touched the 'This Is Anfield' sign as usual, and this gesture seemed to take them aback. We rerecorded me going through the ritual time after time from all sorts of angles before setting off again.

Several months later, the series aired on TV worldwide. Each week it would start its run in Canada and get to the UK the following Friday. Some kind soul in Canada sent me a clip she'd filmed off her TV. That was a real eye-opener as I realized that my name was spelled wrong in the titles. They had my surname as 'Septhon' instead of 'Sephton'! As luck would have it, the following morning I received a disclaimer to sign from the club's solicitor. I refused point-blank until they corrected my name. To my amazement, Channel 5 sorted it out before the first episode was broadcast on the Friday night here. I must have had more clout than I thought!

The day after my second contribution was broadcast (episode five in the series), Liverpool had a home game. Sometime after the final whistle, I was wandering along the front of the Kop taking my two-way radio back to reception. Jamie Carragher and some other players were warming down by running up and down the pitch. They and I drew level, and the players all stopped dead. Jamie shouted across the Kop wall, 'Oi, George! How come you're in that programme more than I am?'

I was taken aback but gathered my thoughts and, deciding to act dumb, stroked my chin and said, 'Which programme's that, Jamie?' And then, before he had a chance to reply, followed up with, 'Oh, you mean the Brendan Rodgers show!'

To be fair, Brendan had been the central character in the series, having taken over as manager mid-filming. He had also been portrayed as something of an egotist. Even so, the reaction of Jamie and the rest of the players lined up alongside him surprised me. They all started laughing. Eventually, they got back to their warm-down, and I went home. I was a bit wary of upsetting anyone at the club and was hoping the encounter wasn't reported back to Brendan. Suffice to say, I didn't get the sack. Recently, Jamie described Brendan in glowing terms on Sky TV, but, all in all, I don't think he ever generated the same level of respect as some of the managerial giants who have guided the club in my lifetime.

It was around 5.30 p.m., and I was on my way into Liverpool city centre when my phone rang. It was Jimmy Swords, one of the drivers who worked for my employers Winners. My first thought was that there was a problem with one of the company vehicles. I was heading for the launch party of the Liverpool Irish Festival and really didn't want any sort of hassle, but I pulled over and answered. Jimmy was excited, going on hysterically: 'You're on *The Chase*!'

The Chase is the ITV teatime quiz show that pits teams of contestants against the finest quiz brains in the country. 'I'm sorry, Jimmy. You must have got it wrong. I was on *Eggheads* a while ago, but I've not been on *The Chase*.'

'No, no. You're not on the show. You're a question!' I couldn't believe what I was hearing and didn't understand what was happening. Just in case, I phoned Liz at home and asked her to record the programme when it was on the plus-one channel an hour after the first transmission. I texted my three kids to tell them the same.

When I eventually got home a few hours later, I watched the recorded programme. Sure as night follows day, there it was! The question: 'Stadium announcer George Sephton is known as the Voice of . . . (A) Anfield (B) Old Trafford or (C) White Hart Lane?'

The answer is of course (A), and I'm pleased to say that the contestant and the chaser (Paul Sinha) both got the right answer. What a buzz that was!

Gotye's remarkable 'Somebody That I Used to Know' smashed it in 2012. I'm proud to say, however, that I had a hand in the Christmas number one that year! It was 'He Ain't Heavy, He's My Brother' by The Justice Collective. My MP Steve Rotheram phoned me at work in the autumn to tell me about the project, which had been organized by my friend Peter Hooton from the band The Farm. He had got together some of the great and good of contemporary English music to record a version of the song that had been a huge hit for The

Hollies, and which had been played over the PA at Goodison before the derby game in September. The likes of Mel C, Glenn Tilbrook, Robbie Williams, Paloma Faith and Holly Johnson all contributed, as did Gerry Marsden and Paul McCartney. It was due for release on 17 December, and my job was to plug it mercilessly both at Anfield and on social media. I had a couple of demo copies but made sure to buy a couple of copies as well. I didn't even bother to unwrap my purchases, instead storing them away for safekeeping. I was so pleased that the song made the number one slot at Christmas. A few days later, I got a message: 'Have you seen the cover of "He Ain't Heavy"?' I took the cellophane off one of the CD singles and discovered my name in the credits, just under Paul McCartney! Stunned doesn't come close! I believe my eldest granddaughter Holly proudly told everyone at school that her grandad had the number one single at Christmas!

Sculptor Tom Murphy's wonderful memorial to the victims of Hillsborough was unveiled in St John's Gardens facing the entrance to the Mersey Tunnel the day before the twenty-fourth anniversary of the disaster. It is a magnificent piece of work that should be a port of call for Scousers and tourists alike.

Tom said, 'Hillsborough means a lot to people in the city. It's not just the tragedy of the people who died, but the legacy of the people who were there and were traumatized by it. I think this is the most important sculpture I've done. This monument is about being a human being. It is about saying, "We have not forgotten you. We will remember you."'

2013–14

Hitting forty is a huge milestone in anyone's life. An even bigger milestone in my life was when my eldest child hit the big four-o. Rob had been living down south since the early nineties, but he and his family came home for the celebrations. I thought that we had to have a celebration meal at Anfield, and the Boot Room Sports Café is a really good place to eat.

All fourteen of us gathered at Anfield for the big night. When we arrived, Alan Herr, then a tour guide, called me over and showed me a picture on his phone. The picture was taken in the summer of 1981 in the old Main Stand trophy room, just before the royal wedding of Charles and Diana. It showed me (with my perm), my two sons (Rob was nearly eight and Laurie was six) wearing their Radio City European Cup T-shirts and Karen Manning, Bob Paisley's PA, who, sadly for everyone at Anfield, was about to leave her job and move to London. Karen is now Karen Gilbert, married with one grown-up son and living in Kent. She had been in the Boot Room not long before we arrived and had got into conversation with Alan. She had showed him some pictures from her time at Anfield, and the one I just described was amongst them. Suffice to say that I was soon in touch with Karen and her family, and we've met up several times since. In 2018, she was taken on a guided tour of the new Main Stand and was thrilled to see so many pictures of her old boss. Like all of us, she was very fond of Bob.

Rob enjoyed his little party, and I have to put on record my gratitude to his four favourite players who all signed and dedicated birthday cards for him: Kenny Dalglish, Jan Mølby, Robbie Fowler and Ronnie Whelan. The icing on the cake!

From my point of view, it was so gratifying to see all of my extended family in one place. Rob and his wife Sue live in Crawley with their daughter Edith, who was born in 2011. Rob has a daughter, Holly, from a previous relationship, and she was my first grandchild, born in 1998. Laurie lives in Widnes with his wife Pam, and at that time they had two daughters, Amber who was born in 2008 and her sister Harper, who was born on the Island of Mauritius in 2011. Maya then came along in 2014. Kim is married to Mike Brennan, and they had two sons at that time: my eldest grandson Stephen, born in the early hours of the morning after the general election in 2010, and Thomas, who was born just after Edith in 2011. Since then, their family has grown, with Rory arriving in 2014 and Cora in 2017. They are such a great bunch, and Liz and I love the bones of each and every one of them.

On 2 September, I attended a dinner at Anfield hosted by my friend Colin Murray to commemorate the 100th anniversary of the birth of Bill Shankly. Some of Shankly's family were there, and the creation of the Shankly Foundation was announced. The menu was the same as that served at Shankly's retirement dinner thirty-nine years before.

Former player Ian Callaghan said, 'I never had a cross word with him. From a personal point of view, he was a very special man. I pinch myself today thinking I played for this man for fourteen seasons.' Cally then said that Shankly had promised 'to make Liverpool Football Club great – and he did. He took to the Liverpool people. It was a great relationship. Liverpool FC were a Second Division club going nowhere when he arrived.'

On 30 September 2013, I was sitting at my desk in the Winners' office and toying with the idea of going home for lunch when my phone rang. It was Liz: 'Are you coming home soon? I've got some news!' She wouldn't elaborate. I drove home at speed, fearing the worst.

The news was awful. Laurie had been diagnosed with Parkinson's disease. The poor lad was only thirty-eight. I had previously thought of Parkinson's as an old man's disease, but believe me I've had my eyes opened over the subsequent years.

> Robin Thicke's controversial but catchy 'Blurred Lines' topped the charts in 2013.

The overall aim of the season appeared to be to qualify for the Champions League for the first time since 2009. It was probably a reasonable and realistic step on the club's way back to the top of the pile where we belonged, but, to an old Kopite like me, it seemed slightly lacking in ambition.

We secured qualification on 20 April, but for a brief period we were actually in with a chance of winning the league. The wheels fell off when we lost at home to Chelsea on 27 April, following an eleven-game winning streak. Rumours were rife that Chelsea would field a team of youngsters, as they were heading to a Champions League semi-final the following week. They didn't – they put out a strong side, including, incidentally, a promising young Egyptian by the name of Mohamed Salah!

Demba Ba scored a breakaway goal near the end of the first half after Steven Gerrard inexplicably slipped and lost the ball. People have given Steven some terrible stick since, but I've heard a theory that it was the topspin on Mamadou Sakho's pass that did for him. And Jamie Carragher is of the opinion that if Alisson Becker had been in goal, it would have been saved! Chelsea's Willian killed the game late on. Four days later, we threw away a comfortable lead at Crystal Palace, drawing 3–3.

We scored a record number of goals that season and reached the last home game still with a chance of winning the title. Recently, while clearing out the pictures folder on my laptop, I found an innocuous-looking photograph that I took in the Anfield Road car park on that day. It's of a strange-looking vehicle (which could be an overgrown quad bike) towing a trailer loaded with several semi-circular, royal-blue wooden structures. It was the podium, ready for the presentation of the Premier League trophy. Similar arrangements had been made at Manchester City's Etihad Stadium, and I believe the trophy itself was in a helicopter somewhere between there and Anfield. When I went back to my car after the game, our podium was being towed away, unused.

2014–15

Hopes were high at the start of the new season, even though the prolific Luis Suárez had been sold to Barcelona. Transfers the other way during July were plentiful, with the likes of Adam Lallana, Emre Can, Dejan Lovren, Divock Origi and Rickie Lambert coming in. The first four of those had star quality, and Rickie had been scoring freely for Southampton and was a lifelong Reds fan, which I hoped would add an edge to his play. Divock was loaned back to Lille for the season. I was quite disappointed, to be honest, because I'd been impressed by what I'd seen during his games for the Belgian side on TV. August brought the arrival of Alberto Moreno and, more significantly, Mario Balotelli. I confess I was beyond excited when Mario arrived. I got that one wrong!

There were some star names in the out tray, too: apart from Suárez, there was Pepe Reina, Martin Kelly, Conor Coady and, sadly, Daniel Agger. Martin and Conor have had long careers at other clubs. Pepe was still a star keeper, and I was sorry to see Daniel go. He was a dedicated Red from way back, and I once heard him say that he wouldn't ever play for another

English club. He went home to Denmark and played out the rest of his career there.

Despite the transfer activity, Liverpool had the worst start to a season for several years, struggling in the Premier League and falling at the first hurdle in the Champions League group stage. Beaten twice by Real Madrid and once by Basel, we ended up third in our group and were consigned to the Europa League in the new year.

> The joyous 'Happy' by the ubiquitous Pharrell Williams was everyone's favourite in 2014.

I'd warned my boss Gary Winn before Christmas that I was hoping to give up the 'day job' before too long. To be fair on both of us, I hung around long enough for him to find and train a replacement. He recruited a good guy who was more than a replacement for me and took to the job like the proverbial duck to water. Looking back, I now wonder, like most folk of my age, how I ever found time to go to work!

Liverpool v. Crystal Palace, Anfield, 16 May 2015

Steven Gerrard endured a disappointing final home match with Liverpool as Crystal Palace ruined his Anfield farewell with a 3–1 win in the Premier League. His legacy will always be the 'Triumph of Istanbul', but he produced many memories over the years: the screamer against West Ham at the Millennium Stadium; the rocket against Olympiakos that kept us in the Champions League in 2005; the sending off against United in March 2015 when Brendan kept him on the bench while he was champing at the bit, and he flattened Ander Herrera thirty-eight seconds after joining the fray. The bottom line is that he was a fearless, loyal and inspirational leader. But in his 709th appearance for Liverpool, he couldn't produce one last moment of brilliance at a stadium he had illuminated so many times during his seventeen-year Liverpool career. Instead, it was a fairly low-key performance in a result that ended Liverpool's slim hopes of qualifying for the Champions League.

During the final minute of the match, the Kop sang 'Steven Gerrard is Red'. I put on an extra play of 'You'll Never Walk Alone' at the end, as well as a couple of Genesis tracks (he's apparently a fan) and 'Stevie' by Kasabian. I was sad to see him go. The following day, I was invited to Salford Quays to take part in a discussion programme on BBC Radio 5. Presenter Jonathan Overend asked me how I felt. I told him I feared for the future of my club. He was shocked. I told him that the Scouse heart had been torn out of Liverpool FC. Now we have Trent Alexander-Arnold and Curtis Jones in the squad and an honorary Scouser as manager.

The funeral of Brian Hall took place at St Lawrence's Church in Longridge, Lancashire, on 24 July. Fellow footballers turned out to pay tribute to the sixty-eight-year-old who had sadly lost his battle against leukaemia. I was really struck by the numbers of the great and good who had come out to pay their respects.

Brian played 224 games for the Reds between 1969 and 1976 and scored twenty-one goals, winning two league championships, an FA Cup and two UEFA Cup winners' medals. He returned to Liverpool in 1991 to head the club's public relations department before retiring twenty years later. I had many dealings with him in that role, and I can echo everything positive that's been said about the guy.

Priscilla Maria Veronica White OBE, better known as Cilla Black, was an English singer and TV presenter. She passed away at her Spanish retreat on 1 August, and it's fair to say that the city of Liverpool was in shock. She always said that she wanted to be remembered as a singer, and that's how I always thought of her. She made some wonderful records, and I still listen to them today. I met her three or four times over the years and was sad to hear of her death, so I was glad of the opportunity to make my own small tribute in the book of condolence at Liverpool Town Hall.

I had to attend a production meeting at The Cavern a couple of days later. The production meeting was with the guys from a German film company called Florian Films who were embarking on a documentary about the true history of the song 'You'll Never Walk Alone' and wanted to know if I would take part. Of course I would.

2015–16

The first home game of the new season was against Bournemouth. An hour or so before kick-off, I received a call from Craig in PR. He had King Kenny with him. Earlier in the summer, I'd left a congratulations card with a request for Kenny to sign it. My son's friend Stu was getting married, and the guy idolized Kenny Dalglish. I'd not heard any more about the card and had reached the conclusion that I'd probably asked Kenny for too many favours in the 'please sign this' department. Nothing could be further from the truth. Kenny had kept the card safe until he got to Anfield and hadn't signed it because I hadn't thought to include the bride's name!

I suddenly realized I didn't know and made a frantic call to Rob. I rang Craig back with the details, and two days later I got the precious card through my letter box. Stu was thrilled when one of the cards being read out at his wedding turned out to be from his hero! I don't know of anyone else of the stature of Sir Kenneth Dalglish who would go to so much trouble for a fan.

After a disappointing run of form, Brendan Rodgers was shown the door on Saturday, 4 October within an hour of the final whistle after a 1–1 draw with Everton at Goodison Park. Four days later, the rising star of German football management, the charismatic Jürgen Klopp, was given the manager's job at Anfield. He'd been in charge at Borussia Dortmund, where he'd enjoyed a fair amount of success, but was now looking for a new challenge. The two clubs have a similar fan base (they even sing 'You'll Never Walk Alone' before games), and Jürgen appeared to be a perfect fit. His first game in charge was an away draw against Spurs in the Premier League. His second was a Europa League game against Rubin Kazan at Anfield the following Thursday.

After the game, I was hanging around in the Main Stand reception as usual, waiting for the traffic to subside. Suddenly, Jürgen appeared from the corridor leading from the dressing rooms and went past me up the stairs to the temporary press room. I decided that I couldn't miss the opportunity and followed him. 'Herr Klopp,' I shouted.

When he stopped, I held out my right hand and got as far as, 'Hello, my name's George,' before he interrupted me. His eyes lit up.

'Ah, yes! You are the famous Voice of Anfield!'

He shook my hand firmly. I was stunned. I managed, 'Welcome to Anfield,' before he went off to his press conference.

When I turned around, there were three club stewards standing there. Two were open-mouthed. The third wasn't. 'Do you know what,' he said. 'I work at Melwood during the day. That guy has been here a week and he knows everyone's name. Not just the players but the academy kids, the office staff, the tea lady, the stewards and the office cat! Brendan Rodgers was here three years and he still didn't know my name!'

We knew we were in a period of change, but we didn't realize what was on the horizon.

Mark Ronson's ultimate foot-tapper 'Uptown Funk', featuring Bruno Mars, sold in the millions in 2015.

League Cup Final – Liverpool v. Manchester City, Wembley Stadium, 28 February 2016

I'd more or less given up on ever going to a big final again. However, Liverpool got to the League Cup final against arch-rivals Manchester City, and out of the blue I was offered a trip to the match. I'm not quite sure why, but I think I came out top in the attendance records for the casual match-day staff. I was entitled to a pensioner's ticket and a free seat on one of the staff coaches. It was a good trip spoiled only when some halfwit let off a flare inside the services on the M6 Toll road just as I'd put my card in the cash machine and couldn't escape.

It was nice not having to drive through the streets of London, but I had a rude awakening in the stadium itself. I came to realize how spoiled I am at Anfield. First, the battle for refreshments. Then, having found my seat, I stood patiently waiting for kick-off. The teams lined up, the referee blew his whistle and I settled down into my seat to watch the game. It dawned on me very quickly that everyone else was still standing. I know I'm an old grouch, but I can't understand the logic of spending a fair amount of money on a seat and then not using it! City took the lead, but Liverpool fought back to take the match to extra time and penalties. Penalty shoot-outs are often a lottery, and on this particular day City had the winning ticket! By the end of extra time and penalties, I was exhausted and staggered back to the coach.

UEFA Europa League Quarter-final – Liverpool v. Borussia Dortmund, Anfield, 14 April 2016

This game ranks highly in the recent history of Liverpool matches, although it tends to slip under the radar a bit, because, in the end, it didn't lead to silverware. Borussia Dortmund were the visitors – Jürgen's old team and one of Germany's big guns. We had drawn the away leg 1–1, so a win or a 0–0 draw would see us through. Henrikh Mkhitaryan and Pierre-Emerick Aubameyang put the Germans in control within the first nine minutes. Early in the second half, Divock Origi pulled one back, but Marco Reus soon scored to make it 3–1. We then witnessed a Liverpool comeback that ranks up there with the best. Philippe Coutinho gave us faint hope, then, of all people, Mamadou Sakho equalized. In the last few minutes, you would have sworn Liverpool were playing with fifteen men. They swamped Dortmund, overran them! And in the ninetieth minute, Borussia collapsed under sheer weight of Liverpool's attacking, Dejan Lovren scoring the winner. Dortmund brought with them their famous 'Yellow Wall' of spectators, and 'You'll Never Walk Alone' that night was sung at full belt by all four sides of the stadium.

It was a day of mixed emotions on 26 April 2016. The jury in the second Hillsborough inquest had been out deliberating for a few days, and I was in turmoil. I wanted to be there in the coroner's court when the verdicts were announced, but there was no room, and, in any case, I had been invited to Ken Dodd's 'Good Turns Club' at the Devonshire House Hotel in Edge Lane in Liverpool and was being collected from home at 11.30 a.m. Luckily, the announcement was made just before my car came. The jury decided that the ninety-six people who died in the Hillsborough Disaster in 1989 were unlawfully killed, and a catalogue of failings by police and the ambulance services had contributed to their deaths. The verdict vindicated the bereaved families. The families and friends of the ninety-six who were at the court were euphoric. They sang 'You'll Never Walk Alone' at the top of their voices for all the world to hear. We'd campaigned for years for truth and justice. The truth was now ours.

It was late in the 2015–16 season that someone on my Facebook timeline sent me a video accompanied with the standard 'Have you seen this?' The video was a brief TV piece about Manel Vich, the voice of the Camp Nou!

I watched in amazement as I discovered that he had been reading out the teams for Barcelona since 1956 and was coming to the end of his sixtieth season in the post! He made me look like a complete beginner! Not only that but he'd had run-ins with the Franco regime, who had forbidden the use of his native Catalan. On 3 September 1972, he had made a standard lost child announcement in his mother tongue during a match between Barcelona and Deportivo, 'A child has been lost. He is at the door of the tribune,' which had caused an angry reaction from the minister of the interior Tomas Goni, who was present at the stadium, and Vich did not use Catalan again at the magnificent Camp Nou until 26 August 1975. Like many others in my profession, he'd started out in hospital radio, but his ambition was always to work as the stadium announcer for his beloved Barca. He succeeded magnificently and missed only four games in six decades.

I remarked to my wife that during the close season, I'd get in touch with Manel in the hope of organizing some sort of exchange visit. No more than a fortnight later, I heard that he had passed away. I only wish I'd heard about him earlier!

My friend Andreas (Andy), who runs the Liverpool supporters' club in Enköping, invited me to pay them a visit over the May Day bank holiday weekend. This was my first time in Sweden, and it turned out to be a great trip. Scandinavians are very hospitable people, but this lot took the biscuit!

I was collected at the airport and driven to a very nice hotel. The following day, I was taken to Andy's house, where I found the most amazing collection of memorabilia. Then it was on to the supporters' club, where I spoke to the locals, answered a few questions and drew the usual raffle, before being given a typical Scandinavian lunch and settling down to watch Liverpool's game at Swansea live on a cinema-size screen. After that, it was back to the hotel for a rest, and then I was taken to dinner at a terrific restaurant just around the corner. That would have kept me happy, but the following day Andy suggested that as my flight wasn't till the evening, we should have a look around Stockholm. It transpires that Andy is friendly with the head of the ground staff at the national stadium, who had agreed to give me a tour. When we arrived, however, the CEO had heard that someone from Liverpool was on his way and had decided he would do the tour instead. It was like a royal visit! It's a fabulous place, and I had the full works, concluding with a look round the dressing rooms. I had some pictures taken sitting in Zlatan Ibrahimović's place holding his captain's armband. Not only that but I came away with a Sweden shirt! It doesn't get much better than this, I thought. Wrong! Half an hour later, we were having lunch in the Abba Museum, somewhere I never thought I'd see. If you're an Abba fan, which of course I am, it's an unbelievable experience. The band are fully supportive of the museum, so some of the exhibits are priceless. It was a happy George who got back to Arlanda Airport that night for my flight home!

UEFA Europa League Final – Liverpool v. Sevilla, St Jakob-Park, 18 May 2016

Sevilla regard the Europa League as their property nowadays, and this game demonstrated why. Liverpool were in the lead and looking comfortable, but the Spaniards made a superb comeback early in the second half and were lucky to benefit from all the contentious decisions to win 3–1. This was Liverpool's second final defeat that season, after they had lost to Manchester City in the Capital One Cup.

Once again, I watched the game from the settee in my living room. I had more or less given up hope of attending another European final, but this time the opportunity to go was dangled in front of me and then snatched away again. I received a call from Anfield to say that someone from UEFA had asked if there was anyone available who was familiar with the music played on the match days at Anfield. There was, of course, someone to fit the bill. A guy who had played the match-day music at Anfield for forty-five years! They wanted me to attend the fan party in Basel before the game and play my usual set to the Reds fans – wow!

I quickly packed an overnight bag and found my passport. Before phoning Liz to tell her the good news, I got my usual match-day box of tricks together: duplicate memory sticks with more than enough music on there, CDR back-ups of the same music in case the decks in Basel's main square didn't have USB ports, a couple of 'proper' CDs with some stadium rock just in case I had to fill in for a long while, a water bottle, CD cleaning tissues, paracetamol, a selection of batteries, some chocolate biscuits and a packet of jelly babies. The last two items were to keep my blood sugar at a decent level because of my diabetes. Later that same day, I got another call. I wasn't needed after all. My music was, but I wasn't. My initial inclination was to say, 'Sort your own music out!' but I'm not made that way. I duly compiled a CD of LFC music and off it went. People think I have no feelings!

Tenerife in the Canary Islands is home to a sizeable ex-pat community of Liverpool fans, and in June Phil Neal and I were invited over by the supporters' club organizer, John Knowles. It was a wonderful break. John and his crew looked after us over the three days we were there, and Phil and I were made very welcome. When it came to my turn to speak on the Saturday night, it suddenly hit me that I was standing on a rock in the middle of the Atlantic with a replica European Cup and the ex-captain of England. Surreal.

Phil is probably the Liverpool player I've had most contact with over the years. It was he who saved me from the clutches of a UEFA official in 1985 at the Heysel Stadium, and his son Ashley has been a neighbour of mine for the best part of twenty years. Nowadays, Ashley runs a very successful driving school. He is the same age as Laurie, and they used to play in the same junior league when they were much younger, so Phil and I were often on the same Sunday morning touchline. Phil was managing Bolton Wanderers around the time I was heavily involved in junior football, and I sent a few promising lads to him for trials. Phil's trophy haul at Liverpool is unsurpassed:

eight league championships, four League Cups, four European Cups, one UEFA Cup and one UEFA Super Cup. Not to mention fifty appearances for his country.

Ian St John had just celebrated his seventy-eighth birthday, and a tribute night was held for him at the Devonshire Hotel on 10 June, which also raised money for a couple of worthwhile charities. I was ill-prepared but eventually made a speech I was proud of. The crowd had a few drinks before I got on stage but were very good to me. The Saint was a boyhood hero, and it was weird talking about him when he was in the crowd listening to me. I told them about my poor old dad who was a lifelong Red but crippled with arthritis by the time of the 1965 FA Cup final. I spoke of Ian's wonderful flying header and how my dad had turned to me and said, 'This is the greatest day of my life!' I then reminded Ian of the day in 2011 when he had presented me with the Tom Saunders Memorial Award. 'So, Ian,' I concluded, 'for making the greatest day of my dad's life and the greatest day of mine, thank you!'

2016–17

To my amazement, I received an email from the staffing department at Liverpool FC to say that I had to attend an induction course! On the eve of my forty-fifth season with the Reds, I thought that I might have got the hang of things by now!

I rang up to query the request: 'Is this a joke?'

'No, all the casual staff have to attend. But you'll get paid.'

Easily swung by the offer of money, as ever, I calmed down and booked myself in.

The course was divided into three sessions. The first was by way of a welcome to the new Main Stand, an introduction to the new people who would be working there (average age about twelve from what I could see) and a general pep talk (plus motivational video) to make people aware of their responsibilities to the Liverpool supporters who would henceforth be known as 'customers'.

The second session was due to take place on the Tuesday following this inspirational event. On the intervening Sunday, I met up with two Swedish friends of mine, Erin and Jenni, who are huge Liverpool fans. They'd booked to visit Liverpool and watch the home game against Burnley. Sadly, the new Main Stand wasn't ready, so the game was played away at Turf Moor. As they'd paid for plane fares and a hotel, they decided to come anyway, and a friend of mine managed to get them tickets for the game and transport up to Burnley.

We met near their hotel and had a coffee in Bold Street. After a long chat, the sharing of some pictures and a general catch-up, we were about to go our separate ways. I had to get home for Sunday lunch. 'What are you doing with the rest of your day?' I asked. Turns out they were off to Anfield to spend some kronor in the club store, so I offered them a lift, as it was no more than two minutes out of my way. On the way up to the ground, I discovered that they hadn't seen inside the new club museum. Sunday lunch could wait! I took them in and gave them the full tour. Some of the guys on duty took the girls' picture with one of the European Cups, as well as one or two with the 'virtual' Steven Gerrard. They were chuffed.

Two days later, I was back at Anfield for the second leg of the induction course. We all assembled in the Centenary Stand for coffee and were then told not to get comfy as we all had to go on a short trip – around the museum! Several of the staff were curious to know why I needed to be shown around somewhere I had been doing the guiding myself only two days previously. 'Don't ask!' was the best I could come up with.

Another week and the third (and final, thank God) section of the induction course. This time we had another motivational talk and then one of those absurd team-bonding games that some lunatic in an HR department far, far away in an alternate universe had come up with. I was easily the oldest person on my table for the task, which involved lots of glue and cutting out to make a jigsaw. Think *Blue Peter* for adults and you've got the idea. During the induction course, I turned from an inductee into a VIP and received an invitation to the official opening of the new Main Stand. It came on headed notepaper from Ian Ayre's PA. I was as pleased as punch.

There had been two 'test runs' involving crowds of five and ten thousand volunteers to make sure that the new Main Stand could handle the numbers it would be accommodating, but the official opening involved about 120 people only. I was delighted to be there. After a welcome coffee, we all sat in the front few rows of the lower tier and listened to the speeches from John Henry, Tom Werner and Jürgen Klopp.

The American owners in particular were justifiably proud. After the speeches, we were treated to a tour of the new building, and when we reached the sixth floor and took in the view over the city and the local area, I found myself standing between John Henry and Ann O'Byrne, who was then the deputy mayor with responsibility for regeneration on Liverpool City Council. I looked both of them in the eye in turn and said, 'Thank you – just thank you!'

What had happened to my beloved old stadium was wonderful. It was nothing like some of the sterile new heaps of concrete that had appeared at other clubs. More to the point, the Anfield district had also been transformed. I was very impressed. And that's an understatement.

Next came lunch in the boardroom. By this time, I had got chatting to Linda Pizzuti, John Henry's wife. On the way in, I cheekily asked her for a selfie. She obliged, of course. The boardroom itself is mightily impressive. If you visualize some of those five-star restaurants featured on TV cookery programmes then ratchet them up another two or three stars, then you have a reasonable idea of how grand the place is. All this, of course, in a venue that overlooks the Anfield pitch.

At this point, the day took a comic turn. When all the guests sat down to lunch, droves of waiting staff suddenly appeared. Their brief was to cater to our every need, but I realized that several of them had been on my induction course earlier in the week. Back then, I was just another member of the workforce being put through his paces alongside the rest of the casual staff, but now they were waiting on me hand and foot and wondering why I was suddenly a VIP! I suspect a lot of them thought I was probably a plant, placed there as some sort of spy for the management. I smiled serenely and didn't spoil their illusions. In fact, I thoroughly enjoyed the whole experience. I don't suppose I'll ever be invited into the inner sanctum again.

When the afternoon was over, I headed back to my car and happened to bump into Jason Judge, who was the stadium manager at the time. I was pleased to see him, because I'd realized that I hadn't received my access pass for the first home game the next day. Jason apologized and said it was on his desk ready. I also asked about my car park pass, and it was then that I discovered that my car park privileges had been taken away. The following day, I had to take the bus to Anfield for the first time in decades. Talk about back down to earth with a bump!

On 16 September, I was back at the Devonshire House Hotel, this time for a tribute night for Tommy Smith and Tommy Lawrence. I was lucky enough to have been around for both of their careers. I remember bumping into Smithy in a coffee bar in Maghull in 1965 when he was on the eve of flying out to play in a European game for the Reds. Now here he was in the depths of Alzheimer's, a shell of the Anfield Iron we all revered. Tommy Lawrence was in fine form on the night, and there was a wonderful moment when he came over to shake Smithy's hand. A broad smile of recognition crossed the latter's face at the arrival of his namesake. Priceless. Sadly, neither of them are with us any longer.

On 3 October, I was at yet another dinner, this time just as a guest. After a wonderful meal, a couple of ex-players took to the stage. I was sitting next to Jimmy Case's better half. Jimmy was talking with Phil Neal and Phil Thompson and regaling the crowd, as usual, with all sorts of stories. Suddenly, I realized a felt a bit light-headed. My first thought was that I was having a hypoglycaemic attack, but I'd just had a three-course meal, so it couldn't be that. I said, 'Excuse me for five minutes. I need some fresh air!'

The next thing I remember is coming to on the floor and a sea of faces looking at me. A voice said, 'There's an ambulance on its way. Don't worry, George!' I later found out that voice belonged to Gill Brockenhurst, a trained first-aider. As luck would have it, I landed at her feet!

I have no memory of the ride in the ambulance, but I do have vague memories of lying on a bed in A & E at the Royal Liverpool Hospital, trying to open my eyes. When I did, the whole room was spinning around and around, and I had to shut them again. Then there was a voice: 'I'm here, Dad.' It was Laurie, who had been ferried from Widnes by his brother-in-law. Sometime later, Liz and Kim arrived. This is all still a blur – it wasn't until the next day that the sequence of events was explained to me. Laurie had apparently arrived at the Royal at the same time as the ambulance and had seen what he thought was a dead body being wheeled in. It was me. Fortunately, he had soon discovered that I was still alive!

All sorts of blood samples were taken, and I was told later that a doctor had asked me how much I'd had to drink. I'd said that I didn't drink, but my speech had been slurred, so the staff had taken my answer with a pinch of salt. We realized later that after I'd passed out, I'd hit my head on the sharp corner of a table on my way to the floor. I was concussed.

The blood tests came back quite quickly, and the first thing the medics noticed was a distinct lack of alcohol! At this point, it was assumed that I'd had a stroke. I was taken for a brain scan, but, again, I have no actual memory of the journey. Before you crack the usual joke, yes, they did find a brain. The scan was clear, though, so it wasn't a stroke! They then tested for a heart attack. Again, all clear. Eventually, it was discovered that I was completely dehydrated because of a reaction to a new diabetic medication that I had been given. I was put on a potassium drip, and by the next morning I was as right as rain.

Liz rang to say she was coming to visit me in the ward where I'd been admitted overnight, but while she was on her way down, the duty doctor came to give me the once-over. Poor doctor. She gave me all the usual tests to detect stroke symptoms and so on, but when she got to the 'squeeze my hand, push me away, pull me towards you' bit, I was so determined to prove my fitness for discharge that I must have come close to breaking both her arms. 'Do you want to go home, Mr Sephton?'

'Yes, please!'

Liz drove me back to Anfield to collect my car. When we got there, I was told that the staff had put my cash and valuables in the safe. Heading in to collect them, I bumped into Phil Neal and Jimmy Case. I can still see the looks on their faces – a mixture of shock and amazement. They were pleased to see me, but I looked a bit rough to say the least, with quite a few chunks of cotton wool covering the site of blood tests and intravenous drips.

The following Monday, I went to my GP and had a brief chat: 'I'm not taking any more of those new tablets!'

'No, Mr Sephton. I wouldn't either, if I were you!' Panic over.

I've developed a keen interest in Parkinson's disease. There's nothing you can really do for the sufferer other than support them and, in a broader sense, help raise money for research into the illness, so I decided to run a fundraising event and booked the best lounge in the new Main Stand. Social media is brilliant on these occasions – publicity is a given.

I booked Jan Mølby to speak and my neighbour Lee Martin to sing. Bookings came in steadily, although not as many as I would have liked, but then Laurie's friends rallied round and booked two tables. A couple of contacts on Facebook booked several places and then stopped answering my emails. I've never forgiven them for that. It ate into the funds. I'm a trusting soul, and when someone says they're coming, I take them at their word.

I cobbled together a leaflet asking for donations in the form of raffle prizes and spent three whole days wandering around Liverpool One, leaving them with every shop that could possibly supply a prize. My efforts resulted in one small goody bag from a perfumier in Church Street, where the manageress took pity on me. Her dad had Parkinson's, apparently. But the guys at the club museum were generous, as were the LFC Foundation, who found me a signed shirt.

On the night, we had a decent crowd. Sarah Green from Parkinson's UK came with two young volunteers, and they worked miracles selling the raffle tickets. I found out that the volunteers normally ended up sitting in a corner like naughty schoolgirls with a couple of sandwiches after these events. Not on my watch! Because of the people who hadn't shown up, there were meals going begging, and I made sure that Sarah and the girls sat with the rest of the guests and had a proper dinner. The museum had lent me the Champions League trophy for the night and everyone, including the girls, took turns having a picture taken with it. Thanks to their efforts, and the generosity of people like TV producer Colin McKeown, the night raised nearly two and a half grand.

Drake's 'One Dance' was the top seller in 2016.

I think it's fair to say that I didn't enjoy large chunks of 2017. As I said earlier, I'd been stripped of my car park pass in August 2016. This, sadly, coincided with a growing problem with my mobility. I was starting to find that I had little strength in my legs, which slowly developed into severe pain.

After my car park pass was withdrawn, my wonderful friends at Hotel Tia said that I could park in front of their building until the renovations were complete. I was very grateful, but by the turn of the year I was even struggling to get down Anfield Road to the ground! After the Manchester City game on New Year's Eve, it took me the best part of an hour to get to my car. I was stopping every 100 yards or so.

After that trauma, I decided I had to change my plans. There is no free parking available anywhere near the ground other than in the official car parks. But, after a couple of trial runs, I discovered that I could park in a side road directly opposite the Asda in Walton. If I left home early, I could get in pole position at the end of the road, about forty yards from a bus stop. I could then wait at the stop until either an Anfield-bound bus or a taxi went past and get on whichever came first. Mostly it was a taxi that saved me. It was more expensive, but the bonus was that a taxi could get very close to the Shankly Gates, and I could hobble through there to reception and take the lift up to my floor.

The third or fourth time I arrived this way, I casually mentioned my routine to Tony Burke, one of the long-standing staff members in the match control room. Sometime later, without my knowledge or prompting, he buttonholed the head of health and safety and gave him an impromptu ear-bashing along the lines of, 'George has been here all these years and he still has to park in the street.'

The response was, 'I didn't know!' To his eternal credit, my car park privileges were not only restored but enhanced, and since then I've had a space directly opposite the Shankly Gates.

To complete my upturn in fortune, I managed to persuade my GP to prescribe a drug called gabapentin. Several people had told me that it would help with my walking problems. They were right. It can be quite addictive, but I took it long enough to get me mobile again. I'm never going to run in the Olympic Games, but at least I'm on the move.

Results on the pitch at this time were variable to say the least. In the third round of the FA Cup, we drew with lowly Plymouth and scraped through 1–0 after the replay at Home Park. It wasn't to be our year. Wolves beat us 2–1 at Anfield in the fourth round. In the league, we went down to Leicester, Swansea, Hull and Stoke but beat Arsenal, Spurs and Everton.

Looking back, I suppose the season should be noted as the one that saw the arrival of Trent Alexander-Arnold. He obviously had the raw talent, but Jürgen has brought him through the system and turned him into a world-class player. And he's a Scouser! His mural in Sybil Road near Anfield is now a tourist attraction. He's also generous with his time and money. A couple of Christmases ago, he arranged for several local families who couldn't otherwise have managed it to be treated to Christmas dinner at the Hotel Tia while their children were given some wonderful presents, all out of Trent's pocket.

The summer break was welcome, and the 2017–18 season promised improvement. We had, after all, qualified for the Champions League again. And the appointment of Peter Moore as CEO was a breath of fresh air.

2017–18

I experienced a serious candidate for the most surreal experience of my adult life at Liverpool's Philharmonic Hall on 29 October when I attended the world premiere of a new movie called *Shankly: Nature's Fire*. When my invitation arrived, I vaguely remembered having recorded a short interview for the production team, but I didn't know if I was actually in the film. I was – two and a half years after I'd spoken to them. I took Laurie and was glad I did.

Sitting in the stalls in the Phil, it was weird to see myself on the big screen. I couldn't help but reflect that three months earlier I had sat in the same seats watching Paul McCartney congratulating the 2017 graduates from the Liverpool Institute for Performing Arts. More to the point, sixty years ago, Paul McCartney, George Harrison and one or two others had been sitting there (as was I) at our school speech day. If someone had predicted where we'd all end up, you would have told them they were crazy. But it's a funny old world.

The film's press release described it as follows:

Shankly: Nature's Fire is a film that searches for the soul of British football. It is a poignant and nostalgic journey into the origins of the world's favourite game, and a study of Britain in the twentieth century and of the rise and fall of the industrial heartlands where the sport meant so much to so many. It is also about how heroes still matter – and how legends are born that transcend generations. Few people have made such an impact through sport as Bill Shankly. In exploring his life, the film looks at why this man – and his singular vision to make Liverpool the greatest football club in the world – came to leave such a legacy in his adopted home city. Following the basic arc of a biopic, the film also interweaves a contemporary narrative of Liverpool now, of fans today and how they still rally around Shankly's name. With extensive archive, mixed with interviews and observational footage, the film gives contemporary viewers a real sense of Shankly's personality and the time of his reign.

There was an impressive array of contributors, including Ian St John, Denis Law, Roger Hunt, Kevin Keegan, Steven Gerrard and Irvine Welsh, as well as some of Shankly's family members, fans and, I'm proud to say, me!

Ed Sheeran's 'Shape of You' helped him to world domination in 2017.

FA Cup Third Round – Liverpool v. Everton, Anfield, 5 January 2018

Following a win against Everton in the league, the Reds hosted them for the second time in less than thirty days, this time in the third round of the FA Cup. I arrived at Anfield very early for the match. Looking back, it may just have been my usual derby game pre-match nerves that persuaded me to leave home so promptly. Anyway, I had half an hour to kill, so I went right through the Kenny Dalglish Stand car park and across Lower Breck Road to say hello to my friends in the Homebaked Café, the wonderful community café that arose from the ashes of Mitchell's Bakery, a family-run business that had been there for eighty years but which had closed down a few years previously. I used to rely on them for my pre-match meal in the seventies.

As soon as I opened the door, I heard someone in the far corner say in a loud voice, 'Here's George!' The voice belonged to one of the staff who was looking after a customer with a familiar face, Stan Collymore. I hadn't spoken to Stan for years, so we had a good chat, mostly about derby games. Stan had played in or attended quite a few over the years: apart from the Merseyside derby, there was the Milan derby, the Glasgow derby, the north London derby and a derby game in Turkey that sounded more like a medieval battle than a football match. I finished my coffee and looked at my watch.

'Nice to see you, Stan, but I'm afraid I'll have to go!'

He asked me if I could spare a couple more minutes to do a quick interview with the camera crew he had with him, so we did a quick Q and A and off I went.

Before we parted, we swapped business cards. It was only when I got to my seat in the DJ room next to match-day control that I looked closely at Stan's card. I thought he was working for Sky Sports, but it turned out he was presenting a football programme for the Russia Today TV channel.

The match itself was memorable for the moment that Virgil van Dijk scored the winner on his debut in a 2–1 victory.

FA Cup Fourth Round – Liverpool v. West Bromwich Albion, Anfield, 27 January 2018

This loss to West Brom in the fourth round of the FA Cup was noteworthy for being the first time in the Premier League that a referee had referred to a pitchside monitor to help him make his decision when he awarded Liverpool a penalty that Roberto Firmino ultimately missed. It was not the only video assistant referee (VAR) decision that day. Referee Craig Pawson also ruled out an Albion goal and delayed awarding West Brom's third goal until VAR had confirmed it.

At this point, VAR was still in the experimental stages and decisions weren't being communicated to spectators, or me for that matter. The only way I knew what was happening was by keeping an eye on the TV screen in my room. BT Sport had better connections than I did. During the second half, I jokingly poked my head into the match control room and asked, 'Anyone know what's going on?'

UEFA Champions League Semi-final – Liverpool v. AS Roma, Anfield, 24 April 2018

For the first time in eleven years, Liverpool had reached the Champions League semi-finals, and Roma stood between us and a place in the biggest club game in world football. They came to Anfield having dumped the favourites Barcelona out of the competition, partly thanks to a solid back line and a world-class keeper, Alisson Becker. But he conceded five goals at Anfield and another two in the return leg.

Mo Salah was on fire, and he scored two goals in the first half to put the Reds in a good position. We then scored another three in the second half, and it looked like we had at least one-and-three-quarter feet in the Champions League final. But Liverpool always like to make their fans sweat, and so it was that night. Roma scored two late goals to give them more than a little hope, and we couldn't uncork the champagne just yet.

Despite the slightly disappointing end to the match, the atmosphere that night was as good as it gets. Italian fans are always loud and colourful, but the Liverpool fans were up to the challenge, and Anfield was at its noisy best.

However, the win was overshadowed by the senseless and devastating attack on Sean Cox, an innocent Irish fan looking forward to seeing his beloved Reds in action. He appears to be on a long and slow road to recovery, but the sickening violence inflicted on him brought back some nightmarish memories of the worst football hooliganism of the past. I thought that we'd seen the last of it, but, sadly, I was wrong. A group of Roma fans arrived in the areas wearing no club colours and marched quietly up Venmore Street, which runs up from Robson Street and emerges in Lower Breck Road, opposite the Kop and near the Albert Pub. They then, without warning, laid into anyone in a red scarf who happened to be passing. Poor Sean sustained life-changing head injuries.

We lost 4–2 in Rome a couple of weeks later, but we were through by an incredible 7–6 margin.

UEFA Champions League Final – Liverpool v. Real Madrid, NSC Olimpiyskiy, 26 May 2018

Liverpool were robbed in Kiev. No ifs, buts or maybes. Loris Karius made a monumental error to gift Real one of their goals, but the damage was done earlier in the match thanks to a vicious tackle by Sergio Ramos on Mo Salah. Ramos has enough red cards to paper the walls of his lounge, but he got away scot-free with this one. He pulled Mo to the floor using a technique that bore more than a passing resemblance to one of the throws that used to be taught at my sons' ju-jitsu lessons.

I wasn't in Kiev but watching at home. A couple of weeks earlier, a complete stranger had walked up to me in a pub, pushed a piece of paper with his phone number on it into my top pocket and said, 'If you hear of any spare tickets, can you give me a ring?'

My reply was simple: 'Don't hold your breath!'

Simon Ellis-Jones and Neil Mellor put on another of their 'Evening With' events on 7 June at the Sidings Club in Hoylake. Simon is an experienced video journalist who is now working as a senior studio producer at LFCTV. Neil Mellor, meanwhile, is the ex-Liverpool striker who made his mark in Reds' football history in late 2004 when he scored a goal against Olympiacos on the road to Istanbul. This time the guest was Sam Quek, who won a gold medal at the Rio Olympics as part of the Great Britain hockey team. She turned out to be a terrific interviewee for Simon.

Luckily for me, Sam came and sat at my table when the interview was over. I knew she was a Liverpool fan but wasn't sure if she would know who the hell I was – she did! Sam had to do some signings and pose for a few selfies. Before she did, however, she reached into her handbag and fished out a small wooden box that turned out to be the case in which she kept her Olympic gold medal! She passed it over for me to have a closer look. I was stunned. I never, ever thought I'd get my hands on one of them.

When she was finished talking to (almost) everybody in the place, I looked at my watch and realized that it was time to hit the road. Hoylake to Aintree is a fair trip late at night. I went over to say goodnight and asked if I could have a picture. 'Of course,' she said and promptly hung her gold medal around my neck – blimey! My friend Ron took a couple of pictures, and I said my thanks and headed to my car. I turned as I got to the door, and she was grinning like the proverbial Cheshire Cat! I wondered what was tickling her until she said, 'You're getting very comfy with that, aren't you?' I was so taken with the experience that I was calmly walking off with her medal still around my neck! I apologized and handed back her precious gong. Embarrassed or what!

2018–19

We began the season with a comfortable win at home against West Ham. It was a run-of-the-mill day for me, but there was a notable piece of music on my playlist. I'd been sent a professional-looking CD from a young local singer–songwriter called Megan Louise. I've got to know her since and heard her described as 'England's Taylor Swift'.

I'm proud to be the first person to have given her some sort of platform and found out later that playing the track had some positive consequences. One of her family made a video of Megs listening to herself on the Anfield PA. Several months later, the video popped up on Granada TV in the North West in a short profile feature. She told me some time later that a boy at school who had been calmly ignoring her saw the programme and was impressed by her sudden fame. All of a sudden, he was returning her calls and wanted to get to know her. Her ardour had cooled by now, but I was quietly chuffed to know that my interest in her music had boosted her street cred.

UEFA Champions League Group C – Liverpool v. Red Star Belgrade, Anfield, 24 October 2018

More than forty years after Red Star swept Shankly's side from the old European Cup, the roles were reversed, and Klopp's Reds saw off the team from Belgrade, moving Liverpool to top of their Champions League group. Luckily, I arrived very early, and no sooner had I turned off the engine in the car park than I saw that I had a message on my phone. It was from Chris Holding, Elvis Costello's tour manager. I hadn't heard from him in a while. He told me that he was bringing Elvis to the match and wondered if I could play one of his tracks at half-time. I have an ongoing problem with people asking me to play specific tracks when I'm already at Anfield with my playlist set in stone. I thought this was yet another instance. I told Chris that I had just parked up at Anfield and that if he'd only asked me an hour earlier, I would have brought a Costello CD with me.

'No problem,' he said. 'I'll be there in ten minutes.' True to his word, he arrived near the Shankly Gates with a shrink-wrapped copy of Elvis's new CD, and it was the deluxe edition. Just then, the man himself arrived – Elvis Costello. I hadn't seen him in the flesh since the spring of 2001, when I'd bumped into him three times in quick succession: once at a CD launch in Liverpool, then in his hotel just before the Arsenal cup final in Cardiff, followed by an encounter at Düsseldorf Airport on the way home from the UEFA Cup triumph over Alavés.

Elvis is a diehard Red. We spoke at length about Liverpool's chances and his new album, then I told him a few things that surprised him. As a child, I used to see his dad, Ross McManus, regularly on TV. He didn't think I was old enough! I also complained that he'd never got around to bringing his wife, the jazz musician Diana Krall, to Anfield. I'm a huge fan! They were married in December 2003, and for a while after that I always took one of her CDs to Anfield when there was a game on in the vain hope that I would get it signed. He thought that was hilarious. Anyway, Elvis and I went our separate ways, me clutching my new CD and Elvis heading for the hospitality lounges.

A few weeks later, I got another message from Chris. Elvis was coming to the Napoli game and he was bringing Diana! They were planning to gather at the Hotel Tia and walk up to the ground. Afterwards, they would head back to the hotel.

'Dare I ask?' I said. 'Can I drop in and say hello?'

'Of course,' Chris replied.

UEFA Champions League Group C – Liverpool v. Napoli, Anfield, 11 December 2018

The group was on a knife-edge. We had to beat Napoli 1–0 or win by two clear goals to qualify for the knockout stages. I had a double dose of butterflies. I was keen for Liverpool to go through, but desperate for us not to end up in third place and drop into the Europa League. That would consign us to playing regular Thursday night football and potentially foul up our path to a Premier League trophy. The prospect of meeting Diana Krall was also at the back of my mind.

Just to complicate things further, I'd received a message two days previously from a good friend in London who said he'd requested two tickets for me to see Paul McCartney at the Echo Arena the night after the Napoli game. I'd been told to expect confirmation sometime on the Monday. By the time I got to Anfield, however, there was still no word, and I thought my chance had gone.

The atmosphere at Anfield was brilliant. It starts to build up later nowadays than in the days when the terraces were packed two hours before kick-off. But sometimes, mostly European games under the midweek floodlights, the noise grows to a volume that is guaranteed to intimidate any opposition. This was one of those nights.

Mo Salah scored just after the half-hour mark. Sadio Mané missed a couple of chances before half-time that would have seen us safely through, and in the end it was a world-class save from Alisson that put us through. A 1–0 scoreline was the best and worst of results: it was enough to put us through but also kept everyone on tenterhooks till the end.

During the game, my precious confirmation email turned up with my ticket details to see Paul McCartney the following night. Two down, one to go. After the match, Ron and I hurried down Anfield Road to the Hotel Tia, but there was no sign of Elvis or his good lady! Then, just as I'd decided I must have missed them, in came Mr and Mrs Costello. I'd played Diana's version of 'Jingle Bells' at half-time so was awaiting feedback. Elvis introduced us. I would have been very happy with a polite handshake. What I got instead was a big hug and a broad grin.

Ms Krall squeezed into the other half of my double seat, and we had a long chat, including revelations about her father, who had played football. I asked for a photo and handed my camera to Ron, who took a picture. Then Diana pulled a camera out of her bag and handed it to Ron. She wanted a picture with me. I was gobsmacked! We had a good old natter till they had to go back to their hotel, and I floated home.

The following night at the Echo Arena was amazing. Paul and his band played for three solid hours without a pause. My friend Ian Fryer came with me, and we were sitting behind Liverpool CEO Peter Moore and his wife. I got on well with Peter, and he and Ian had a good old chinwag about Liverpool's season. What a night.

Just to round off the perfect week, Liverpool beat Manchester United 3–1 at Anfield in the Sunday TV game. That was the match that finally put an end to José Mourinho's career at Old Trafford.

Dua Lipa's 'One Kiss' was the song of the year and the song of the Champions League final in Kiev. Reds thought of the song as their own, but its association with the heart-wrenching defeat in the final led to me dropping it from my playlist the following season.

Liverpool v. Manchester City, Etihad Stadium, 3 January 2019

Liverpool were due to face Manchester City at the Etihad, and after the Christmas holiday results, the team were travelling in a positive mood. We were seven points clear at the top of the Premier League and would open up a ten-point gap if we won. It was a classic six-pointer. It was also being billed as the title decider in some quarters. It wasn't, of course, but nevertheless a win for either side would give them a massive boost for the remainder of the season. Sadly, Manchester City won 2–1, ending Liverpool's Premier League unbeaten run.

Well, if the first week of December 2018 was one of the best weeks of my life, this week was definitely one of the worst. I'd been feeling nauseous for about a week, so I went to see my GP the day after a loss to Wolves, fully expecting to come away with some anti-nausea pills. Instead, I was sent for blood tests. Normally, it takes a week or so for the results to come back, but on this occasion the GP rang me later that same day. I had to come to the surgery early the next morning. There were some drastic results from the tests on my liver.

He said, 'I'm sorry to be the bearer of . . .' then stopped before saying 'bad news' and instead changed it to 'worrying news'. By now I was having kittens. Needless to say, I didn't sleep that night.

When I got to my GP's surgery first thing the next morning, I was sent straight to Aintree Hospital with a letter in my hand. I then spent the day being poked and prodded and had thirteen lots of blood taken plus an ultrasound scan. I spoke to two different doctors, and then, late in the day, they decided they had to admit me. After much more of the same the next day, I was told that I was going to need major changes to my medication and would start on insulin at 6 p.m. that night. Then I could go home. The time came and went, and when the night shift came on at 8 p.m. I politely asked if I was actually going to start the new medication that night after all. I was told that the revised start time was now 10 p.m. and then I would have to wait another twenty-four hours to ensure there were no adverse reactions. Great!

Eventually, I got to speak with a doctor face to face on the Friday morning. I repeated my mantra that I wasn't stupid. I was married to a nurse, and I had a blood sugar tester at home, which also, incidentally, backed on to the hospital. He agreed that I shouldn't be taking up a bed and said I'd be released at lunchtime. In the event, it was 2 p.m. when I got out, but by then I didn't care. I was just glad to be going home.

My friend Gerry Firth in Harlow messaged me: 'Have you seen the *Daily Telegraph*?'

No, I hadn't, and it was too late to go and buy one when I got the message. Luckily, Gerry had kept the paper and sent me the back page. Towards the end of a column by Jim White, a highly respected journalist, was the following footnote:

About the only English ground where European nights still have a bit of resonance is Anfield. True, at Premier League games the place frequently resembles the quiet room at the British Library. But, as Bayern Munich will discover tonight, the Champions League brings out a different side to the venerable stadium. It is no coincidence that it is there that the least obtrusive of pre-match announcers holds sway. George Sephton, whose gentle Scouse tones have prevailed since 1971, would no more exhort the locals to 'make some noise' than he would play the new single from the latest *X Factor* winner. The truth is, thanks to his self-effacing style, Anfield can still sound a bit like Newport.

UEFA Champions League Round of 16 – Liverpool v. Bayern Munich, Anfield, 19 February 2019

This was the dreaded night when UEFA introduced VAR to European club football. As I've said previously, we'd had two trial runs of VAR previously, both in 2018: once in the FA Cup against West Bromwich Albion and once against Chelsea in the Carabao Cup. The system was much more complicated now, and, just to finish me off altogether, the decisions were being delivered in two languages! The match itself finished 0–0 with chances aplenty for both sides. There was, however, very little call for the intervention of VAR, but the logistics were still troubling me.

My duties now included interacting with the UEFA official in charge of VAR. In the case of VAR being used, he would radio through to let me know what was being checked. That in itself was problematic, because two-way radio communication in the midst of a noisy crowd is not easy, and it can be very difficult to hear clearly. Once we'd overcome that barrier, my new dedicated keyboard operator on the scoreboard computer had to find the VAR category from her list and frantically key it in. Then she had to find the same topic in the language of the away team! Meanwhile, I had to announce the fact that VAR was in operation, and my interpreter had to do the same over my microphone. When a decision was eventually made, we had to repeat the process. It was basically impossible in the time available. Eventually, common sense prevailed, and nowadays the whole VAR process is operated remotely and communication is visual. We have a replica of the big purple-and-blue screen you see on TV or stadium scoreboards. And there's a dedicated VAR operator with his own keyboard, screens and microphone.

After being appointed CEO at Anfield on 1 June 2017, Peter Moore was a breath of fresh air on the admin side of the club in the same way that Jürgen was on the footballing side. I'd first met him in the spring of 2018, and we were in frequent contact via social media after that. He turned up at the 'Run for the 96' charity 5k that year and promised to come over to my corner of Anfield and see what happened in my room. In the end, we settled for the day of the Chelsea game.

It occurred to me that I wasn't sure if he'd be escorted over there, and I wondered if he knew the security code for the match-day control room. I messaged him the code and thought no more about it until about thirty minutes before he was due, when someone told me that rather than sending him a private message, I'd inadvertently tweeted the code to nearly 40,000 people! I have never been so embarrassed in my entire life. Luckily the guys from the maintenance department sorted the problem quickly, and Peter was more amused than annoyed! Despite the hiccup, it was good to see him on my 'perch', and he took a genuine interest in the strange layout of the screens and keyboards over there.

UEFA Champions League Semi-final – Liverpool v. Barcelona, Anfield, 7 May 2019

Barcelona, the greatest club on the planet, were due at Anfield for the second leg of the Champions League semi-final. Barca had won the first leg a week earlier 3–0, and, with no away goal in the bank, the consensus was that Liverpool were already out of the competition. We could beat the Spaniards 4–1, and they would still go through on the away goals rule. What were the chances? I mean, Barcelona always score, don't they? To make matters worse, Mo Salah and Roberto Firmino were both unavailable, and Barca had Lionel Messi in their team.

I was ambivalent about this game. I couldn't honestly see a way through and was far more concerned about the Premier League than the Champions League. Istanbul was still fresh in the memory, but a whole generation of Liverpool fans hadn't seen their beloved team win the league. To someone of my generation, it niggled me that teams could get into the Champions League without actually being the champions in their own country. Nevertheless, we were going to give it a go.

For whatever reason, everything clicked on the night. The crowd seemed to appear from nowhere in the twenty minutes before kick-off. The rendition of 'You'll Never Walk Alone' was stirring. The Champions League anthem was louder than normal. The atmosphere burst into life, and the stadium was rocking. Divock Origi scored early on, and that set the ball rolling. Andy Robertson was crocked in the first half, and Gini Wijnaldum came on at half-time and scored two goals. We were level! Surely we couldn't be heading for the final. We needed another goal, and we needed to keep a clean sheet. Then a stroke of genius from Trent Alexander-Arnold caught everyone napping from a quickly taken corner. Everyone, that is, except Divock Origi, who appeared from between two surprised Barcelona defenders and looped the ball into the net. We hung on and the final whistle brought the loudest roar I've heard at Anfield for many years.

People continually ask me to compare the atmosphere that night with the Saint-Étienne game in the seventies or the Chelsea semi-final in 2005. I am sure as sure that this was better. There is occasionally a lot of noise in my corner of the stadium, and sometimes a thunder-like rumble when the crowd stamp their feet in the stand behind me. I've been over the corner between the Kop and the Kenny Dalglish Stand for twenty years now, and that night was the first time that my room physically shook. For a short while, I thought I was going to fall to the concrete below.

After the match, the entire squad lined up in front of the Kop just as I put on 'You'll Never Walk Alone' again, and they joined in the singing with the same level of energy they'd just put into the game. After they were finished, I was waiting for the crowd to drift away. I'd used up all the music that I'd brought. I then realized my John Lennon CD was lying on the desk in front of me. Someone had suggested 'Imagine' would be an ideal song to play that night, but I hadn't used it pre-match. Now was the perfect time. On it went and, much to my amazement, the whole Kop joined in. It was a magic moment. I heard later that grown men were in tears. And not just inside Anfield. One report came in from a casino in Sydney, Australia!

The following morning, Piers Morgan on ITV said that 'whoever put that on was a genius'. Radio 4 called to ask if I would do an interview with Evan Davis on their *PM* programme. While I was at Radio Merseyside to do that one, I recorded an interview for Paul Salt's *Drivetime* programme. During both interviews, I used the same line, paraphrased from a quote by the late Brian Clough: 'I wouldn't say it was my favourite night at Anfield, but it's definitely up there in the top one!'

Liverpool v. Wolverhampton Wanderers, Anfield, 12 May 2019

The final home game of the season took place, as usual, at the exact same time as all the other final-day Premier League matches. We went into the game against Wolves in second place in the league, while leaders Manchester City took on Brighton at the Amex Stadium on the south coast. If we won and City lost, we would take the title. Brighton scored early in game, and the news quickly spread around the Anfield stands. Sadly, that brief glimmer of optimism didn't last long. City soon equalized and then took the lead. We duly beat Wolves, but it was to no avail. We finished an incredible season second in the league with a monumental ninety-seven points, enough to take the title most years.

I make no secret of the fact that I don't like rugby. Pelé once described football as the 'beautiful game', and in my humble opinion rugby is the diametric opposite. Ironic, then, that

Anfield was chosen as the venue for the 2019 'Magic Weekend'. This consists of a two-day event where every team in rugby league's Super League plays a match on a neutral ground, three games per day.

Previously, I'd been politely asked to stay away when the occasional rugby game was played at Anfield, but this time the good old HR computer requested my presence. The Super League were providing an announcer/DJ, and I was to operate the scoreboard. I had a crash course in rugby league scoring and off we went. I did have a TV monitor to check my figures, but I'm pleased to say that during six games over two long days there was only one instance when my scoreboard and the TV caption were different. And even then it was the TV people who had it wrong!

One thing that did fascinate me that weekend was the use of the video referee in rugby. When there was a problem, the referee on the pitch would clearly ask for help, and the replays were shown on the big screens inside the stadium. Not only that but the conversations between the on-pitch referee and the video referee were clearly audible to everyone in the ground. We already knew that VAR was to be used at every Premier League game from August 2019 onwards, so those of us involved in professional football were all on red alert. Rugby had obviously got it right, but only time would tell if football would be able to follow in their footsteps.

UEFA Champions League Final – Liverpool v. Tottenham Hotspur, Metropolitano Stadium, 1 June 2019

It's noon on the day of the 2019 Champions League final. I'm an emotional wreck. I've never been so desperate for Liverpool to win a game. I'm one of the few people, it seems, who isn't happy with coming second in the Premier League. I subscribe to the Shankly maxim of 'first is first and second is nowhere'! I am heartily sick of hearing about Manchester City's 'unprecedented' domestic Treble of Premier League, FA Cup and League Cup. If Liverpool win tonight, it will hopefully keep the keyboard warriors quiet for a while.

More to the point, I'm writing this at my desk in Liverpool. Social media and all the TV channels are full of the grinning faces of Liverpool fans who are on the ground in Madrid and looking forward to the game. The loyal hard core of dedicated lifelong Reds are, for the most part, over there, but alongside them are many, many people who have been to very few, if any, games this season. My inbox is also full of messages from Reds fans who can't understand why I'm not in Madrid. Well, I can tell you – I don't understand either. I would kill to be at the game, but for the fourth European final in succession I have suddenly turned into the invisible man. This year in particular I can claim to have played my part in creating the famous Anfield atmosphere that helped to propel the team into the final. At this moment in time, I'm feeling like the kid with his nose pushed up against the sweet-shop window.

An incident on the Thursday prior to the Champions League final had finished me off completely. I knew that people had been asking some of the senior guys at the club why I wasn't being taken to Madrid. I had also received several messages from complete strangers asking me if I knew of any spare tickets anywhere. The answer was always the same: 'If I could find a spare ticket, I'd use it myself!' People assumed that I was automatically given a ticket – I wish!

Anyway, I had an overnight bag packed and ready in case the miracle happened and I was invited to the final, although I wasn't holding my breath. Late on the Thursday afternoon, my phone rang and I saw the magic words 'private number' on the display. I said to Liz, 'This is the call I've been waiting for!'

Sure enough, it was one of the senior managers at Anfield. 'Hi, George,' he said. 'I believe you're coming down in the morning to pick up your car park passes for the concerts?'

'I am,' I said. I was fully expecting the next words from him to be something along the lines of, 'While you're here, you can pick up your travel documents for Madrid.' How wrong can you be! He was actually ringing to say that I wasn't needed for the concerts that were happening that summer at Anfield. I was shocked. I'd been looking forward to them all year, and HR had booked me in to attend several months previously. Moreover, Liz and I had moved our holiday to accommodate the Take That gig, and I was now being told that I was being deprived of three fees that I could ill afford to lose. Not to mention the fact that I'd cancelled a speaking engagement on the evening of the P!nk concert and was really looking forward to seeing Bon Jovi in action. I don't lose my temper very often, and I really don't like arguments. I'm definitely one for the quiet life. On this occasion, however, I lost it. Within the space of a minute, I'd been deprived of any chance of going to the Champions League final in Madrid, a fair amount of money and the opportunity to see some great gigs.

So it was that I ended up watching the historic 2019 Champions League final in my living room with Liz. The Reds beat Spurs 2–0 to secure their sixth European Cup victory and the club's first since 2005. They took the lead after just two minutes through Mo Salah's penalty but didn't seal the win until three minutes from time when Divock Origi scored the vital goal. The relief of putting the Kiev disaster behind us and finally lifting the 'Klopp can't win a final' hoodoo was wonderful, but it was tempered by the fact that I wasn't there.

The morning after the final, the squad returned to Liverpool and paraded the trophy through the city. Liz and I wanted to see it but didn't fancy hanging around for hours, so we went down to Allerton Road and parked up not far from the start of the parade. It was a real carnival atmosphere, and it turned out to be one of the great occasions in the footballing life of the city. Kim bravely took her four young children down to the Pier Head and told me later it was worth the wait.

Laurie, however, didn't go to see the parade. I rang him to ask why not.

'Well, I'm going to the players' party tonight,' he said. I was stunned. Literally speechless. After I recovered my composure, I asked him how he'd managed to wangle that. It turned out that one of his neighbours was a member of staff down at Melwood. He had two tickets for the event, but his wife was an Everton fan and refused to use hers.

I was slightly taken aback, but on the other hand I was thrilled for Laurie. He'd had a rough couple of years and really deserved a treat. Later that evening, pictures started arriving on my mobile phone: Laurie with Virgil van Dijk, then with Andy Robertson, then with Jordan Henderson, and then up close and personal with Jürgen Klopp! Finally, there was a wonderful picture of him holding old 'Jug Ears' itself – the European Cup. I was chuffed for him!

I'm very lucky to be married to a woman who likes football, and we both follow women's football, so we were excited to watch the Women's World Cup during the summer of 2019. The standard of the women's game has come on in leaps and bounds in the past few years. It was sad that the England team came home empty-handed, but it was fascinating to watch the games.

With the spectre of regular VAR looming over the Premier League, I took a professional interest in its effect on this tournament. I was shocked at the number of VAR decisions early in the group games and slightly taken aback by the way things changed later on. Maybe I'm being cynical, but things seemed to change drastically for the better after the referees had a meeting where they were lectured by Pierluigi Collina, the best referee in the history of football. I was, however, still wary of what VAR would bring to the table in the Premier League.

I haven't spoken to Paul McCartney since 1958 when we were at school together. I have, on the other hand, regularly come across his younger brother Mike ('Our Kid'). Early in June, he telephoned me out of the blue to invite me to the relaunch of his wonderful album *McGear*. I had been a star-struck lad in my twenties when I'd had a drink with him and one or two others at a bar opposite Radio City's old studios in Stanley Street in early 1975 for the launch of the original album – on vinyl, of course. In June 2019, he was relaunching it on CD, as well as releasing a box set and a remastered vinyl version. The album is a gem, with some clever songs backed by some top-drawer musicians, who basically made up his brother's band Wings. To put the icing on the cake, the launch was taking place at our old school, and more specifically in the art room, where I'd spent many a frustrating hour trying to persuade the teacher, Stan Reed, that I could actually draw!

2019–20

Liverpool v. Norwich City,
Anfield, 9 August 2019

Norwich were the first visitors to Anfield for the new season. The match was notable for two reasons. First, it was being played on a Friday night. When I first started at Anfield, I used to buy one of those student diaries every summer then enter up the fixtures for the coming season. Nowadays, I still buy a student diary, but I also buy a bottle of Tipp-Ex (other correction fluids are available!) and stand by for the fixtures to be rearranged. Today, football can be played on any day of the week. Second, this was the first Premier League season with VAR in force at every game.

To be honest, I was dreading the new season. Whenever a goal was scored, I had to more or less simultaneously announce the goal and change the scoreboard. The two keyboards involved were six feet apart, and things were sometimes complicated by doubt about whom the actual goalscorer had been. Now I would have to do all that while waiting to see if the goal had been legitimate and, possibly, backtrack. I was convinced I couldn't cope.

When push came to shove, I was saved from all this by the arrival of a clever young guy by the name of Joel Lampkin, who had been seconded from LFCTV! Nobody had thought to tell me that he was coming or that the scoreboard had been revamped, but I was so relieved you wouldn't believe it! He had an assistant by the name of Bayley Gibson-Leeming, who, despite his aristocratic name, is a Salford lad! Moreover, he's that rarest of creatures: a Salfordian who loves Liverpool FC. The three of us get on like a house on fire. I feel like their grandad sometimes, but we do our jobs well.

I got a message from Elvis Costello's tour manager Chris Holding to say that Elvis was sixty-five on the day of the Arsenal game on 26 August and was desperate to spend it at Anfield with his family. However, I have no particular influence and came to the conclusion that my (and their) only hope was to go straight to the top and ask the CEO. God bless him. Peter was brilliant and pushed the boat out on Elvis's behalf. On the day, they were his special guests: best seats in the house, the biggest cake you've ever seen, and a signed and framed shirt.

After the game, I went back to my car, where Rob and his wife Sue were waiting for me. I texted Chris to see if he and Elvis were close to leaving. They weren't. Never mind, I thought. But just as I was about to set off home, I received a text: 'Diana wants to see you!' This was an invitation I couldn't refuse. I apologized to Rob and Sue then headed into the Main Stand. Technically speaking, my pass doesn't allow me access to the Main Stand, but I managed to blag my way up to the boardroom, where Elvis and Diana thanked me for my help. I needed no thanks. I was just so pleased that it had all worked out.

I was invited to the launch of Michael Owen's new book *Reboot* on 5 September. I was keen to go but didn't fancy wrestling with the new Runcorn–Widnes bridge and then finding my way to the upmarket hotel in the wilds of the Cheshire countryside. However, I was on the guest list, and it sounded like a very civilized event. I was right. Michael was interviewed by Steve Bower, one of the main commentators on *Match of the Day*.

I first saw Michael in a red shirt as a fourteen-year-old, and I followed his career avidly. I was disappointed by some of the abuse that came his way after he left Anfield, something the book addresses head-on.

A headline popped up on my timeline to say that vinyl records were about to outsell CDs for the first time in decades. To someone of my age, this was quite something. I got my first records in the early fifties. We're talking about 78 rpm shellac (breakable!) records at that time. Then a friend of a friend of my dad's brought some of the newfangled 45 rpm records back from a trip to the United States. My parents were never technically minded (we were very late in the day getting our first TV), but somehow, we had a big, new stereogram, which would play the seven-inch records. The old shellac 78s eventually disappeared. Seven-inch vinyl became the norm until the early nineties when CDs took over. Recently, soulless downloads have been the thing, but vinyl is making a comeback in a big way. Too late for me, which is probably just as well, as I wouldn't fancy having to lug a box of heavy records up to Anfield these days.

Liverpool v. Manchester City, Anfield, 10 November 2019

By the time Manchester City came to Anfield in the Premier League, Liverpool already had a substantial lead over the team who had pipped us at the post the previous season. Regardless, this was always going to be a pivotal game. By a stroke of good luck, this match was the first time my grandson Thomas had attended a first-team game at Anfield. He's a huge fan of Mo Salah and was blessed to be in the Anfield Road stand when Mo scored in front of him. The final score was 3–1. Job done.

FIFA Club World Cup – Liverpool v. Flamengo, Khalifa International Stadium, 21 December 2019

Liverpool beat the Brazilian champions Flamengo 1–0 after extra time to win the FIFA Club World Cup. There were several keyboard warriors on social media decrying the victory, but I was probably prouder than I've ever been of my club. Champions of the world! How good does that sound.

'Someone You Loved' by unlikely Scottish superstar Lewis Capaldi was the biggest song of 2019.

Liverpool FC went into the new year with a huge lead in the Premier League. Even though everyone around me was going around with smug smiles, I couldn't help but have a dreadful sense of foreboding hanging over me. I kept telling myself that we couldn't possibly let the lead go. Could we? Surely not!

But then things started to happen. I lost two friends in quick succession. After the last match of 2019 (home to Wolves), a guy called Moneeb Noordeane returned to his home in the south of England after watching his beloved Reds and died from a heart attack. For many years, he and his friend Mike Wheeler were always to be found standing next to the Shankly Gates before nearly every game, and until my arrival time was changed in 2019, I always stopped for a chat with the pair of them on my way into Anfield. Moneeb was a very quiet, respectful and cheerful guy who lived for his regular trips north. I was sad to hear of his passing.

Later in January, following news of a novel coronavirus taking hold in the Wuhan region of China, my old friend Alan Munnerley died at his home in Skipton after a long battle with cancer. He and Moneeb had both been expected to be around to see their beloved Reds lift the Premier League trophy in May. Maybe that's why I have a sense of foreboding, I thought. Am I going to have a coronary before the end of the season? How wrong I was. It was Covid-19 that was going to curse everyone's life in 2020.

On 24 January, Sky and BT Sport issued the rearranged fixture list for March. My poor, long-suffering wife was coming up to a special birthday (her eightieth), and we had arranged a family meal for the evening of 21 March. But Sky had moved the Crystal Palace game to the evening of the 21st, so we quickly rearranged everything for Sunday, 22 March. This caused us a bit of a problem at first, because it was Mother's Day, and getting a table was not easy. Nevertheless, we succeeded, booking a nice country pub called the Wayfarer in Parbold. Problem solved? Not quite! Liverpool's youth team got through the fourth round of the FA Cup and were drawn away to Chelsea in round five. If we won, our sixth-round game would be on the big day. I confess I watched the Chelsea match in a state of trepidation. I couldn't win. In the end, Chelsea beat us and at least the birthday bash could go ahead. In theory!

Andreas Frege is a German singer, songwriter and actor. He is best known as the lead vocalist of Die Toten Hosen, a German punk rock band, and goes by the stage name of Campino. I'd first become aware of him during the making of the documentary *You'll Never Walk Alone* several months earlier. He's a big Liverpool fan, a friend of Jürgen Klopp's and, luckily, a mate of my friend Graham Agg. Graham is a Scouser who speaks fluent German and organizes the annual exchange visits between Liverpool and Borussia Mönchengladbach fans. He also established the German Reds, the German branch of the Liverpool Supporters Club. Graham rang me, and we both arranged to meet Campino at the Philharmonic pub in town. He can only be described as a lovely man. He's half English so speaks the language perfectly. We had a long and wide-ranging chat, and he had brought some of his band's CDs, which will all find their way on to my match-day playlist. He was, incidentally, very happy to be able to have a quiet drink. Back home, he is continually mobbed by fans.

Terry Sylvester is a name that rings loud bells with anyone who was around during the sixties. He was in a terrific Liverpool band called The Escorts and then joined The Hollies as a replacement for Graham Nash when the latter went off to the USA to take a new musical direction with David Crosby and Stephen Stills. Terry was a perfect fit for The Hollies and made his mark with them. I met him when he wrote, sang on and produced 'Never Gonna Stop', a record that Liverpool FC released in the seventies. He moved down south and also ended up living in America. We hadn't seen each other for a very long time, but I managed to get him tickets for the home game against Southampton on 1 February. We met up early on the Saturday morning in the Anfield Road car park and had a good chat. Suffice to say, we've both aged a little since the sixties.

Around this time, I had the flu. My bones were aching, I had a dreadful hacking cough and I was sneezing continually. If I had been in that state in March or April, I would have been frightened to death. On the way home from an FA Cup replay against Shrewsbury Town, I had a coughing fit that was so violent that I actually passed out. Luckily, the symptoms went away. Covid-19 was already in the UK at that time, so I consoled myself later that I might now be immune. But I still took the lockdown very seriously, as did the rest of my family.

Liverpool's campaign for their first Premier League title in years was also causing me stress. Several media outlets realized that there was basically only one person at Anfield who was involved in the 1990 triumph and still at the club – me! I was very flattered to get some requests for interviews from people I looked up to. In particular, I regard the BBC as the benchmark for news and sport reporting. I was, therefore, tickled pink when the delightful Katie Gornall phoned me out of the blue. She arrived at Anfield with a cameraman on 12 February, and we did an interview in my room in the Kenny Dalglish Stand. It was quite surreal. The following day, a crew turned up at my house and turned my living room into a studio, much to the consternation of my dog, who sat in silence right through the set-up and sound checks until we started the actual interview, at which point she started a sort of low howl and had to be locked in my car with a treat while the interview was completed.

The annual reunion dinner for Liobians (Liverpool Institute Old Boys) takes place in one of the sumptuous lounges in the Main Stand. It's normally held on the first Friday in March, but since the advent of Friday night football, the organizers have booked two consecutive Fridays and plumped for one of the two after the Premier League have published their fixtures in June. This year I had a dilemma, as Elvis Costello had invited me to his concert in Liverpool the same night. I reluctantly but politely declined on the grounds that I only get to see some of my old friends once a year, and it's sadly true that the attendances fall away every year. I'd hate to pass up the chance to see one of the old gang for the last time.

The event started out as being for any old boys who played football for the school. As time went on, the numbers were dwindling and non-footballers started to attend, including me since 2002. My Evertonian friend Ken Georgeson and I then started to organize reunions for our year (1957 entrants) in 2007 and succeeded in tracking down about fifty people who had fallen off the radar. Quite a few of them started to come, and a few people from other years too, so the numbers stabilized and then increased slightly. I did my bit, and I hope the event will now outlive me. My dream would be to see some of the ex-students from LIPA there one day. Apart from the two Beatles, the place churned out several people who made their mark on the world: the newsreader Peter Sissons, Bill Kenwright the Everton chairman, actors and so on.

One memorable year, I was the after-dinner speaker – a proud moment. The following year, I found myself sitting next to a guy who was older than me and introduced himself as Ron. After we finished eating, he was called to the top table to address the throng. Ron was, in fact, Ron Oxburgh, now Lord Oxburgh, one-time chairman of Shell and previously a member of Maggie Thatcher's war cabinet during the Falklands conflict.

Liverpool v. Watford,
Vicarage Road, 29 February 2020

The Reds were almost unbeatable at this point in the season. That is we were unbeatable until this visit to Vicarage Road when we were somehow steamrollered and went down 3–0 to a Watford side fighting relegation. Post-mortems were inevitable, but events outside football would soon eclipse all other topics of conversation.

Ragnhild Lund Ansnes and her husband Jostein are part owners of the Hotel Tia in Anfield Road. When Tage Herstad first introduced me to Ragnhild back in 2008, she was still working for TV2 in Norway and living in Trondheim. Nowadays, the Ansnes family, like the Herstads, have upped sticks and moved to Liverpool. She is a very busy woman and devotes herself to her various roles, running the hotel, writing some exceptional books about Liverpool FC, looking after her family and organizing all sorts of events. She founded the Liverpool Hearts website and set up Livergirls, an international organization to create a sisterhood of female Liverpool fans worldwide.

I was very pleased to be invited to the Livergirls get-together at Anfield on 8 March. I was the DJ and went for an all-female playlist with a party feel. I also played some background music when we were eating. Peter Moore and Phil Thompson were listed as speakers, along with Vicky Jepson, the manager of Liverpool Women, and Lizzi Doyle, producer of *The Anfield Wrap*.

This was around the time when people were just starting to avoid handshaking and hugging in social situations. I arrived early and set up before disappearing off to the executive lounge to say hello to some of the guests. Peter arrived and greeted me with his usual firm handshake accompanied by his trademark broad grin. His equally gregarious wife Debbie, close behind, said, 'Are we still hugging?'

'Oh yes, definitely,' was my immediate response.

The speakers were all a joy to listen to. Peter in particular is the most accomplished speaker I've ever heard in the flesh. If you weren't a Liverpool fan beforehand, you would be by the time you'd heard what he had to say. I like Vicky Jepson very much. She works hard for her team, and although I'd met her previously, I hadn't heard her backstory. Likewise, Lizzi Doyle's description of her career path to date was frankly exhausting and inspiring. Phil Thompson is someone I've known since 1971 and whose progress from skinny young reserve at Anfield to captaining Liverpool, playing for England, managing the Reds and proving to be a top-class pundit has been astonishing. I've heard most of his stories before, but he's very entertaining, and the crowd were hanging on his every word.

Between the day of the dinner and the end of March, the pandemic got significantly worse. On 11 March, Liverpool played the second leg of their Champions League game against Atlético Madrid at Anfield. The 3–2 defeat was, it turns out, the least of our worries. Several thousand *madrileños* flew to Liverpool to support their team in the middle of the outbreak in Spain that had left large chunks of that country in lockdown. The Spanish visitors had not been checked at either end of their flight and had mixed freely with the locals in pubs and clubs all over Liverpool. As time went on, it became clear that it was a serious error to play that game. I was horrified. After the match, I had to pass through the crowds of Spaniards heading back to their coaches. I was in close proximity to several hundred of them and confess I was mightily relieved when I realized on 25 March that fourteen days had passed since my close encounter and that I hadn't caught the virus.

Rumours were rife that there would eventually be a ban on large crowds, and Reds fans were hoping that Liverpool would get the two wins they needed to sew up the Premier League before it came into effect. Our hopes were dashed on Thursday, 12 March when the FA, Premier League and English Football League decided to suspend their games until at least the beginning of April.

It was becoming clear that Liz's birthday bash was unlikely to go ahead. Rob and his family were booked to head north from Crawley on 21 March. Their journey would involve them getting a crowded train to Victoria via Gatwick Airport. That service is invariably packed to the gunnels. They would then have to get the Tube to Euston before travelling on another busy train to Liverpool. It was basically an invitation to contract the virus. In addition, several of our old friends who were due to attend the meal were in the 'vulnerable' group who had already been advised to stay indoors. We reluctantly decided that we had to call it off.

I'd been doing interviews for the media since the turn of the year, but before long I was telling journalists, radio presenters, TV reporters, bloggers and a few students that there was a queue forming. A couple of interviews were completed via Zoom, Skype and email, but several needed my physical presence. The last of these was for the German TV company ZDF. They spent some time trying (and failing) to get permission to film inside my room at Anfield. I didn't want them to film in my house after the previous debacle with my dog, so I arranged to meet them at the Homebaked Café. I'd already done one interview in there, and I'd seen several clips of the place on TV. Then came the first announcement about social distancing from the government. People like me who were over seventy with underlying health issues should stay at home if possible. I messaged ZDF to say I couldn't meet them at the Homebaked Café after all. In the end, we compromised and met in 96 Avenue in the open air, with no handshakes or physical contact. We did the interview, and the resultant twenty-minute film was terrific.

The prime minister eventually announced the compulsory lockdown on Monday, 23 March, to start the following morning – Liz's birthday! The long-awaited party for family and friends was now a distant dream. On the day of her birthday, Liz blew out the candles on her cake in our living room with me filming her on my phone while the dog looked at us as if we were crazy. Several online conversations took place, and local family members left gifts on the doorstep. Rob's present to his mum was a week away with his family in Tenerife. That, too, bit the dust.

Tuesday, 24 March was significant for another reason. The first victim of Covid-19 in Liverpool was local singer Cy Tucker, who had once performed alongside The Beatles and had been a part of the local music scene since the sixties. When I first saw Terry Sylvester back in 1965, he was a member of The Escorts. That band were regulars at the Mardi Gras Club on the same bill as Cy Tucker and the Friars. Terry went on to great things with The Hollies, and Cy, a postman by trade, stayed in Liverpool. Such is life.

On 2 April, my old friend Paul Quirk died at his home in Parbold after a short battle with cancer. I had first met Paul Quirk in the early nineties when he was running Quirk's Records in Ormskirk. Paul and his shop manager Wendy were always great fun to talk to, and Paul was a dedicated Red! For many years, he was the chairman of the Entertainment Retailers Association, a prime mover behind Record Store Day in the UK and a mentor to countless people across the industry. Every record collector in England owes him!

Three days later, the prime minister, who had been ill with the virus for several days, was moved to intensive care. I'm no fan of Boris Johnson, but I wouldn't wish the illness on anyone. He survived, of course, but I sincerely hope that he emerged with a better appreciation of the NHS in general and its nursing staff in particular. Only time will tell.

The first week in May brought a sea change in the pandemic. Some European countries were starting to ease their lockdowns. In Spain, players in La Liga could train in limited numbers. The French football season was abandoned, but the Bundesliga in Germany was preparing to restart. At the same time, discussions were going on between clubs in the Premier League. Rumours and counter-rumours were appearing every day on social media and in tabloid headlines, but it was obvious that moves were afoot in the corridors of power to at least do something to get football going again. Whichever way the dice fell, it seemed to be a racing certainty that I wouldn't be back inside Anfield before 2021. I was feeling

317

the strain, but someone pointed out that if I was DJing at Anfield in 2021, then I would almost certainly still be alive! True. I decided to be grateful for small mercies. I was also quite settled into being at home, although I occasionally had an overwhelming urge to shake someone's hand or go into a shop or sit at a pavement café with a coffee and watch the world go by!

On 10 May, the prime minister, still looking rather pale, addressed the nation on TV and announced that the lockdown was being eased. At the same time, a series of contradictory, misleading and frankly untrue headlines were to be found on the sports pages of the newspapers: the Premier League season would definitely be voided; the Premier League would definitely not be voided. The Premier League would resume soon; the Premier League would not resume for months. Matches would be played at neutral grounds; matches would not be played at neutral grounds!

It seemed the Premier League were committed to finishing the season but were reliant on a majority of the twenty clubs voting to go ahead. My mindset remained the same. I and every other Liverpool fan around the world wanted Liverpool to finish the job and win the league. It was the only fair outcome. To have it taken from us at this late stage would be nothing less than criminal. Having said that, voices from inside the boardrooms of other clubs were making worrying noises, and I knew we wouldn't be safely installed as worthy champions any time soon.

After weeks of deliberation, the Premier League announced that matches would recommence on 17 June, with all games played behind closed doors. That would be weird, but at least we would get to play and win the title legitimately. Overall, I was pleased, although I did have some worries. If we played at neutral grounds, I wouldn't be there when the great title-winning day came. And if we played our four remaining home games at Anfield, would there be room for me? I'd been sharing my room at Anfield with the VAR guys since August, and there certainly wasn't space for all of us to adhere to the social-distancing guidelines.

Senior people at the league headquarters were adamant that Liverpool would have to play at neutral grounds while the title was still mathematically undecided. The thinking was that Liverpool fans would turn up in their droves to be as close to the stadium as possible for the derby match and the home game against Crystal Palace. Then the assistant chief constable of Merseyside Police issued a statement: 'We have no objections to any of the Everton or Liverpool home fixtures being played at their respective grounds.' So there!

Ten days later, I was back inside Anfield for our first technical rehearsal. The strict rules about games being played behind closed doors limited the numbers allowed in the stadium, but I was included! On 7 June, a few of us part-timers arrived at Anfield for a briefing. Between then and the first home game of Project Restart, we got together at the ground five times, including one full-scale friendly match against Blackburn, which we won 6–0. When Liverpool finally played their first proper league game, it was the rearranged derby match against Everton at Goodison Park. The goalless draw didn't surprise me, to be honest. Carlo Ancelotti is a very experienced Italian manager, steeped in *catenaccio* football, and he had three months to plan for the game. It was always going to be 0–0! Four days later and Crystal Palace came to Anfield. Palace have been a thorn in our side more than once over the years, but that night Liverpool were in form and crushed them 4–0. We were on the brink.

Thursday, 25 June was the greatest, weirdest, craziest day of my life. I spent five hours sitting in front of my laptop watching the Chelsea v. Man City game on BT Sport while simultaneously being watched by BT Sport via Skype. In the studio, you could see the 'Fan Wall' on various monitors on the left-hand side of the background. Over to the right, there was a group of four Reds watching intently: me, DJ Spoony, Jamie Webster and Chelcee Grimes – two musicians and two DJs. It was double nerve-racking. Once in a while my concentration lapsed, and I forgot I was being watched! When Chelsea scored their first, my shouts of 'get in' were recorded and broadcast at half-time. Ditto my joy at the final whistle. It's hard to describe that moment! Thirty years melted away. We were champions again – at last!

That night a good-natured and very happy crowd of Liverpool fans descended on Anfield. Strictly speaking, they were breaking lockdown regulations, but I for one forgave them unconditionally. If I hadn't been glued to my webcam, I would have joined them! The following night, a crowd gathered at the Liverpool Waterfront that, I'm convinced, had very little to do with Liverpool FC. The media, of course, pounced on the opportunity to vilify Reds fans, even though the troublemakers who ended up in front of the magistrates later didn't have Liverpool addresses, and there was a distinct lack of red shirts in the news footage.

Liverpool v. Chelsea, Anfield, 22 July 2020

The final home game of the season was something else, a 5–3 win over Chelsea followed by the most spectacular presentation ceremony in the history of English football. Peter Moore had told the Livergirls dinner in March that Liverpool have a billion followers around the world. Well, I was one of only 300 people inside Anfield when Jordan Henderson picked up the trophy. I couldn't have felt more privileged.

On 31 July, it was announced that Peter Moore would not be staying at Anfield after the end of his contract in August. The news brought me right back down to earth with a bump. I will miss his presence. He's a good man and has been wonderful for the Reds. Billy Hogan has big shoes to fill, and I hope there's room in his plans for me.

2020–21

The new season began on 12 September, my fiftieth! Half a century working for Liverpool Football Club! Who knows what the campaign will bring. But after the previous one, nothing will ever surprise us again – I hope!

Epilogue

These Are a Few of My Favourite Things

Desert Island Discs

Someone messaged me a couple of years ago to say that I should only play modern music, so nothing before the eighties. 'OK,' I replied, 'so you don't want "You'll Never Walk Alone"? Or "Ring of Fire"? Or "Fields of Anfield Road"? Or most of the supporters' other favourites?' I didn't get a reply.

Liverpool supporters are, and always have been, the most inventive in the business. When I first started going to Anfield, two years before the Tannoy system was installed, the most famous sound to come from the terraces was the 'Kop Roar'. It rose and fell and was a deafening and intimidating wall of sound when Liverpool had a corner kick. Then came 'You'll Never Walk Alone' in 1963. The following year, an obscure American band called The Routers released 'Let's Go', and its hand-clapping riff became the 'St John Chant'. Fifty-six years later and I'm still playing it occasionally. It's had several reincarnations as the 'Torres Chant', the 'Suárez Chant' and, most notably, the 'Fowler Chant'. A gentle folk song by The Sandpipers called 'Guantanamera' has had similar longevity:

'One da da da da, there's only one da da da da' has serenaded many players down the years. From the same era, came the ludicrous 'Asia Minor' by B. Bumble and the Stingers (yes, really!) that still occasionally rears its head as 'We are the famous, the famous Kopites!' Ritchie Valens's 'La Bamba' is even older and was in full throttle when Rafa Benítez had a team containing several Spaniards. 'We Love You Liverpool!' started out in a West End musical (*Bye Bye Birdie*) in the sixties as 'We Love You Conrad'. In the seventies, it was Chicory Tip's 'Son of My Father' that was adapted to include several of our big names. And we're still adopting and adapting hit songs today. In the twenty-first century, we changed 'The Fields of Athenry' to 'The Fields of Anfield Road'. James's classic 'Sit Down' scanned neatly when substituted with 'Mo Salah'. And the most recent is 'Allez Allez Allez', which has done well for young Jamie Webster but started out as an Italian disco hit in 1985 called 'Summer Is Ending' by a band called Righeira. It was then picked up by Napoli fans before moving on to Anfield. 'Dirty Old Town' by folk singer Ewan MacColl, Kirsty MacColl's dad, is now the 'Virgil van Dijk Song'.

Along the way, there have been clever songs that have fallen by the wayside. The Baha Men's 'Who Let the Dogs Out?' turned into 'Who Led the Reds Out?' during Gérard Houllier's time. And the Boney M hit 'Brown Girl in the Ring' became 'We Are Liverpool'.

However, the tune that made the biggest impact in my life, because I was heavily involved in promoting the Anfield version, was a soppy American song, 'The Ballad of the Green Berets' by Barry Sadler. Craig Johnston bought the rights to it, rewrote the lyrics and released it as 'Pride of Merseyside' with a vocalist called (amazingly!) Joe Fagin. Joe was well known for singing the theme tune to the Geordie TV comedy series *Auf Wiedersehen, Pet*. Craig made sure I had several copies and kept me up to speed with release dates after the original promotional copies arrived. He had one particularly annoying day. I was flitting from office to office sorting out a network problem, and he couldn't track me down to tell me he'd left some copies for me. The fact that several receptionists refused to believe he actually was Craig Johnston didn't help either. They were all flabbergasted when I got back to base and told them he definitely was!

The Big Match

There have been some big occasions at Anfield in my time. The European Cup semi-final against Inter Milan in 1965, the Saint-Étienne game in 1977, the Chelsea semi-final in 2005, the 4–3 defeat of Borussia Dortmund, the two seven-goal thrillers against Newcastle, and a few more. But nothing will ever surpass the Barcelona semi-final in the Champions League in 2019.

The First XI

To be honest, I find it difficult when people ask me to pick an all-time Liverpool team from my time working at the club. It is nigh on impossible, and I usually avoid answering the question. However, Ray Clemence is still the best keeper I've seen for Liverpool, although Bruce Grobbelaar more than made his mark. I remember Tommy Lawrence with fondness, and Alisson Becker will go down as a Liverpool great.

When it comes to the outfield players . . . well, you have to start with Kenny Dalglish. If you include Kenny, you have to have Ian Rush alongside him. And you can't ignore Mo Salah, can you? Or Sadio Mané? And definitely not Robbie Fowler! So it goes on. I haven't even mentioned John Barnes yet.

Virgil van Dijk is the best centre-back we've ever had, but who would you play alongside him? You can't separate Mark Lawrenson and Alan Hansen. And you can't ignore Phil Thompson and Emlyn Hughes. And what about Tommy Smith? Or Jamie Carragher? Trent Alexander-Arnold will end his career as an Anfield icon. Steven Gerrard already is, and he lined up alongside the likes of Xabi Alonso. I give up. If I struggled on for a while, I could probably come up with a squad of about thirty-six, but there is no way on planet Earth that I could narrow it down to just eleven players. The only way I might eventually be able to come up with an all-time XI is if I have a long and peaceful retirement.

My plans for retirement so far include two aims. The first is simply to get back to Anfield. The second is to spend a lot of time listening to my CD collection!

In the meantime, thanks for buying the book, and remember: We Are Liverpool and You'll Never Walk Alone!

Acknowledgements

Thank you to Sir Kenny Dalglish and Elvis Costello OBE for their kind and generous words. David Luxton, whose help and advice have been invaluable. Peter Hooton of The Farm, who set the ball rolling (no pun intended!) with this book. Ed Faulkner and everyone at Allen & Unwin and Atlantic Books who have worked so hard for me. Gemma Bodinetz, Deborah Aydon and Sara Ogle, who brought my two favourite theatres back to life. Mark Featherstone-Witty who, with Sir Paul McCartney, has done the same for my old school. Tage and Kamilla Herstad, Jostein and Ragnhild Lund Ansnes, who made the Hotel Tia a special place. Keith Wilson, who encouraged me to write long ago. Peter Robinson, who took a chance on me all those years ago. Liverpool fans, who are still the best in the world. All the musicians, in Liverpool and beyond, who (along with the people listed above) make life worthwhile. Gerry Marsden who lit up all of our lives for six decades and whose name will be remembered for many years to come.

Plate Section Photography Credits

Page 1 – Bill Shankly (Mirrorpix via Getty Images)

Page 2 – Kevin Keegan (Liverpool FC via Getty Images); Bob Paisley (Bob Thomas / Bob Thomas Sports Photography via Getty Images)

Page 3 – Phil Neal's goal (David Cannon / David Cannon Collection via Getty Images); Juventus terrace (Bob Thomas / Bob Thomas Sports Photography via Getty Images)

Page 4 – Floral tribute at Anfield (Liverpool FC via Getty Images); Kenny Dalglish (Bob Thomas / Bob Thomas Sports Photography via Getty Images); standing Kop (Liverpool FC via Getty Images)

Page 5 – The Miracle of Istanbul (Mike Hewitt / Getty Images Sport Classic via Getty Images)

Page 6 – George Sephton with 'Saint' Ian St John (Frank Carlyle); George Sephton's 40th anniversary at Anfield (Paul Cooper)

Page 7 – George Sephton (Stuart James, *The Athletic*)

Page 8 – 'You'll Never Walk Alone' team rendition (Laurence Griffiths / Getty Images Sport via Getty Images); lifting the Premier League trophy (Phil Noble / AFP via Getty Images)

All other featured images courtesy of the author

Index

INDEX

INDEX